FIXED INCOME
ANALYSIS
WORKBOOK

CFA Institute is the premier association for investment professionals around the world, with more than 150,000 CFA charterholders worldwide in 165+ countries and regions. Since 1963 the organization has developed and administered the renowned Chartered Financial Analyst® Program. With a rich history of leading the investment profession, CFA Institute has set the highest standards in ethics, education, and professional excellence within the global investment community and is the foremost authority on investment profession conduct and practice. Each book in the CFA Institute Investment Series is geared toward industry practitioners along with graduate-level finance students and covers the most important topics in the industry. The authors of these cutting-edge books are themselves industry professionals and academics and bring their wealth of knowledge and expertise to this series.

FIXED INCOME ANALYSIS WORKBOOK

Fourth Edition

James F. Adams, PhD, CFA

Donald J. Smith, PhD

WILEY

Cover image: Background © maxkrasnov/iStock.com
Cover design: Wiley

Published by John Wiley & Sons, Inc., Hoboken, New Jersey.
The First, Second, and Third Editions of this book were published by Wiley in 2000, 2011, and 2015, respectively.
Published simultaneously in Canada.

For general information on our other products and services or for technical support, please contact our Customer
Care Department within the United States at (800) 762-2974, outside the United States at (317) 572-3993, or
fax (317) 572-4002.

Wiley publishes in a variety of print and electronic formats and by print-on-demand. Some material included with
standard print versions of this book may not be included in e-books or in print-on-demand. If this book refers to
media such as a CD or DVD that is not included in the version you purchased, you may download this material at
http://booksupport.wiley.com. For more information about Wiley products, visit www.wiley.com.

ISBN 978-1-119-62744-9 (Paper)
ISBN 978-1-119-64687-7 (ePDF)
ISBN 978-1-119-62818-7 (ePub)

Printed in the United States of America.
SKY10031612_112421

CONTENTS

PART I

LEARNING OBJECTIVES, SUMMARY OVERVIEW, AND PROBLEMS

CHAPTER 1

FIXED-INCOME SECURITIES: DEFINING ELEMENTS

LEARNING OUTCOMES

After completing this chapter, you will be able to do the following:

- describe basic features of a fixed-income security;
- describe content of a bond indenture;
- compare affirmative and negative covenants and identify examples of each;
- describe how legal, regulatory, and tax considerations affect the issuance and trading of fixed-income securities;
- describe how cash flows of fixed-income securities are structured;
- describe contingency provisions affecting the timing and/or nature of cash flows of fixed-income securities and identify whether such provisions benefit the borrower or the lender.

SUMMARY OVERVIEW

This chapter provides an introduction to the salient features of fixed-income securities while noting how these features vary among different types of securities. Important points include the following:

- The three important elements that an investor needs to know when investing in a fixed-income security are: (1) the bond's features, which determine its scheduled cash flows and thus the bondholder's expected and actual return; (2) the legal, regulatory, and tax considerations that apply to the contractual agreement between the issuer and the bondholders; and (3) the contingency provisions that may affect the bond's scheduled cash flows.
- The basic features of a bond include the issuer, maturity, par value (or principal), coupon rate and frequency, and currency denomination.

- Issuers of bonds include supranational organizations, sovereign governments, non-sovereign governments, quasi-government entities, and corporate issuers.
- Bondholders are exposed to credit risk and may use bond credit ratings to assess the credit quality of a bond.
- A bond's principal is the amount the issuer agrees to pay the bondholder when the bond matures.
- The coupon rate is the interest rate that the issuer agrees to pay to the bondholder each year. The coupon rate can be a fixed rate or a floating rate. Bonds may offer annual, semi-annual, quarterly, or monthly coupon payments depending on the type of bond and where the bond is issued.
- Bonds can be issued in any currency. Bonds such as dual-currency bonds and currency option bonds are connected to two currencies.
- The yield to maturity is the discount rate that equates the present value of the bond's future cash flows until maturity to its price. Yield to maturity can be considered an estimate of the market's expectation for the bond's return.
- A plain vanilla bond has a known cash flow pattern. It has a fixed maturity date and pays a fixed rate of interest over the bond's life.
- The bond indenture or trust deed is the legal contract that describes the form of the bond, the issuer's obligations, and the investor's rights. The indenture is usually held by a financial institution called a trustee, which performs various duties specified in the indenture.
- The issuer is identified in the indenture by its legal name and is obligated to make timely payments of interest and repayment of principal.
- For asset-backed securities, the legal obligation to repay bondholders often lies with a separate legal entity—that is, a bankruptcy-remote vehicle that uses the assets as guarantees to back a bond issue.
- How the issuer intends to service the debt and repay the principal should be described in the indenture. The source of repayment proceeds varies depending on the type of bond.
- Collateral backing is a way to alleviate credit risk. Secured bonds are backed by assets or financial guarantees pledged to ensure debt payment. Examples of collateral-backed bonds include collateral trust bonds, equipment trust certificates, mortgage-backed securities, and covered bonds.
- Credit enhancement can be internal or external. Examples of internal credit enhancement include subordination, overcollateralization, and reserve accounts. A bank guarantee, a surety bond, a letter of credit, and a cash collateral account are examples of external credit enhancement.
- Bond covenants are legally enforceable rules that borrowers and lenders agree on at the time of a new bond issue. Affirmative covenants enumerate what issuers are required to do, whereas negative covenants enumerate what issuers are prohibited from doing.
- An important consideration for investors is where the bonds are issued and traded, because it affects the laws, regulation, and tax status that apply. Bonds issued in a particular country in local currency are domestic bonds if they are issued by entities incorporated in the country and foreign bonds if they are issued by entities incorporated in another country. Eurobonds are issued internationally, outside the jurisdiction of any single country, and are subject to a lower level of listing, disclosure, and regulatory requirements than domestic or foreign bonds. Global bonds are issued in the Eurobond market and at least one domestic market at the same time.
- Although some bonds may offer special tax advantages, as a general rule, interest is taxed at the ordinary income tax rate. Some countries also implement a capital gains tax. There may be specific tax provisions for bonds issued at a discount or bought at a premium.

- An amortizing bond is a bond whose payment schedule requires periodic payment of interest and repayment of principal. This differs from a bullet bond, whose entire payment of principal occurs at maturity. The amortizing bond's outstanding principal amount is reduced to zero by the maturity date for a fully amortized bond, but a balloon payment is required at maturity to retire the bond's outstanding principal amount for a partially amortized bond.
- Sinking fund agreements provide another approach to the periodic retirement of principal, in which an amount of the bond's principal outstanding amount is usually repaid each year throughout the bond's life or after a specified date.
- A floating-rate note, or floater, is a bond whose coupon is set based on some reference rate plus a spread. FRNs can be floored, capped, or collared. An inverse FRN is a bond whose coupon has an inverse relationship to the reference rate.
- Other coupon payment structures include bonds with step-up coupons, which pay coupons that increase by specified amounts on specified dates; bonds with credit-linked coupons, which change when the issuer's credit rating changes; bonds with payment-in-kind coupons that allow the issuer to pay coupons with additional amounts of the bond issue rather than in cash; and bonds with deferred coupons, which pay no coupons in the early years following the issue but higher coupons thereafter.
- The payment structures for index-linked bonds vary considerably among countries. A common index-linked bond is an inflation-linked bond, or linker, whose coupon payments and/or principal repayments are linked to a price index. Index-linked payment structures include zero-coupon-indexed bonds, interest-indexed bonds, capital-indexed bonds, and indexed-annuity bonds.
- Common types of bonds with embedded options include callable bonds, putable bonds, and convertible bonds. These options are "embedded" in the sense that there are provisions provided in the indenture that grant either the issuer or the bondholder certain rights affecting the disposal or redemption of the bond. They are not separately traded securities.
- Callable bonds give the issuer the right to buy bonds back prior to maturity, thereby raising the reinvestment risk for the bondholder. For this reason, callable bonds have to offer a higher yield and sell at a lower price than otherwise similar non-callable bonds to compensate the bondholders for the value of the call option to the issuer.
- Putable bonds give the bondholder the right to sell bonds back to the issuer prior to maturity. Putable bonds offer a lower yield and sell at a higher price than otherwise similar non-putable bonds to compensate the issuer for the value of the put option to the bondholders.
- A convertible bond gives the bondholder the right to convert the bond into common shares of the issuing company. Because this option favors the bondholder, convertible bonds offer a lower yield and sell at a higher price than otherwise similar non-convertible bonds.

PROBLEMS

1. A 10-year bond was issued four years ago. The bond is denominated in US dollars, offers a coupon rate of 10% with interest paid semi-annually, and is currently priced at 102% of par. The bond's:
   A. tenor is six years.
   B. nominal rate is 5%.
   C. redemption value is 102% of the par value.

2. A sovereign bond has a maturity of 15 years. The bond is *best* described as a:
   A. perpetual bond.
   B. pure discount bond.
   C. capital market security.

3. A company has issued a floating-rate note with a coupon rate equal to the three-month Libor + 65 basis points. Interest payments are made quarterly on 31 March, 30 June, 30 September, and 31 December. On 31 March and 30 June, the three-month Libor is 1.55% and 1.35%, respectively. The coupon rate for the interest payment made on 30 June is:
   A. 2.00%.
   B. 2.10%.
   C. 2.20%.

4. The legal contract that describes the form of the bond, the obligations of the issuer, and the rights of the bondholders can be *best* described as a bond's:
   A. covenant.
   B. indenture.
   C. debenture.

5. Which of the following is a type of external credit enhancement?
   A. Covenants
   B. A surety bond
   C. Overcollaterization

6. An affirmative covenant is *most likely* to stipulate:
   A. limits on the issuer's leverage ratio.
   B. how the proceeds of the bond issue will be used.
   C. the maximum percentage of the issuer's gross assets that can be sold.

7. Which of the following *best* describes a negative bond covenant? The issuer is:
   A. required to pay taxes as they come due.
   B. prohibited from investing in risky projects.
   C. required to maintain its current lines of business.

8. A South African company issues bonds denominated in pound sterling that are sold to investors in the United Kingdom. These bonds can be *best* described as:
   A. Eurobonds.
   B. global bonds.
   C. foreign bonds.

9. Relative to domestic and foreign bonds, Eurobonds are *most likely* to be:
   A. bearer bonds.
   B. registered bonds.
   C. subject to greater regulation.

10. An investor in a country with an original issue discount tax provision purchases a 20-year zero-coupon bond at a deep discount to par value. The investor plans to hold the bond until the maturity date. The investor will *most likely* report:
    A. a capital gain at maturity.
    B. a tax deduction in the year the bond is purchased.
    C. taxable income from the bond every year until maturity.

11. A bond that is characterized by a fixed periodic payment schedule that reduces the bond's outstanding principal amount to zero by the maturity date is *best* described as a:
    A. bullet bond.
    B. plain vanilla bond.
    C. fully amortized bond.

12. If interest rates are expected to increase, the coupon payment structure *most likely* to benefit the issuer is a:
    A. step-up coupon.
    B. inflation-linked coupon.
    C. cap in a floating-rate note.
13. Investors who believe that interest rates will rise *most likely* prefer to invest in:
    A. inverse floaters.
    B. fixed-rate bonds.
    C. floating-rate notes.
14. A 10-year, capital-indexed bond linked to the Consumer Price Index (CPI) is issued with a coupon rate of 6% and a par value of 1,000. The bond pays interest semi-annually. During the first six months after the bond's issuance, the CPI increases by 2%. On the first coupon payment date, the bond's:
    A. coupon rate increases to 8%.
    B. coupon payment is equal to 40.
    C. principal amount increases to 1,020.
15. The provision that provides bondholders the right to sell the bond back to the issuer at a predetermined price prior to the bond's maturity date is referred to as:
    A. a put provision.
    B. a make-whole call provision.
    C. an original issue discount provision.
16. Which of the following provisions is a benefit to the issuer?
    A. Put provision
    B. Call provision
    C. Conversion provision
17. Relative to an otherwise similar option-free bond, a:
    A. putable bond will trade at a higher price.
    B. callable bond will trade at a higher price.
    C. convertible bond will trade at a lower price.
18. Which type of bond *most likely* earns interest on an implied basis?
    A. Floater
    B. Conventional bond
    C. Pure discount bond
19. Clauses that specify the rights of the bondholders and any actions that the issuer is obligated to perform or is prohibited from performing are:
    A. covenants.
    B. collaterals.
    C. credit enhancements.
20. Which of the following type of debt obligation *most likely* protects bondholders when the assets serving as collateral are non-performing?
    A. Covered bonds
    B. Collateral trust bonds
    C. Mortgage-backed securities
21. Which of the following *best* describes a negative bond covenant? The requirement to:
    A. insure and maintain assets.
    B. comply with all laws and regulations.
    C. maintain a minimum interest coverage ratio.

22. Contrary to positive bond covenant, negative covenants are *most likely*:
    A. costlier.
    B. legally enforceable.
    C. enacted at time of issue.
23. A five-year bond has the following cash flows:

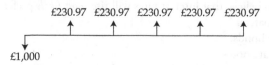

    £230.97   £230.97   £230.97   £230.97   £230.97

    £1,000

    The bond can *best* be described as a:
    A. bullet bond.
    B. fully amortized bond.
    C. partially amortized bond.
24. Investors seeking some general protection against a poor economy are *most likely* to select a:
    A. deferred coupon bond.
    B. credit-linked coupon bond.
    C. payment-in-kind coupon bond.
25. The benefit to the issuer of a deferred coupon bond is *most likely* related to:
    A. tax management.
    B. cash flow management.
    C. original issue discount price.
26. Which of the following bond types provides the *most* benefit to a bondholder when bond prices are declining?
    A. Callable
    B. Plain vanilla
    C. Multiple put
27. Which type of call bond option offers the *greatest* flexibility as to when the issuer can exercise the option?
    A. A Bermuda call
    B. A European call
    C. An American call
28. Which of the following *best* describes a convertible bond's conversion premium?
    A. Bond price minus conversion value
    B. Par value divided by conversion price
    C. Current share price multiplied by conversion ratio

CHAPTER 2

FIXED-INCOME MARKETS: ISSUANCE, TRADING, AND FUNDING

LEARNING OUTCOMES

After completing this chapter, you will be able to do the following:

- describe classifications of global fixed-income markets;
- describe the use of interbank offered rates as reference rates in floating-rate debt;
- describe mechanisms available for issuing bonds in primary markets;
- describe secondary markets for bonds;
- describe securities issued by sovereign governments;
- describe securities issued by non-sovereign governments, quasi-government entities, and supranational agencies;
- describe types of debt issued by corporations;
- describe structured financial instruments;
- describe short-term funding alternatives available to banks;
- describe repurchase agreements (repos) and the risks associated with them.

SUMMARY OVERVIEW

Debt financing is an important source of funds for households, governments, government-related entities, financial institutions, and non-financial companies. Well-functioning fixed-income markets help ensure that capital is allocated efficiently to its highest and best use globally. Important points include the following:

- The most widely used ways of classifying fixed-income markets include the type of issuer; the bonds' credit quality, maturity, currency denomination, and type of coupon; and where the bonds are issued and traded.

- Based on the type of issuer, the four major bond market sectors are the household, non-financial corporate, government, and financial institution sectors.
- Investors make a distinction between investment-grade and high-yield bond markets based on the issuer's credit quality.
- Money markets are where securities with original maturities ranging from overnight to one year are issued and traded, whereas capital markets are where securities with original maturities longer than one year are issued and traded.
- The majority of bonds are denominated in either euros or US dollars.
- Investors make a distinction between bonds that pay a fixed rate versus a floating rate of interest. The coupon rate of floating-rate bonds is often expressed as a reference rate plus a spread. Interbank offered rates, such as Libor, historically have been the most commonly used reference rates for floating-rate debt and other financial instruments but are being phased out to be replaced by alternative reference rates.
- Based on where the bonds are issued and traded, a distinction is made between domestic and international bond markets. The latter includes the Eurobond market, which falls outside the jurisdiction of any single country and is characterized by less reporting, regulatory, and tax constraints. Investors also make a distinction between developed and emerging bond markets.
- Fixed-income indexes are used by investors and investment managers to describe bond markets or sectors and to evaluate performance of investments and investment managers.
- The largest investors in bonds include central banks; institutional investors, such as pension funds, hedge funds, charitable foundations and endowments, insurance companies, mutual funds and ETFs, and banks; and retail investors, typically by means of indirect investments.
- Primary markets are markets in which issuers first sell bonds to investors to raise capital. Secondary markets are markets in which existing bonds are subsequently traded among investors.
- There are two mechanisms for issuing a bond in primary markets: a public offering, in which any member of the public may buy the bonds, or a private placement, in which only an investor or small group of investors may buy the bonds either directly from the issuer or through an investment bank.
- Public bond issuing mechanisms include underwritten offerings, best effort offerings, shelf registrations, and auctions.
- When an investment bank underwrites a bond issue, it buys the entire issue and takes the risk of reselling it to investors or dealers. In contrast, in a best-efforts offering, the investment bank serves only as a broker and sells the bond issue only if it is able to do so. Underwritten and best effort offerings are frequently used in the issuance of corporate bonds.
- The underwriting process typically includes six phases: the determination of the funding needs, the selection of the underwriter, the structuring and announcement of the bond offering, pricing, issuance, and closing.
- A shelf registration is a method for issuing securities in which the issuer files a single document with regulators that describes and allows for a range of future issuances.
- An auction is a public offering method that involves bidding, and that is helpful in providing price discovery and in allocating securities. It is frequently used in the issuance of sovereign bonds.
- Most bonds are traded in over-the-counter (OTC) markets, and institutional investors are the major buyers and sellers of bonds in secondary markets.
- Sovereign bonds are issued by national governments primarily for fiscal reasons. They take different names and forms depending on where they are issued, their maturities, and their

coupon types. Most sovereign bonds are fixed-rate bonds, although some national governments also issue floating-rate bonds and inflation-linked bonds.

- Local governments, quasi-government entities, and supranational agencies issue bonds, which are named non-sovereign, quasi-government, and supranational bonds, respectively.
- Companies raise debt in the form of bilateral loans, syndicated loans, commercial paper, notes, and bonds.
- Commercial paper is a short-term unsecured security that is used by companies as a source of short-term and bridge financing. Investors in commercial paper are exposed to credit risk, although defaults are rare. Many issuers roll over their commercial paper on a regular basis.
- Corporate bonds and notes take different forms depending on the maturities, coupon payment, and principal repayment structures. Important considerations also include collateral backing and contingency provisions.
- Medium-term notes are securities that are offered continuously to investors by an agent of the issuer. They can have short-term or long-term maturities.
- The structured finance sector includes asset-backed securities, collateralized debt obligations, and other structured financial instruments. All of these seemingly disparate financial instruments share the common attribute of repackaging risks.
- Many structured financial instruments are customized instruments that often combine a bond and at least one derivative. The redemption and often the coupons of these structured financial instruments are linked via a formula to the performance of the underlying asset(s). Thus, the bond's payment features are replaced with non-traditional payoffs that are derived not from the issuer's cash flows but from the performance of the underlying asset(s). Capital protected, yield enhancement, participation, and leveraged instruments are typical examples of structured financial instruments.
- Financial institutions have access to additional sources of funds, such as retail deposits, central bank funds, interbank funds, large-denomination negotiable certificates of deposit, and repurchase agreements.
- A repurchase agreement is similar to a collateralized loan. It involves the sale of a security (the collateral) with a simultaneous agreement by the seller (the borrower) to buy the same security back from the purchaser (the lender) at an agreed-on price in the future. Repurchase agreements are a common source of funding for dealer firms and are also used to borrow securities to implement short positions.

PROBLEMS

1. In most countries, the bond market sector with the smallest amount of bonds outstanding is *most likely* the:
   A. government sector.
   B. financial corporate sector.
   C. non-financial corporate sector.
2. The distinction between investment grade debt and non-investment grade debt is *best* described by differences in:
   A. tax status.
   B. credit quality.
   C. maturity dates.

3. A bond issued internationally, outside the jurisdiction of the country in whose currency the bond is denominated, is *best* described as a:
   A. Eurobond.
   B. foreign bond.
   C. municipal bond.

4. When classified by type of issuer, asset-backed securities are part of the:
   A. corporate sector.
   B. structured finance sector.
   C. government and government-related sector.

5. Compared with developed markets bonds, emerging markets bonds *most likely*:
   A. offer lower yields.
   B. exhibit higher risk.
   C. benefit from lower growth prospects.

6. With respect to floating-rate bonds, a reference rate such as the London interbank offered rate (Libor) is *most likely* used to determine the bond's:
   A. spread.
   B. coupon rate.
   C. frequency of coupon payments.

7. The variability of the coupon rate on a Libor-based floating-rate bond is *most likely* due to:
   A. periodic resets of the reference rate.
   B. market-based reassessments of the issuer's creditworthiness.
   C. changing estimates by the Libor administrator of borrowing capacity.

8. Which of the following statements is *most accurate*? An interbank offered rate:
   A. is a single reference rate.
   B. applies to borrowing periods of up to 10 years.
   C. is used as a reference rate for interest rate swaps.

9. An investment bank that underwrites a bond issue *most likely*:
   A. buys and resells the newly issued bonds to investors or dealers.
   B. acts as a broker and receives a commission for selling the bonds to investors.
   C. incurs less risk associated with selling the bonds than in a best efforts offering.

10. In major developed bond markets, newly issued sovereign bonds are *most* often sold to the public via a(n):
    A. auction.
    B. private placement.
    C. best efforts offering.

11. Which of the following describes privately placed bonds?
    A. They are non-underwritten and unregistered.
    B. They usually have active secondary markets.
    C. They are less customized than publicly offered bonds.

12. A mechanism by which an issuer may be able to offer additional bonds to the general public without preparing a new and separate offering circular *best* describes:
    A. the grey market.
    B. a shelf registration.
    C. a private placement.

13. Which of the following statements related to secondary bond markets is *most accurate*?
    A. Newly issued corporate bonds are issued in secondary bond markets.
    B. Secondary bond markets are where bonds are traded between investors.
    C. The major participants in secondary bond markets globally are retail investors.

14. A bond market in which a communications network matches buy and sell orders initiated from various locations is *best* described as an:
    A. organized exchange.
    B. open market operation.
    C. over-the-counter market.
15. A liquid secondary bond market allows an investor to sell a bond at:
    A. the desired price.
    B. a price at least equal to the purchase price.
    C. a price close to the bond's fair market value.
16. Corporate bond secondary market trading *most often* occurs:
    A. on a book-entry basis.
    B. on organized exchanges.
    C. prior to settlement at $T + 1$.
17. Sovereign bonds are *best* described as:
    A. bonds issued by local governments.
    B. secured obligations of a national government.
    C. bonds backed by the taxing authority of a national government.
18. Which factor is associated with a more favorable quality sovereign bond credit rating?
    A. Issued in local currency, only
    B. Strong domestic savings base, only
    C. Issued in local currency of country with strong domestic savings base
19. Which type of sovereign bond has the lowest interest rate risk for an investor?
    A. Floaters
    B. Coupon bonds
    C. Discount bonds
20. Agency bonds are issued by:
    A. local governments.
    B. national governments.
    C. quasi-government entities.
21. The type of bond issued by a multilateral agency such as the International Monetary Fund (IMF) is *best* described as a:
    A. sovereign bond.
    B. supranational bond.
    C. quasi-government bond.
22. A bond issued by a local government authority, typically without an explicit funding commitment from the national government, is *most likely* classified as a:
    A. sovereign bond.
    B. quasi-government bond
    C. non-sovereign government bond.
23. Which of the following statements relating to commercial paper is *most accurate*?
    A. There is no secondary market for trading commercial paper.
    B. Only the strongest, highly rated companies issue commercial paper.
    C. Commercial paper is a source of interim financing for long-term projects.
24. Eurocommerical paper is *most likely*:
    A. negotiable.
    B. denominated in euro.
    C. issued on a discount basis.

25. For the issuer, a sinking fund arrangement is *most similar* to a:
    A. term maturity structure.
    B. serial maturity structure.
    C. bondholder put provision.
26. When issuing debt, a company may use a sinking fund arrangement as a means of reducing:
    A. credit risk.
    B. inflation risk.
    C. interest rate risk.
27. Which of the following is a source of wholesale funds for banks?
    A. Demand deposits
    B. Money market accounts
    C. Negotiable certificates of deposit
28. A characteristic of negotiable certificates of deposit is:
    A. they are mostly available in small denominations.
    B. they can be sold in the open market prior to maturity.
    C. a penalty is imposed if the depositor withdraws funds prior to maturity.
29. A repurchase agreement is *most* comparable to a(n):
    A. interbank deposit.
    B. collateralized loan.
    C. negotiable certificate of deposit.
30. The repo margin is:
    A. negotiated between counterparties.
    B. established independently of market-related conditions.
    C. structured on an agreement assuming equal credit risks to all counterparties.
31. The repo margin on a repurchase agreement is *most likely* to be lower when:
    A. the underlying collateral is in short supply.
    B. the maturity of the repurchase agreement is long.
    C. the credit risk associated with the underlying collateral is high.

CHAPTER 3

INTRODUCTION TO FIXED-INCOME VALUATION

LEARNING OUTCOMES

After completing this chapter, you will be able to do the following:

- calculate a bond's price given a market discount rate;
- identify the relationships among a bond's price, coupon rate, maturity, and market discount rate (yield-to-maturity);
- define spot rates and calculate the price of a bond using spot rates;
- describe and calculate the flat price, accrued interest, and the full price of a bond;
- describe matrix pricing;
- calculate annual yield on a bond for varying compounding periods in a year;
- calculate and interpret yield measures for fixed-rate bonds and floating-rate notes;
- calculate and interpret yield measures for money market instruments;
- define and compare the spot curve, yield curve on coupon bonds, par curve, and forward curve;
- define forward rates and calculate spot rates from forward rates, forward rates from spot rates, and the price of a bond using forward rates;
- compare, calculate, and interpret yield spread measures.

SUMMARY OVERVIEW

This chapter covers the principles and techniques that are used in the valuation of fixed-rate bonds, as well as floating-rate notes and money market instruments. These building blocks are used extensively in fixed income analysis. The following are the main points made in the chapter:

- The market discount rate is the rate of return required by investors given the risk of the investment in the bond.
- A bond is priced at a premium above par value when the coupon rate is greater than the market discount rate.

- A bond is priced at a discount below par value when the coupon rate is less than the market discount rate.
- The amount of any premium or discount is the present value of the "excess" or "deficiency" in the coupon payments relative to the yield-to-maturity.
- The yield-to-maturity, the internal rate of return on the cash flows, is the implied market discount rate given the price of the bond.
- A bond price moves inversely with its market discount rate.
- The relationship between a bond price and its market discount rate is convex.
- The price of a lower-coupon bond is more volatile than the price of a higher-coupon bond, other things being equal.
- Generally, the price of a longer-term bond is more volatile than the price of shorter-term bond, other things being equal. An exception to this phenomenon can occur on low-coupon (but not zero-coupon) bonds that are priced at a discount to par value.
- Assuming no default, premium and discount bond prices are "pulled to par" as maturity nears.
- A spot rate is the yield-to-maturity on a zero-coupon bond.
- A yield-to-maturity can be approximated as a weighted average of the underlying spot rates.
- Between coupon dates, the full (or invoice, or "dirty") price of a bond is split between the flat (or quoted, or "clean") price and the accrued interest.
- Flat prices are quoted to not misrepresent the daily increase in the full price as a result of interest accruals.
- Accrued interest is calculated as a proportional share of the next coupon payment using either the actual/actual or 30/360 methods to count days.
- Matrix pricing is used to value illiquid bonds by using prices and yields on comparable securities having the same or similar credit risk, coupon rate, and maturity.
- The periodicity of an annual interest rate is the number of periods in the year.
- A yield quoted on a semi-annual bond basis is an annual rate for a periodicity of two. It is the yield per semi-annual period times two.
- The general rule for periodicity conversions is that compounding more frequently at a lower annual rate corresponds to compounding less frequently at a higher annual rate.
- Street convention yields assume payments are made on scheduled dates, neglecting weekends and holidays.
- The current yield is the annual coupon payment divided by the flat price, thereby neglecting as a measure of the investor's rate of return the time value of money, any accrued interest, and the gain from buying at a discount and the loss from buying at a premium.
- The simple yield is like the current yield but includes the straight-line amortization of the discount or premium.
- The yield-to-worst on a callable bond is the lowest of the yield-to-first-call, yield-to-second-call, and so on, calculated using the call price for the future value and the call date for the number of periods.
- The option-adjusted yield on a callable bond is the yield-to-maturity after adding the theoretical value of the call option to the price.
- A floating-rate note (floater, or FRN) maintains a more stable price than a fixed-rate note because interest payments adjust for changes in market interest rates.
- The quoted margin on a floater is typically the specified yield spread over or under the reference rate, which often is Libor.
- The discount margin on a floater is the spread required by investors, and to which the quoted margin must be set, for the FRN to trade at par value on a rate reset date.

- Money market instruments, having one year or less time-to-maturity, are quoted on a discount rate or add-on rate basis.
- Money market discount rates understate the investor's rate of return (and the borrower's cost of funds) because the interest income is divided by the face value or the total amount redeemed at maturity, not by the amount of the investment.
- Money market instruments need to be converted to a common basis for analysis.
- A money market bond equivalent yield is an add-on rate for a 365-day year.
- The periodicity of a money market instrument is the number of days in the year divided by the number of days to maturity. Therefore, money market instruments with different times-to-maturity have annual rates for different periodicities.
- In theory, the maturity structure, or term structure, of interest rates is the relationship between yields-to-maturity and times-to-maturity on bonds having the same currency, credit risk, liquidity, tax status, and periodicity.
- A spot curve is a series of yields-to-maturity on zero-coupon bonds.
- A frequently used yield curve is a series of yields-to-maturity on coupon bonds.
- A par curve is a series of yields-to-maturity assuming the bonds are priced at par value.
- In a cash market, the delivery of the security and cash payment is made on a settlement date within a customary time period after the trade date—for example, "$T+3$."
- In a forward market, the delivery of the security and cash payment is made on a predetermined future date.
- A forward rate is the interest rate on a bond or money market instrument traded in a forward market.
- An implied forward rate (or forward yield) is the breakeven reinvestment rate linking the return on an investment in a shorter-term zero-coupon bond to the return on an investment in a longer-term zero-coupon bond.
- An implied forward curve can be calculated from the spot curve.
- Implied spot rates can be calculated as geometric averages of forward rates.
- A fixed-income bond can be valued using a market discount rate, a series of spot rates, or a series of forward rates.
- A bond yield-to-maturity can be separated into a benchmark and a spread.
- Changes in benchmark rates capture macroeconomic factors that affect all bonds in the market—inflation, economic growth, foreign exchange rates, and monetary and fiscal policy.
- Changes in spreads typically capture microeconomic factors that affect the particular bond—credit risk, liquidity, and tax effects.
- Benchmark rates are usually yields-to-maturity on government bonds or fixed rates on interest rate swaps.
- A G-spread is the spread over or under a government bond rate, and an I-spread is the spread over or under an interest rate swap rate.
- A G-spread or an I-spread can be based on a specific benchmark rate or on a rate interpolated from the benchmark yield curve.
- A Z-spread (zero-volatility spread) is based on the entire benchmark spot curve. It is the constant spread that is added to each spot rate such that the present value of the cash flows matches the price of the bond.
- An option-adjusted spread (OAS) on a callable bond is the Z-spread minus the theoretical value of the embedded call option.

PROBLEMS

1. A portfolio manager is considering the purchase of a bond with a 5.5% coupon rate that pays interest annually and matures in three years. If the required rate of return on the bond is 5%, the price of the bond per 100 of par value is *closest* to:
   A. 98.65.
   B. 101.36.
   C. 106.43.

2. A bond with two years remaining until maturity offers a 3% coupon rate with interest paid annually. At a market discount rate of 4%, the price of this bond per 100 of par value is *closest* to:
   A. 95.34.
   B. 98.00.
   C. 98.11.

3. An investor who owns a bond with a 9% coupon rate that pays interest semi-annually and matures in three years is considering its sale. If the required rate of return on the bond is 11%, the price of the bond per 100 of par value is *closest* to:
   A. 95.00.
   B. 95.11.
   C. 105.15.

4. A bond offers an annual coupon rate of 4%, with interest paid semi-annually. The bond matures in two years. At a market discount rate of 6%, the price of this bond per 100 of par value is *closest* to:
   A. 93.07.
   B. 96.28.
   C. 96.33.

5. A bond offers an annual coupon rate of 5%, with interest paid semi-annually. The bond matures in seven years. At a market discount rate of 3%, the price of this bond per 100 of par value is *closest* to:
   A. 106.60.
   B. 112.54.
   C. 143.90.

6. A zero-coupon bond matures in 15 years. At a market discount rate of 4.5% per year and assuming annual compounding, the price of the bond per 100 of par value is *closest* to:
   A. 51.30.
   B. 51.67.
   C. 71.62.

7. Consider the following two bonds that pay interest annually:

Bond	Coupon Rate	Time-to-Maturity
A	5%	2 years
B	3%	2 years

At a market discount rate of 4%, the price difference between Bond A and Bond B per 100 of par value is *closest* to:
   A. 3.70.
   B. 3.77.
   C. 4.00.

The following information relates to Questions 8 and 9

Bond	Price	Coupon Rate	Time-to-Maturity
A	101.886	5%	2 years
B	100.000	6%	2 years
C	97.327	5%	3 years

8. Which bond offers the lowest yield-to-maturity?
   A. Bond A
   B. Bond B
   C. Bond C
9. Which bond will *most likely* experience the smallest percent change in price if the market discount rates for all three bonds increase by 100 basis points?
   A. Bond A
   B. Bond B
   C. Bond C

---

10. Suppose a bond's price is expected to increase by 5% if its market discount rate decreases by 100 basis points. If the bond's market discount rate increases by 100 basis points, the bond price is *most likely* to change by:
    A. 5%.
    B. less than 5%.
    C. more than 5%.

The following information relates to Questions 11 and 12

Bond	Coupon Rate	Maturity (years)
A	6%	10
B	6%	5
C	8%	5

All three bonds are currently trading at par value.

11. Relative to Bond C, for a 200 basis point decrease in the required rate of return, Bond B will *most likely* exhibit a(n):
    A. equal percentage price change.
    B. greater percentage price change.
    C. smaller percentage price change.
12. Which bond will *most likely* experience the greatest percentage change in price if the market discount rates for all three bonds increase by 100 basis points?
    A. Bond A
    B. Bond B
    C. Bond C

13. An investor considers the purchase of a 2-year bond with a 5% coupon rate, with interest paid annually. Assuming the sequence of spot rates shown below, the price of the bond is *closest* to:

Time-to-Maturity	Spot Rates
1 year	3%
2 years	4%

   A. 101.93.
   B. 102.85.
   C. 105.81.

14. A 3-year bond offers a 10% coupon rate with interest paid annually. Assuming the following sequence of spot rates, the price of the bond is *closest* to:

Time-to-Maturity	Spot Rates
1 year	8.0%
2 years	9.0%
3 years	9.5%

   A. 96.98.
   B. 101.46.
   C. 102.95.

The following information relates to Questions 15–17

Bond	Coupon Rate	Time-to-Maturity	Time-to-Maturity	Spot Rates
X	8%	3 years	1 year	8%
Y	7%	3 years	2 years	9%
Z	6%	3 years	3 years	10%

All three bonds pay interest annually.

15. Based upon the given sequence of spot rates, the price of Bond X is *closest* to:
   A. 95.02.
   B. 95.28.
   C. 97.63.

16. Based upon the given sequence of spot rates, the price of Bond Y is *closest* to:
   A. 87.50.
   B. 92.54.
   C. 92.76.

17. Based upon the given sequence of spot rates, the yield-to-maturity of Bond Z is *closest* to:
   A. 9.00%.
   B. 9.92%.
   C. 11.93%

18. Bond dealers *most* often quote the:
    A. flat price.
    B. full price.
    C. full price plus accrued interest.

The following information relates to Questions 19–21

Bond G, described in the exhibit below, is sold for settlement on 16 June 2020.

Annual Coupon	5%
Coupon Payment Frequency	Semi-annual
Interest Payment Dates	10 April and 10 October
Maturity Date	10 October 2022
Day Count Convention	30/360
Annual Yield-to-Maturity	4%

19. The full price that Bond G settles at on 16 June 2020 is *closest* to:
    A. 102.36.
    B. 103.10.
    C. 103.65.
20. The accrued interest per 100 of par value for Bond G on the settlement date of 16 June 2020 is *closest* to:
    A. 0.46.
    B. 0.73.
    C. 0.92.
21. The flat price for Bond G on the settlement date of 16 June 2020 is *closest* to:
    A. 102.18.
    B. 103.10.
    C. 104.02.

---

22. Matrix pricing allows investors to estimate market discount rates and prices for bonds:
    A. with different coupon rates.
    B. that are not actively traded.
    C. with different credit quality.
23. When underwriting new corporate bonds, matrix pricing is used to get an estimate of the:
    A. required yield spread over the benchmark rate.
    B. market discount rate of other comparable corporate bonds.
    C. yield-to-maturity on a government bond having a similar time-to-maturity.
24. A bond with 20 years remaining until maturity is currently trading for 111 per 100 of par value. The bond offers a 5% coupon rate with interest paid semi-annually. The bond's annual yield-to-maturity is *closest* to:
    A. 2.09%.
    B. 4.18%.
    C. 4.50%.

25. The annual yield-to-maturity, stated for with a periodicity of 12, for a 4-year, zero-coupon bond priced at 75 per 100 of par value is *closest* to:
    A. 6.25%.
    B. 7.21%.
    C. 7.46%.
26. A 5-year, 5% semi-annual coupon payment corporate bond is priced at 104.967 per 100 of par value. The bond's yield-to-maturity, quoted on a semi-annual bond basis, is 3.897%. An analyst has been asked to convert to a monthly periodicity. Under this conversion, the yield-to-maturity is *closest* to:
    A. 3.87%.
    B. 4.95%.
    C. 7.67%.

The following information relates to Questions 27–30

A bond with 5 years remaining until maturity is currently trading for 101 per 100 of par value. The bond offers a 6% coupon rate with interest paid semi-annually. The bond is first callable in 3 years, and is callable after that date on coupon dates according to the following schedule:

End of Year	Call Price
3	102
4	101
5	100

27. The bond's annual yield-to-maturity is *closest* to:
    A. 2.88%.
    B. 5.77%.
    C. 5.94%.
28. The bond's annual yield-to-first-call is *closest* to:
    A. 3.12%.
    B. 6.11%.
    C. 6.25%.
29. The bond's annual yield-to-second-call is *closest* to:
    A. 2.97%.
    B. 5.72%.
    C. 5.94%.
30. The bond's yield-to-worst is *closest* to:
    A. 2.88%.
    B. 5.77%.
    C. 6.25%.

31. A two-year floating-rate note pays 6-month Libor plus 80 basis points. The floater is priced at 97 per 100 of par value. Current 6-month Libor is 1.00%. Assume a 30/360 day-count convention and evenly spaced periods. The discount margin for the floater in basis points (bps) is *closest* to:
    A. 180 bps.
    B. 236 bps.
    C. 420 bps.

32. An analyst evaluates the following information relating to floating rate notes (FRNs) issued at par value that have 3-month Libor as a reference rate:

Floating Rate Note	Quoted Margin	Discount Margin
X	0.40%	0.32%
Y	0.45%	0.45%
Z	0.55%	0.72%

Based only on the information provided, the FRN that will be priced at a premium on the next reset date is:
    A. FRN X.
    B. FRN Y.
    C. FRN Z.

33. A 365-day year bank certificate of deposit has an initial principal amount of USD 96.5 million and a redemption amount due at maturity of USD 100 million. The number of days between settlement and maturity is 350. The bond equivalent yield is *closest* to:
    A. 3.48%.
    B. 3.65%.
    C. 3.78%.

34. The bond equivalent yield of a 180-day banker's acceptance quoted at a discount rate of 4.25% for a 360-day year is *closest* to:
    A. 4.31%.
    B. 4.34%.
    C. 4.40%.

35. Which of the following statements describing a par curve is *incorrect*?
    A. A par curve is obtained from a spot curve.
    B. All bonds on a par curve are assumed to have different credit risk.
    C. A par curve is a sequence of yields-to-maturity such that each bond is priced at par value.

36. A yield curve constructed from a sequence of yields-to-maturity on zero-coupon bonds is the:
    A. par curve.
    B. spot curve.
    C. forward curve.

37. The rate, interpreted to be the incremental return for extending the time-to-maturity of an investment for an additional time period, is the:
    A. add-on rate.
    B. forward rate.
    C. yield-to-maturity.

The following information relates to Questions 38 and 39

Time Period	Forward Rate
"0y1y"	0.80%
"1y1y"	1.12%
"2y1y"	3.94%
"3y1y"	3.28%
"4y1y"	3.14%

All rates are annual rates stated for a periodicity of one (effective annual rates).

38. The 3-year implied spot rate is *closest* to:
    A. 1.18%.
    B. 1.94%.
    C. 2.28%.
39. The value per 100 of par value of a two-year, 3.5% coupon bond, with interest payments paid annually, is *closest* to:
    A. 101.58.
    B. 105.01.
    C. 105.82.

40. The spread component of a specific bond's yield-to-maturity is *least likely* impacted by changes in:
    A. its tax status.
    B. its quality rating.
    C. inflation in its currency of denomination.
41. The yield spread of a specific bond over the standard swap rate in that currency of the same tenor is *best* described as the:
    A. I-spread.
    B. Z-spread.
    C. G-spread.

The following information relates to Question 42

Bond	Coupon Rate	Time-to-Maturity	Price
UK Government Benchmark Bond	2%	3 years	100.25
UK Corporate Bond	5%	3 years	100.65

Both bonds pay interest annually. The current three-year EUR interest rate swap benchmark is 2.12%.

42. The G-spread in basis points (bps) on the UK corporate bond is *closest* to:
    A. 264 bps.
    B. 285 bps.
    C. 300 bps.

43. A corporate bond offers a 5% coupon rate and has exactly 3 years remaining to maturity. Interest is paid annually. The following rates are from the benchmark spot curve:

Time-to-Maturity	Spot Rate
1 year	4.86%
2 years	4.95%
3 years	5.65%

The bond is currently trading at a Z-spread of 234 basis points. The value of the bond is *closest* to:

A. 92.38.

B. 98.35.

C. 106.56.

44. An option-adjusted spread (OAS) on a callable bond is the Z-spread:

A. over the benchmark spot curve.

B. minus the standard swap rate in that currency of the same tenor.

C. minus the value of the embedded call option expressed in basis points per year.

CHAPTER 4

INTRODUCTION TO ASSET-BACKED SECURITIES

LEARNING OUTCOMES

After completing this chapter, you will be able to do the following:

- explain benefits of securitization for economies and financial markets;
- describe securitization, including the parties involved in the process and the roles they play;
- describe typical structures of securitizations, including credit tranching and time tranching;
- describe types and characteristics of residential mortgage loans that are typically securitized;
- describe types and characteristics of residential mortgage-backed securities, including mortgage pass-through securities and collateralized mortgage obligations, and explain the cash flows and risks for each type;
- define prepayment risk and describe the prepayment risk of mortgage-backed securities;
- describe characteristics and risks of commercial mortgage-backed securities;
- describe types and characteristics of non-mortgage asset-backed securities, including the cash flows and risks of each type;
- describe collateralized debt obligations, including their cash flows and risks.

SUMMARY OVERVIEW

- Securitization involves pooling debt obligations, such as loans or receivables, and creating securities backed by the pool of debt obligations called asset-backed securities (ABS). The cash flows of the debt obligations are used to make interest payments and principal repayments to the holders of the ABS.
- Securitization has several benefits. It allows investors direct access to liquid investments and payment streams that would be unattainable if all the financing were performed through banks. It enables banks to increase loan originations at economic scales greater than if they used only their own in-house loan portfolios. Thus, securitization contributes to lower costs

of borrowing for entities raising funds, higher risk-adjusted returns to investors, and greater efficiency and profitability for the banking sector.

- The parties to a securitization include the seller of the collateral (pool of loans), the servicer of the loans, and the special purpose entity (SPE). The SPE is bankruptcy remote, which plays a pivotal role in the securitization.

- A common structure in a securitization is subordination, which leads to the creation of more than one bond class or tranche. Bond classes differ as to how they will share any losses resulting from defaults of the borrowers whose loans are in the collateral. The credit ratings assigned to the various bond classes depend on how the credit rating agencies evaluate the credit risks of the collateral and any credit enhancements.

- The motivation for the creation of different types of structures is to redistribute prepayment risk and credit risk efficiently among different bond classes in the securitization. Prepayment risk is the uncertainty that the actual cash flows will be different from the scheduled cash flows as set forth in the loan agreements because borrowers may choose to repay the principal early to take advantage of interest rate movements.

- Because of the SPE, the securitization of a company's assets may include some bond classes that have better credit ratings than the company itself or its corporate bonds. Thus, the company's funding cost is often lower when raising funds through securitization than when issuing corporate bonds.

- A mortgage is a loan secured by the collateral of some specified real estate property that obliges the borrower to make a predetermined series of payments to the lender. The cash flow of a mortgage includes (1) interest, (2) scheduled principal payments, and (3) prepayments (any principal repaid in excess of the scheduled principal payment).

- The various mortgage designs throughout the world specify (1) the maturity of the loan; (2) how the interest rate is determined (i.e., fixed rate versus adjustable or variable rate); (3) how the principal is repaid (i.e., whether the loan is amortizing and if it is, whether it is fully amortizing or partially amortizing with a balloon payment); (4) whether the borrower has the option to prepay and if so, whether any prepayment penalties might be imposed; and (5) the rights of the lender in a foreclosure (i.e., whether the loan is a recourse or non-recourse loan).

- In the United States, there are three sectors for securities backed by residential mortgages: (1) those guaranteed by a federal agency (Ginnie Mae) whose securities are backed by the full faith and credit of the US government, (2) those guaranteed by a GSE (e.g., Fannie Mae and Freddie Mac) but not by the US government, and (3) those issued by private entities that are not guaranteed by a federal agency or a GSE. The first two sectors are referred to as agency residential mortgage-backed securities (RMBS), and the third sector as non-agency RMBS.

- A mortgage pass-through security is created when one or more holders of mortgages form a pool of mortgages and sell shares or participation certificates in the pool. The cash flow of a mortgage pass-through security depends on the cash flow of the underlying pool of mortgages and consists of monthly mortgage payments representing interest, the scheduled repayment of principal, and any prepayments, net of servicing and other administrative fees.

- Market participants measure the prepayment rate using two measures: the single monthly mortality rate (SMM) and its corresponding annualized rate—namely, the conditional prepayment rate (CPR). For MBS, a measure widely used by market participants to assess effective duration is the weighted average life or simply the average life of the MBS.

- Market participants use the Public Securities Association (PSA) prepayment benchmark to describe prepayment rates. A PSA assumption greater than 100 PSA means that prepayments are assumed to occur faster than the benchmark, whereas a PSA assumption lower than 100 PSA means that prepayments are assumed to occur slower than the benchmark.
- Prepayment risk includes two components: contraction risk and extension risk. The former is the risk that when interest rates decline, the security will have a shorter maturity than was anticipated at the time of purchase because homeowners will refinance at the new, lower interest rates. The latter is the risk that when interest rates rise, fewer prepayments will occur than what was anticipated at the time of purchase because homeowners are reluctant to give up the benefits of a contractual interest rate that now looks low.
- The creation of a collateralized mortgage obligation (CMO) can help manage prepayment risk by distributing the various forms of prepayment risk among different classes of bondholders. The CMO's major financial innovation is that the securities created more closely satisfy the asset/liability needs of institutional investors, thereby broadening the appeal of mortgage-backed products.
- The most common types of CMO tranches are sequential-pay tranches, planned amortization class (PAC) tranches, support tranches, and floating-rate tranches.
- Non-agency RMBS share many features and structuring techniques with agency CMOs. However, they typically include two complementary mechanisms. First, the cash flows are distributed by rules that dictate the allocation of interest payments and principal repayments to tranches with various degrees of priority/seniority. Second, there are rules for the allocation of realized losses, which specify that subordinated bond classes have lower payment priority than senior classes.
- In order to obtain favorable credit ratings, non-agency RMBS and non-mortgage ABS often require one or more credit enhancements. The most common forms of internal credit enhancement are senior/subordinated structures, reserve funds, and overcollateralization. In external credit enhancement, credit support in the case of defaults resulting in losses in the pool of loans is provided in the form of a financial guarantee by a third party to the transaction.
- Commercial mortgage-backed securities (CMBS) are securities backed by a pool of commercial mortgages on income-producing property.
- Two key indicators of the potential credit performance of CMBS are the debt-service-coverage (DSC) ratio and the loan-to-value ratio (LTV). The DSC ratio is the property's annual net operating income divided by the debt service.
- CMBS have considerable call protection, which allows CMBS to trade in the market more like corporate bonds than like RMBS. This call protection comes in two forms: at the structure level and at the loan level. The creation of sequential-pay tranches is an example of call protection at the structure level. At the loan level, four mechanisms offer investors call protection: prepayment lockouts, prepayment penalty points, yield maintenance charges, and defeasance.
- ABS are backed by a wide range of asset types. The most popular non-mortgage ABS are auto loan ABS and credit card receivable ABS. The collateral is amortizing for auto loan ABS and non-amortizing for credit card receivable ABS. As with non-agency RMBS, these ABS must offer credit enhancement to be appealing to investors.
- A collateralized debt obligation (CDO) is a generic term used to describe a security backed by a diversified pool of one or more debt obligations (e.g., corporate and emerging market bonds, leveraged bank loans, ABS, RMBS, and CMBS).

- A CDO involves the creation of an SPE. The funds necessary to pay the bond classes come from a pool of loans that must be serviced. A CDO requires a collateral manager to buy and sell debt obligations for and from the CDO's portfolio of assets to generate sufficient cash flows to meet the obligations of the CDO bondholders and to generate a fair return for the equity holders.
- The structure of a CDO includes senior, mezzanine, and subordinated/equity bond classes.

PROBLEMS

1. Securitization is beneficial for banks because it:
   A. repackages bank loans into simpler structures.
   B. increases the funds available for banks to lend.
   C. allows banks to maintain ownership of their securitized assets.
2. Securitization benefits financial markets by:
   A. increasing the role of intermediaries.
   B. establishing a barrier between investors and originating borrowers.
   C. allowing investors to tailor credit risk and interest rate risk exposures to meet their individual needs.
3. A benefit of securitization is the:
   A. reduction in disintermediation.
   B. simplification of debt obligations.
   C. creation of tradable securities with greater liquidity than the original loans.
4. Securitization benefits investors by:
   A. providing more direct access to a wider range of assets.
   B. reducing the inherent credit risk of pools of loans and receivables.
   C. eliminating cash flow timing risks of an ABS, such as contraction and extension risks.
5. In a securitization, the special purpose entity (SPE) is responsible for the:
   A. issuance of the asset-backed securities.
   B. collection of payments from the borrowers.
   C. recovery of underlying assets from delinquent borrowers.
6. In a securitization, the collateral is initially sold by the:
   A. issuer.
   B. depositor.
   C. underwriter.
7. A special purpose entity issues asset-backed securities in the following structure.

Bond Class	Par Value (€ millions)
A (senior)	200
B (subordinated)	20
C (subordinated)	5

At which of the following amounts of default in par value would Bond Class A experience a loss?
   A. €20 million
   B. €25 million
   C. €26 million

8. In a securitization, time tranching provides investors with the ability to choose between:
   A. extension and contraction risks.
   B. senior and subordinated bond classes.
   C. fully amortizing and partially amortizing loans.

9. The creation of bond classes with a waterfall structure for sharing losses is referred to as:
   A. time tranching.
   B. credit tranching.
   C. overcollateralization.

10. Which of the following statements related to securitization is correct?
   A. Time tranching addresses the uncertainty of a decline in interest rates.
   B. Securitizations are rarely structured to include both credit tranching and time tranching.
   C. Junior and senior bond classes differ in that junior classes can only be paid off at the bond's set maturity.

11. A goal of securitization is to:
   A. separate the seller's collateral from its credit ratings.
   B. uphold the absolute priority rule in bankruptcy reorganizations.
   C. account for collateral's primary influence on corporate bond credit spreads.

12. The last payment in a partially amortizing residential mortgage loan is *best* referred to as a:
   A. waterfall.
   B. principal repayment.
   C. balloon payment.

13. If a mortgage borrower makes prepayments without penalty to take advantage of falling interest rates, the lender will *most likely* experience:
   A. extension risk.
   B. contraction risk.
   C. yield maintenance.

14. Which of the following characteristics of a residential mortgage loan would *best* protect the lender from a strategic default by the borrower?
   A. Recourse
   B. A prepayment option
   C. Interest-only payments

15. William Marolf obtains a 5 million EUR mortgage loan from Bank Nederlandse. A year later the principal on the loan is 4 million EUR and Marolf defaults on the loan. Bank Nederlandse forecloses, sells the property for 2.5 million EUR, and is entitled to collect the 1.5 million EUR shortfall from Marolf. Marolf *most likely* had a:
   A. bullet loan.
   B. recourse loan.
   C. non-recourse loan.

16. Fran Martin obtains a non-recourse mortgage loan for $500,000. One year later, when the outstanding balance of the mortgage is $490,000, Martin cannot make his mortgage payments and defaults on the loan. The lender forecloses on the loan and sells the house for $315,000. What amount is the lender entitled to claim from Martin?
    A. $0.
    B. $175,000.
    C. $185,000.

17. A ballloon payment equal to a mortgage's original loan amount is a characteristic of a:
    A. bullet mortgage.
    B. fully amortizing mortgage.
    C. partially amortizing mortgage.

18. Which of the following statements is correct concerning mortgage loan defaults?
    A. A non-recourse jurisdiction poses higher default risks for lenders.
    B. In a non-recourse jurisdiction, strategic default will not affect the defaulting borrower's future access to credit.
    C. When a recourse loan defaults, the mortgaged property is the lender's sole source for recovery of the outstanding mortgage balance.

19. Which of the following describes a typical feature of a non-agency residential mortgage-backed security (RMBS)?
    A. Senior/subordinated structure
    B. A pool of conforming mortgages as collateral
    C. A guarantee by a government-sponsored enterprise

20. If interest rates increase, an investor who owns a mortgage pass-through security is *most likely* affected by:
    A. credit risk.
    B. extension risk.
    C. contraction risk.

21. Which of the following is *most likely* an advantage of collateralized mortgage obligations (CMOs)? CMOs can
    A. eliminate prepayment risk.
    B. be created directly from a pool of mortgage loans.
    C. meet the asset/liability requirements of institutional investors.

22. The longest-term tranche of a sequential-pay CMO is *most likely* to have the lowest:
    A. average life.
    B. extension risk.
    C. contraction risk.

23. The tranches in a collateralized mortgage obligation (CMO) that are *most likely* to provide protection for investors against both extension and contraction risk are:
    A. planned amortization class (PAC) tranches.
    B. support tranches.
    C. sequential-pay tranches.

24. Support tranches are *most* appropriate for investors who are:
    A. concerned about their exposure to extension risk.
    B. concerned about their exposure to concentration risk.
    C. willing to accept prepayment risk in exchange for higher returns.

25. In the context of mortgage-backed securities, a conditional prepayment rate (CPR) of 8% means that approximately 8% of the outstanding mortgage pool balance at the beginning of the year is expected to be prepaid:
    A. in the current month.
    B. by the end of the year.
    C. over the life of the mortgages.

26. For a mortgage pass-through security, which of the following risks *most likely* increases as interest rates decline?
    A. Balloon
    B. Extension
    C. Contraction

27. Compared with the weighted average coupon rate of its underlying pool of mortgages, the pass-through rate on a mortgage pass-through security is:
    A. lower.
    B. the same.
    C. higher.

28. The single monthly mortality rate (SMM) *most likely:*
    A. increases as extension risk rises.
    B. decreases as contraction risk falls.
    C. stays fixed over time when the standard prepayment model remains at 100 PSA.

29. Credit risk is an important consideration for commercial mortgage-backed securities (CMBS) if the CMBS are backed by mortgage loans that:
    A. are non-recourse.
    B. have call protection.
    C. have prepayment penalty points.

30. Which commercial mortgage-backed security (CMBS) characteristic causes a CMBS to trade more like a corporate bond than a residential mortgage-backed security (RMBS)?
    A. Call protection
    B. Internal credit enhancement
    C. Debt-service coverage ratio level

31. A commercial mortgage-backed security (CMBS) does not meet the debt-to-service coverage at the loan level necessary to achieve a desired credit rating. Which of the following features would *most likely* improve the credit rating of the CMBS?
    A. Subordination
    B. Call protection
    C. Balloon payments

32. If a default occurs in a non-recourse commercial mortgage-backed security (CMBS), the lender will *most likely:*
    A. recover prepayment penalty points paid by the borrower to offset losses.
    B. use only the proceeds received from the sale of the property to recover losses.
    C. initiate a claim against the borrower for any shortfall resulting from the sale of the property.

33. Which of the following investments is least subject to prepayment risk?
    A. Auto loan receivable–backed securities
    B. Commercial mortgage-backed securities (CMBS)
    C. Non-agency residential mortgage-backed securities (RMBS)

34. An excess spread account incorporated into a securitization is designed to limit:
    A. credit risk.
    B. extension risk.
    C. contraction risk.
35. Which of the following *best* describes the cash flow that owners of credit card receivable asset-backed securities receive during the lockout period?
    A. No cash flow
    B. Only principal payments collected
    C. Only finance charges collected and fees
36. Which type of asset-backed security is not affected by prepayment risk?
    A. Auto loan ABS
    B. Residential MBS
    C. Credit card receivable ABS
37. In auto loan ABS, the form of credit enhancement that *most likely* serves as the first line of loss protection is the:
    A. excess spread account.
    B. sequential pay structure.
    C. proceeds from repossession sales.
38. In credit card receivable ABS, principal cash flows can be altered only when the:
    A. lockout period expires.
    B. excess spread account is depleted.
    C. early amortization provision is triggered.
39. The CDO tranche with a credit rating status between senior and subordinated bond classes is called the:
    A. equity tranche.
    B. residual tranche.
    C. mezzanine tranche.
40. The key to a CDO's viability is the creation of a structure with a competitive return for the:
    A. senior tranche.
    B. mezzanine tranche.
    C. subordinated tranche.
41. When the collateral manager fails pre-specified risk tests, a CDO is:
    A. deleveraged by reducing the senior bond class.
    B. restructured to reduce its most expensive funding source.
    C. liquidated by paying off the bond classes in order of seniority.
42. Collateralized mortgage obligations (CMOs) are designed to:
    A. eliminate contraction risk in support tranches.
    B. distribute prepayment risk to various tranches.
    C. eliminate extension risk in planned amortization tranches.

CHAPTER 5

UNDERSTANDING FIXED INCOME RISK AND RETURN

LEARNING OUTCOMES

After completing this chapter, you will be able to do the following:

- calculate and interpret the sources of return from investing in a fixed-rate bond;
- define, calculate, and interpret Macaulay, modified, and effective durations;
- explain why effective duration is the most appropriate measure of interest rate risk for bonds with embedded options;
- define key rate duration and describe the use of key rate durations in measuring the sensitivity of bonds to changes in the shape of the benchmark yield curve;
- explain how a bond's maturity, coupon, and yield level affect its interest rate risk;
- calculate the duration of a portfolio and explain the limitations of portfolio duration;
- calculate and interpret the money duration of a bond and price value of a basis point (PVBP);
- calculate and interpret approximate convexity and distinguish between approximate and effective convexity;
- estimate the percentage price change of a bond for a specified change in yield, given the bond's approximate duration and convexity;
- describe how the term structure of yield volatility affects the interest rate risk of a bond;
- describe the relationships among a bond's holding period return, its duration, and the investment horizon;
- explain how changes in credit spread and liquidity affect yield-to-maturity of a bond and how duration and convexity can be used to estimate the price effect of the changes.

SUMMARY OVERVIEW

This chapter covers the risk and return characteristics of fixed-rate bonds. The focus is on the widely used measures of interest rate risk—duration and convexity. These statistics are used extensively in fixed income analysis. The following are the main points made in the chapter:

- The three sources of return on a fixed-rate bond purchased at par value are: (1) receipt of the promised coupon and principal payments on the scheduled dates, (2) reinvestment of coupon payments, and (3) potential capital gains, as well as losses, on the sale of the bond prior to maturity.
- For a bond purchased at a discount or premium, the rate of return also includes the effect of the price being "pulled to par" as maturity nears, assuming no default.
- The total return is the future value of reinvested coupon interest payments and the sale price (or redemption of principal if the bond is held to maturity).
- The horizon yield (or holding period rate of return) is the internal rate of return between the total return and purchase price of the bond.
- Coupon reinvestment risk increases with a higher coupon rate and a longer reinvestment time period.
- Capital gains and losses are measured from the carrying value of the bond and not from the purchase price. The carrying value includes the amortization of the discount or premium if the bond is purchased at a price below or above par value. The carrying value is any point on the constant-yield price trajectory.
- Interest income on a bond is the return associated with the passage of time. Capital gains and losses are the returns associated with a change in the value of a bond as indicated by a change in the yield-to-maturity.
- The two types of interest rate risk on a fixed-rate bond are coupon reinvestment risk and market price risk. These risks offset each other to a certain extent. An investor gains from higher rates on reinvested coupons but loses if the bond is sold at a capital loss because the price is below the constant-yield price trajectory. An investor loses from lower rates on reinvested coupon but gains if the bond is sold at a capital gain because the price is above the constant-yield price trajectory.
- Market price risk dominates coupon reinvestment risk when the investor has a short-term horizon (relative to the time-to-maturity on the bond).
- Coupon reinvestment risk dominates market price risk when the investor has a long-term horizon (relative to the time-to-maturity)—for instance, a buy-and-hold investor.
- Bond duration, in general, measures the sensitivity of the full price (including accrued interest) to a change in interest rates.
- Yield duration statistics measuring the sensitivity of a bond's full price to the bond's own yield-to-maturity include the Macaulay duration, modified duration, money duration, and price value of a basis point.
- Curve duration statistics measuring the sensitivity of a bond's full price to the benchmark yield curve are usually called "effective durations."
- Macaulay duration is the weighted average of the time to receipt of coupon interest and principal payments, in which the weights are the shares of the full price corresponding to

each payment. This statistic is annualized by dividing by the periodicity (number of coupon payments or compounding periods in a year).

- Modified duration provides a linear estimate of the percentage price change for a bond given a change in its yield-to-maturity.
- Approximate modified duration approaches modified duration as the change in the yield-to-maturity approaches zero.
- Effective duration is very similar to approximate modified duration. The difference is that approximate modified duration is a yield duration statistic that measures interest rate risk in terms of a change in the bond's own yield-to-maturity, whereas effective duration is a curve duration statistic that measures interest rate risk assuming a parallel shift in the benchmark yield curve.
- Key rate duration is a measure of a bond's sensitivity to a change in the benchmark yield curve at specific maturity segments. Key rate durations can be used to measure a bond's sensitivity to changes in the shape of the yield curve.
- Bonds with an embedded option do not have a meaningful internal rate of return because future cash flows are contingent on interest rates. Therefore, effective duration is the appropriate interest rate risk measure, not modified duration.
- The effective duration of a traditional (option-free) fixed-rate bond is its sensitivity to the benchmark yield curve, which can differ from its sensitivity to its own yield-to-maturity. Therefore, modified duration and effective duration on a traditional (option-free) fixed-rate bond are not necessarily equal.
- During a coupon period, Macaulay and modified durations decline smoothly in a "sawtooth" pattern, assuming the yield-to-maturity is constant. When the coupon payment is made, the durations jump upward.
- Macaulay and modified durations are inversely related to the coupon rate and the yield-to-maturity.
- Time-to-maturity and Macaulay and modified durations are *usually* positively related. They are *always* positively related on bonds priced at par or at a premium above par value. They are *usually* positively related on bonds priced at a discount below par value. The exception is on long-term, low-coupon bonds, on which it is possible to have a lower duration than on an otherwise comparable shorter-term bond.
- The presence of an embedded call option reduces a bond's effective duration compared with that of an otherwise comparable non-callable bond. The reduction in the effective duration is greater when interest rates are low and the issuer is more likely to exercise the call option.
- The presence of an embedded put option reduces a bond's effective duration compared with that of an otherwise comparable non-putable bond. The reduction in the effective duration is greater when interest rates are high and the investor is more likely to exercise the put option.
- The duration of a bond portfolio can be calculated in two ways: (1) the weighted average of the time to receipt of *aggregate* cash flows and (2) the weighted average of the durations of individual bonds that compose the portfolio.
- The first method to calculate portfolio duration is based on the cash flow yield, which is the internal rate of return on the aggregate cash flows. It cannot be used for bonds with embedded options or for floating-rate notes.
- The second method is simpler to use and quite accurate when the yield curve is relatively flat. Its main limitation is that it assumes a parallel shift in the yield curve in that the yields on all bonds in the portfolio change by the same amount.

- Money duration is a measure of the price change in terms of units of the currency in which the bond is denominated.
- The price value of a basis point (PVBP) is an estimate of the change in the full price of a bond given a 1 bp change in the yield-to-maturity.
- Modified duration is the primary, or first-order, effect on a bond's percentage price change given a change in the yield-to-maturity. Convexity is the secondary, or second-order, effect. It indicates the change in the modified duration as the yield-to-maturity changes.
- Money convexity is convexity times the full price of the bond. Combined with money duration, money convexity estimates the change in the full price of a bond in units of currency given a change in the yield-to-maturity.
- Convexity is a positive attribute for a bond. Other things being equal, a more convex bond appreciates in price more than a less convex bond when yields fall and depreciates less when yields rise.
- Effective convexity is the second-order effect on a bond price given a change in the benchmark yield curve. It is similar to approximate convexity. The difference is that approximate convexity is based on a yield-to-maturity change and effective convexity is based on a benchmark yield curve change.
- Callable bonds have negative effective convexity when interest rates are low. The increase in price when the benchmark yield is reduced is less in absolute value than the decrease in price when the benchmark yield is raised.
- The change in a bond price is the product of: (1) the impact per basis-point change in the yield-to-maturity and (2) the number of basis points in the yield change. The first factor is estimated by duration and convexity. The second factor depends on yield volatility.
- The investment horizon is essential in measuring the interest rate risk on a fixed-rate bond.
- For a particular assumption about yield volatility, the Macaulay duration indicates the investment horizon for which coupon reinvestment risk and market price risk offset each other. The assumption is a one-time parallel shift to the yield curve in which the yield-to-maturity and coupon reinvestment rates change by the same amount in the same direction.
- When the investment horizon is greater than the Macaulay duration of the bond, coupon reinvestment risk dominates price risk. The investor's risk is to lower interest rates. The duration gap is negative.
- When the investment horizon is equal to the Macaulay duration of the bond, coupon reinvestment risk offsets price risk. The duration gap is zero.
- When the investment horizon is less than the Macaulay duration of the bond, price risk dominates coupon reinvestment risk. The investor's risk is to higher interest rates. The duration gap is positive.
- Credit risk involves the probability of default and degree of recovery if default occurs, whereas liquidity risk refers to the transaction costs associated with selling a bond.
- For a traditional (option-free) fixed-rate bond, the same duration and convexity statistics apply if a change occurs in the benchmark yield or a change occurs in the spread. The change in the spread can result from a change in credit risk or liquidity risk.
- In practice, there often is interaction between changes in benchmark yields and in the spread over the benchmark.

PROBLEMS

1. A "buy-and-hold" investor purchases a fixed-rate bond at a discount and holds the security until it matures. Which of the following sources of return is *least likely* to contribute to the investor's total return over the investment horizon, assuming all payments are made as scheduled?
   A. Capital gain
   B. Principal payment
   C. Reinvestment of coupon payments

2. Which of the following sources of return is *most likely* exposed to interest rate risk for an investor of a fixed-rate bond who holds the bond until maturity?
   A. Capital gain or loss
   B. Redemption of principal
   C. Reinvestment of coupon payments

3. An investor purchases a bond at a price above par value. Two years later, the investor sells the bond. The resulting capital gain or loss is measured by comparing the price at which the bond is sold to the:
   A. carrying value.
   B. original purchase price.
   C. original purchase price value plus the amortized amount of the premium.

The following information relates to Problems 4–6

An investor purchases a nine-year, 7% annual coupon payment bond at a price equal to par value. After the bond is purchased and before the first coupon is received, interest rates increase to 8%. The investor sells the bond after five years. Assume that interest rates remain unchanged at 8% over the five-year holding period.

4. Per 100 of par value, the future value of the reinvested coupon payments at the end of the holding period is *closest* to:
   A. 35.00.
   B. 40.26.
   C. 41.07.

5. The capital gain/loss per 100 of par value resulting from the sale of the bond at the end of the five-year holding period is *closest* to a:
   A. loss of 8.45.
   B. loss of 3.31.
   C. gain of 2.75.

6. Assuming that all coupons are reinvested over the holding period, the investor's five-year horizon yield is *closest* to:
   A. 5.66%.
   B. 6.62%.
   C. 7.12%.

7. An investor buys a three-year bond with a 5% coupon rate paid annually. The bond, with a yield-to-maturity of 3%, is purchased at a price of 105.657223 per 100 of par value. Assuming a 5-basis point change in yield-to-maturity, the bond's approximate modified duration is *closest* to:
   A. 2.78.
   B. 2.86.
   C. 5.56.

8. Which of the following statements about duration is correct? A bond's:
   A. effective duration is a measure of yield duration.
   B. modified duration is a measure of curve duration.
   C. modified duration cannot be larger than its Macaulay duration (assuming a positive yield-to-maturity).

9. An investor buys a 6% annual payment bond with three years to maturity. The bond has a yield-to-maturity of 8% and is currently priced at 94.845806 per 100 of par. The bond's Macaulay duration is *closest* to:
   A. 2.62.
   B. 2.78.
   C. 2.83.

10. The interest rate risk of a fixed-rate bond with an embedded call option is *best* measured by:
    A. effective duration.
    B. modified duration.
    C. Macaulay duration.

11. Which of the following is *most* appropriate for measuring a bond's sensitivity to shaping risk?
    A. key rate duration
    B. effective duration
    C. modified duration

12. A Canadian pension fund manager seeks to measure the sensitivity of her pension liabilities to market interest rate changes. The manager determines the present value of the liabilities under three interest rate scenarios: a base rate of 7%, a 100 basis point increase in rates up to 8%, and a 100 basis point drop in rates down to 6%. The results of the manager's analysis are presented below:

Interest Rate Assumption	Present Value of Liabilities
6%	CAD510.1 million
7%	CAD455.4 million
8%	CAD373.6 million

The effective duration of the pension fund's liabilities is *closest* to:
   A. 1.49.
   B. 14.99.
   C. 29.97.

13. Which of the following statements about Macaulay duration is correct?
    A. A bond's coupon rate and Macaulay duration are positively related.
    B. A bond's Macaulay duration is inversely related to its yield-to-maturity.
    C. The Macaulay duration of a zero-coupon bond is less than its time-to-maturity.

14. Assuming no change in the credit risk of a bond, the presence of an embedded put option:
    A. reduces the effective duration of the bond.
    B. increases the effective duration of the bond.
    C. does not change the effective duration of the bond.

15. A bond portfolio consists of the following three fixed-rate bonds. Assume annual coupon payments and no accrued interest on the bonds. Prices are per 100 of par value.

Bond	Maturity	Market Value	Price	Coupon	Yield-to-Maturity	Modified Duration
A	6 years	170,000	85.0000	2.00%	4.95%	5.42
B	10 years	120,000	80.0000	2.40%	4.99%	8.44
C	15 years	100,000	100.0000	5.00%	5.00%	10.38

The bond portfolio's modified duration is *closest* to:
    A. 7.62.
    B. 8.08.
    C. 8.20.

16. A limitation of calculating a bond portfolio's duration as the weighted average of the yield durations of the individual bonds that compose the portfolio is that it:
    A. assumes a parallel shift to the yield curve.
    B. is less accurate when the yield curve is less steeply sloped.
    C. is not applicable to portfolios that have bonds with embedded options.

17. Using the information below, which bond has the *greatest* money duration per 100 of par value assuming annual coupon payments and no accrued interest?

Bond	Time-to-Maturity	Price Per 100 of Par Value	Coupon Rate	Yield-to-Maturity	Modified Duration
A	6 years	85.00	2.00%	4.95%	5.42
B	10 years	80.00	2.40%	4.99%	8.44
C	9 years	85.78	3.00%	5.00%	7.54

    A. Bond A
    B. Bond B
    C. Bond C

18. A bond with exactly nine years remaining until maturity offers a 3% coupon rate with annual coupons. The bond, with a yield-to-maturity of 5%, is priced at 85.784357 per 100 of par value. The estimated price value of a basis point for the bond is *closest* to:
    A. 0.0086.
    B. 0.0648.
    C. 0.1295.

19. The "second-order" effect on a bond's percentage price change given a change in yield-to-maturity can be *best* described as:
    A. duration.
    B. convexity.
    C. yield volatility.

20. A bond is currently trading for 98.722 per 100 of par value. If the bond's yield-to-maturity (YTM) rises by 10 basis points, the bond's full price is expected to fall to 98.669. If the bond's YTM decreases by 10 basis points, the bond's full price is expected to increase to 98.782. The bond's approximate convexity is *closest* to:
    A. 0.071.
    B. 70.906.
    C. 1,144.628.

21. A bond has an annual modified duration of 7.020 and annual convexity of 65.180. If the bond's yield-to-maturity decreases by 25 basis points, the expected percentage price change is *closest* to:
    A. 1.73%.
    B. 1.76%.
    C. 1.78%.

22. A bond has an annual modified duration of 7.140 and annual convexity of 66.200. The bond's yield-to-maturity is expected to increase by 50 basis points. The expected percentage price change is *closest* to:
    A. −3.40%.
    B. −3.49%.
    C. −3.57%.

23. Which of the following statements relating to yield volatility is *most* accurate? If the term structure of yield volatility is downward sloping, then:
    A. short-term rates are higher than long-term rates.
    B. long-term yields are more stable than short-term yields.
    C. short-term bonds will always experience greater price fluctuation than long-term bonds.

24. The holding period for a bond at which the coupon reinvestment risk offsets the market price risk is *best* approximated by:
    A. duration gap.
    B. modified duration.
    C. Macaulay duration.

25. When the investor's investment horizon is less than the Macaulay duration of the bond she owns:
    A. the investor is hedged against interest rate risk.
    B. reinvestment risk dominates, and the investor is at risk of lower rates.
    C. market price risk dominates, and the investor is at risk of higher rates.

26. An investor purchases an annual coupon bond with a 6% coupon rate and exactly 20 years remaining until maturity at a price equal to par value. The investor's investment horizon is eight years. The approximate modified duration of the bond is 11.470 years. The duration gap at the time of purchase is *closest* to:
    A. −7.842.
    B. 3.470.
    C. 4.158.

27. A manufacturing company receives a ratings upgrade and the price increases on its fixed-rate bond. The price increase was *most likely* caused by a(n):
    A. decrease in the bond's credit spread.
    B. increase in the bond's liquidity spread.
    C. increase of the bond's underlying benchmark rate.

CHAPTER 6

FUNDAMENTALS OF CREDIT ANALYSIS

LEARNING OUTCOMES

After completing this chapter, you will be able to do the following:

- describe credit risk and credit-related risks affecting corporate bonds;
- describe default probability and loss severity as components of credit risk;
- describe seniority rankings of corporate debt and explain the potential violation of the priority of claims in a bankruptcy proceeding;
- distinguish between corporate issuer credit ratings and issue credit ratings and describe the rating agency practice of "notching";
- explain risks in relying on ratings from credit rating agencies;
- explain the four Cs (Capacity, Collateral, Covenants, and Character) of traditional credit analysis;
- calculate and interpret financial ratios used in credit analysis;
- evaluate the credit quality of a corporate bond issuer and a bond of that issuer, given key financial ratios of the issuer and the industry;
- describe factors that influence the level and volatility of yield spreads;
- explain special considerations when evaluating the credit of high yield, sovereign, and non-sovereign government debt issuers and issues.

SUMMARY OVERVIEW

In this chapter, we introduced readers to the basic principles of credit analysis. We described the importance of the credit markets and credit and credit-related risks. We discussed the role and importance of credit ratings and the methodology associated with assigning ratings, as well as the risks of relying on credit ratings. The chapter covered the key components of credit analysis and the financial measure used to help assess creditworthiness.

We also discussed risk versus return when investing in credit and how spread changes affect holding period returns. In addition, we addressed the special considerations to take into account when doing credit analysis of high-yield companies, sovereign borrowers, and non-sovereign government bonds.

- Credit risk is the risk of loss resulting from the borrower failing to make full and timely payments of interest and/or principal.
- The key components of credit risk are risk of default and loss severity in the event of default. The product of the two is expected loss. Investors in higher-quality bonds tend not to focus on loss severity because default risk for those securities is low.
- Loss severity equals (1 − Recovery rate).
- Credit-related risks include downgrade risk (also called credit migration risk) and market liquidity risk. Either of these can cause yield spreads—yield premiums—to rise and bond prices to fall.
- Downgrade risk refers to a decline in an issuer's creditworthiness. Downgrades will cause its bonds to trade with wider yield spreads and thus lower prices.
- Market liquidity risk refers to a widening of the bid–ask spread on an issuer's bonds. Lower-quality bonds tend to have greater market liquidity risk than higher-quality bonds, and during times of market or financial stress, market liquidity risk rises.
- The composition of an issuer's debt and equity is referred to as its "capital structure." Debt ranks ahead of all types of equity with respect to priority of payment, and within the debt component of the capital structure, there can be varying levels of seniority.
- With respect to priority of claims, secured debt ranks ahead of unsecured debt, and within unsecured debt, senior debt ranks ahead of subordinated debt. In the typical case, all of an issuer's bonds have the same probability of default due to cross-default provisions in most indentures. Higher priority of claim implies higher recovery rate—lower loss severity—in the event of default.
- For issuers with more complex corporate structures—for example, a parent holding company that has operating subsidiaries—debt at the holding company is structurally subordinated to the subsidiary debt, although the possibility of more diverse assets and earnings streams from other sources could still result in the parent having higher effective credit quality than a particular subsidiary.
- Recovery rates can vary greatly by issuer and industry. They are influenced by the composition of an issuer's capital structure, where in the economic and credit cycle the default occurred, and what the market's view of the future prospects is for the issuer and its industry.
- The priority of claims in bankruptcy is not always absolute. It can be influenced by several factors, including some leeway accorded to bankruptcy judges, government involvement, or a desire on the part of the more senior creditors to settle with the more junior creditors and allow the issuer to emerge from bankruptcy as a going concern, rather than risking smaller and delayed recovery in the event of a liquidation of the borrower.
- Credit rating agencies, such as Moody's, Standard & Poor's, and Fitch, play a central role in the credit markets. Nearly every bond issued in the broad debt markets carries credit ratings, which are opinions about a bond issue's creditworthiness. Credit ratings enable investors to compare the credit risk of debt issues and issuers within a given industry, across industries, and across geographic markets.
- Bonds rated Aaa to Baa3 by Moody's and AAA to BBB− by Standard & Poor's (S&P) and/or Fitch (higher to lower) are referred to as "investment grade." Bonds rated lower than that—Ba1 or lower by Moody's and BB+ or lower by S&P and/or Fitch—are referred to

as "below investment grade" or "speculative grade." Below-investment-grade bonds are also called "high-yield" or "junk" bonds.

- The rating agencies rate both issuers and issues. Issuer ratings are meant to address an issuer's overall creditworthiness—its risk of default. Ratings for issues incorporate such factors as their rankings in the capital structure.
- The rating agencies will notch issue ratings up or down to account for such factors as capital structure ranking for secured or subordinated bonds, reflecting different recovery rates in the event of default. Ratings may also be notched due to structural subordination.
- There are risks in relying too much on credit agency ratings. Creditworthiness may change over time, and initial/current ratings do not necessarily reflect the creditworthiness of an issuer or bond over an investor's holding period. Valuations often adjust before ratings change, and the notching process may not adequately reflect the price decline of a bond that is lower ranked in the capital structure. Because ratings primarily reflect the probability of default but not necessarily the severity of loss given default, bonds with the same rating may have significantly different expected losses (default probability times loss severity). And like analysts, credit rating agencies may have difficulty forecasting certain credit-negative outcomes, such as adverse litigation, leveraging corporate transactions, and such low probability/high severity events as earthquakes and hurricanes.
- The role of corporate credit analysis is to assess the company's ability to make timely payments of interest and to repay principal at maturity.
- Credit analysis is similar to equity analysis. It is important to understand, however, that bonds are contracts and that management's duty to bondholders and other creditors is limited to the terms of the contract. In contrast, management's duty to shareholders is to act in their best interest by trying to maximize the value of the company—perhaps even at the expense of bondholders at times.
- Credit analysts tend to focus more on the downside risk given the asymmetry of risk/return, whereas equity analysts focus more on upside opportunity from earnings growth, and so on.
- The "4 Cs" of credit—capacity, collateral, covenants, and character—provide a useful framework for evaluating credit risk.
- Credit analysis focuses on an issuer's ability to generate cash flow. The analysis starts with an industry assessment—structure and fundamentals—and continues with an analysis of an issuer's competitive position, management strategy, and track record.
- Credit measures are used to calculate an issuer's creditworthiness, as well as to compare its credit quality with peer companies. Key credit ratios focus on leverage and interest coverage and use such measures as EBITDA, free cash flow, funds from operations, interest expense and balance sheet debt.
- An issuer's ability to access liquidity is also an important consideration in credit analysis.
- The higher the credit risk, the greater the offered/required yield and potential return demanded by investors. Over time, bonds with more credit risk offer higher returns but with greater volatility of return than bonds with lower credit risk.
- The yield on a credit-risky bond comprises the yield on a default risk–free bond with a comparable maturity plus a yield premium, or "spread," that comprises a credit spread and a liquidity premium. That spread is intended to compensate investors for credit risk—risk of default and loss severity in the event of default—and the credit-related risks that can cause spreads to widen and prices to decline—downgrade or credit migration risk and market liquidity risk.

Yield spread = Liquidity premium + Credit spread.

- In times of financial market stress, the liquidity premium can increase sharply, causing spreads to widen on all credit-risky bonds, with lower-quality issuers most affected. In times of credit improvement or stability, however, credit spreads can narrow sharply as well, providing attractive investment returns.
- Credit curves—the plot of yield spreads for a given bond issuer across the yield curve—are typically upward sloping, with the exception of high premium-priced bonds and distressed bonds, where credit curves can be inverted because of the fear of default, when all creditors at a given ranking in the capital structure will receive the same recovery rate without regard to debt maturity.
- The impact of spread changes on holding period returns for credit-risky bonds is a product of two primary factors: the basis point spread change and the sensitivity of price to yield as reflected by (end-of-period) modified duration and convexity. Spread narrowing enhances holding period returns, whereas spread widening has a negative impact on holding period returns. Longer-duration bonds have greater price and return sensitivity to changes in spread than shorter-duration bonds.

$$\text{Price impact} \approx -(\text{MDur} \times \Delta\text{Spread}) + \tfrac{1}{2}\text{Cvx} \times (\Delta\text{Spread})^2$$

- For high-yield bonds, with their greater risk of default, more emphasis should be placed on an issuer's sources of liquidity, as well as on its debt structure and corporate structure. Credit risk can vary greatly across an issuer's debt structure depending on the seniority ranking. Many high-yield companies have complex capital structures, resulting in different levels of credit risk depending on where the debt resides.
- Covenant analysis is especially important for high-yield bonds. Key covenants include payment restrictions, limitation on liens, change of control, coverage maintenance tests (often limited to bank loans), and any guarantees from restricted subsidiaries. Covenant language can be very technical and legalistic, so it may help to seek legal or expert assistance.
- An equity-like approach to high-yield analysis can be helpful. Calculating and comparing enterprise value with EBITDA and debt/EBITDA can show a level of equity "cushion" or support beneath an issuer's debt.
- Sovereign credit analysis includes assessing both an issuer's ability and willingness to pay its debt obligations. Willingness to pay is important because, due to sovereign immunity, a sovereign government cannot be forced to pay its debts.
- In assessing sovereign credit risk, a helpful framework is to focus on five broad areas: (1) institutional effectiveness and political risks, (2) economic structure and growth prospects, (3) external liquidity and international investment position, (4) fiscal performance, flexibility, and debt burden, and (5) monetary flexibility.
- Among the characteristics of a high-quality sovereign credit are the absence of corruption and/or challenges to political framework; governmental checks and balances; respect for rule of law and property rights; commitment to honor debts; high per capita income with stable, broad-based growth prospects; control of a reserve or actively traded currency; currency flexibility; low foreign debt and foreign financing needs relative to receipts in foreign currencies; stable or declining ratio of debt to GDP; low debt service as a percent of revenue; low ratio of net debt to GDP; operationally independent central bank; track record of low and stable inflation; and a well-developed banking system and active money market.
- Non-sovereign or local government bonds, including municipal bonds, are typically either general obligation bonds or revenue bonds.
- General obligation (GO) bonds are backed by the taxing authority of the issuing non-sovereign government. The credit analysis of GO bonds has some similarities to sovereign

analysis—debt burden per capita versus income per capita, tax burden, demographics, and economic diversity. Underfunded and "off-balance-sheet" liabilities, such as pensions for public employees and retirees, are debt-like in nature.
- Revenue-backed bonds support specific projects, such as toll roads, bridges, airports, and other infrastructure. The creditworthiness comes from the revenues generated by usage fees and tolls levied.

PROBLEMS

1. The risk that a bond's creditworthiness declines is *best* described by:
   A. credit migration risk.
   B. market liquidity risk.
   C. spread widening risk.
2. Stedsmart Ltd and Fignermo Ltd are alike with respect to financial and operating characteristics, except that Stedsmart Ltd has less publicly traded debt outstanding than Fignermo Ltd. Stedsmart Ltd is *most likely* to have:
   A. no market liquidity risk.
   B. lower market liquidity risk.
   C. higher market liquidity risk.
3. In the event of default, the recovery rate of which of the following bonds would *most likely* be the highest?
   A. First mortgage debt
   B. Senior unsecured debt
   C. Junior subordinate debt
4. During bankruptcy proceedings of a firm, the priority of claims was not strictly adhered to. Which of the following is the *least likely* explanation for this outcome?
   A. Senior creditors compromised.
   B. The value of secured assets was less than the amount of the claims.
   C. A judge's order resulted in actual claims not adhering to strict priority of claims.
5. A fixed income analyst is *least likely* to conduct an independent analysis of credit risk because credit rating agencies:
   A. may at times mis-rate issues.
   B. often lag the market in pricing credit risk.
   C. cannot foresee future debt-financed acquisitions.
6. If goodwill makes up a large percentage of a company's total assets, this *most likely* indicates that:
   A. the company has low free cash flow before dividends.
   B. there is a low likelihood that the market price of the company's common stock is below book value.
   C. a large percentage of the company's assets are not of high quality.
7. In order to analyze the **collateral** of a company a credit analyst should assess the:
   A. cash flows of the company.
   B. soundness of management's strategy.
   C. value of the company's assets in relation to the level of debt.

8. In order to determine the **capacity** of a company, it would be *most* appropriate to analyze the:
   A. company's strategy.
   B. growth prospects of the industry.
   C. aggressiveness of the company's accounting policies.

9. A credit analyst is evaluating the creditworthiness of three companies: a construction company, a travel and tourism company, and a beverage company. Both the construction and travel and tourism companies are cyclical, whereas the beverage company is non-cyclical. The construction company has the highest debt level of the three companies. The highest credit risk is *most likely* exhibited by the:
   A. construction company.
   B. beverage company.
   C. travel and tourism company.

10. Based on the information provided in Exhibit 1, the EBITDA interest coverage ratio of Adidas AG is *closest* to:
    A. 7.91x.
    B. 10.12x.
    C. 12.99x.

EXHIBIT 1   Adidas AG Excerpt from Consolidated Income Statement in a given year (€ in millions)

Gross profit	5,730
Royalty and commission income	100
Other operating income	110
Other operating expenses	5,046
Operating profit	894
Interest income	25
Interest expense	113
Income before taxes	806
Income taxes	238
Net income	568

Additional information:
Depreciation and amortization: €249 million

Source: Adidas AG Annual Financial Statements, December 2010

11. The following information is from the annual report of Adidas AG for December 2010:
    • Depreciation and amortization: €249 million
    • Total assets: €10,618 million
    • Total debt: €1,613 million
    • Shareholders' equity: €4,616 million

    The debt/capital ratio of Adidas AG is *closest* to:
    A. 15.19%.
    B. 25.90%.
    C. 34.94%.

12. Funds from operations (FFO) of Pay Handle Ltd increased in 2011. In 2011 the total debt of the company remained unchanged, while additional common shares were issued. Pay Handle Ltd's ability to service its debt in 2011, as compared to 2010, *most likely*:
    A. improved.
    B. worsened.
    C. remained the same.

13. Based on the information in Exhibit 2, Grupa Zywiec SA's credit risk is *most likely*:
    A. lower than the industry.
    B. higher than the industry.
    C. the same as the industry.

EXHIBIT 2   European Food, Beverage, and Tobacco Industry and Grupa Zywiec SA Selected Financial Ratios for 2010

	Total debt/Total capital (%)	FFO/Total debt (%)	Return on capital (%)	Total debt/ EBITDA (x)	EBITDA interest coverage (x)
Grupa Zywiec SA	47.1	77.5	19.6	1.2	17.7
Industry Median	**42.4**	**23.6**	**6.55**	**2.85**	**6.45**

14. Based on the information in Exhibit 3, the credit rating of Davide Campari-Milano S.p.A. is *most likely*:
    A. lower than Associated British Foods plc.
    B. higher than Associated British Foods plc.
    C. the same as Associated British Foods plc.

EXHIBIT 3   European Food, Beverage, and Tobacco Industry; Associated British Foods plc; and Davide Campari-Milano S.p.A. Selected Financial Ratios, 2010

Company	Total debt/total capital (%)	FFO/total debt (%)	Return on capital (%)	Total debt/ EBITDA (x)	EBITDA interest coverage (x)
Associated British Foods plc	0.2	84.3	0.1	1.0	13.9
Davide Campari-Milano S.p.A.	42.9	22.9	8.2	3.2	3.2
European Food, Beverage, and Tobacco Median	**42.4**	**23.6**	**6.55**	**2.85**	**6.45**

15. Holding all other factors constant, the *most likely* effect of low demand and heavy new issue supply on bond yield spreads is that yield spreads will:
    A. widen.
    B. tighten.
    C. not be affected.

16. Credit risk of a corporate bond is *best* described as the:
    A. risk that an issuer's creditworthiness deteriorates.
    B. probability that the issuer fails to make full and timely payments.
    C. risk of loss resulting from the issuer failing to make full and timely payments.

17. The risk that the price at which investors can actually transact differs from the quoted price in the market is called:
    A. spread risk.
    B. credit migration risk.
    C. market liquidity risk.

18. Loss severity is *best* described as the:
    A. default probability multiplied by the loss given default.
    B. portion of a bond's value recovered by bondholders in the event of default.
    C. portion of a bond's value, including unpaid interest, an investor loses in the event of default.

19. The two components of credit risk are default probability and:
    A. spread risk.
    B. loss severity.
    C. market liquidity risk.

20. For a high-quality debt issuer with a large amount of publicly traded debt, bond investors tend to devote *most* effort to assessing the issuer's:
    A. default risk.
    B. loss severity.
    C. market liquidity risk.

21. The expected loss for a given debt instrument is estimated as the product of default probability and:
    A. (1 + Recovery rate).
    B. (1 − Recovery rate).
    C. 1/(1 + Recovery rate).

22. The priority of claims for senior subordinated debt is:
    A. lower than for senior unsecured debt.
    B. the same as for senior unsecured debt.
    C. higher than for senior unsecured debt.

23. A senior unsecured credit instrument holds a higher priority of claims than one ranked as:
    A. mortgage debt.
    B. second lien loan.
    C. senior subordinated.

24. In a bankruptcy proceeding, when the absolute priority of claims is enforced:
    A. senior subordinated creditors rank above second lien holders.
    B. preferred equity shareholders rank above unsecured creditors.
    C. creditors with a secured claim have the first right to the value of that specific property.

25. In the event of default, which of the following is *most likely* to have the highest recovery rate?
    A. Second lien
    B. Senior unsecured
    C. Senior subordinated

26. The process of moving credit ratings of different issues up or down from the issuer rating in response to different payment priorities is *best* described as:
    A. notching.
    B. structural subordination.
    C. cross-default provisions.

27. The factor considered by rating agencies when a corporation has debt at both its parent holding company and operating subsidiaries is *best* referred to as:
    A. credit migration risk.
    B. corporate family rating.
    C. structural subordination.

28. Which type of security is *most likely* to have the same rating as the issuer?
    A. Preferred stock
    B. Senior secured bond
    C. Senior unsecured bond
29. Which of the following corporate debt instruments has the highest seniority ranking?
    A. Second lien
    B. Senior unsecured
    C. Senior subordinated
30. An issuer credit rating usually applies to a company's:
    A. secured debt.
    B. subordinated debt.
    C. senior unsecured debt.
31. The rating agency process whereby the credit ratings on issues are moved up or down from the issuer rating *best* describes:
    A. notching.
    B. pari passu ranking.
    C. cross-default provisions.
32. The notching adjustment for corporate bonds rated Aa2/AA is *most likely*:
    A. larger than the notching adjustment for corporate bonds rated B2/B.
    B. the same as the notching adjustment for corporate bonds rated B2/B.
    C. smaller than the notching adjustment for corporate bonds rated B2/B.
33. Which of the following statements about credit ratings is *most accurate*?
    A. Credit ratings can migrate over time.
    B. Changes in bond credit ratings precede changes in bond prices.
    C. Credit ratings are focused on expected loss rather than risk of default.
34. Which industry characteristic *most likely* has a positive effect on a company's ability to service debt?
    A. Low barriers to entry in the industry
    B. High number of suppliers to the industry
    C. Broadly dispersed market share among large number of companies in the industry
35. When determining the capacity of a borrower to service debt, a credit analyst should begin with an examination of:
    A. industry structure.
    B. industry fundamentals.
    C. company fundamentals.
36. Which of the following accounting issues should *mostly likely* be considered a character warning flag in credit analysis?
    A. Expensing items immediately
    B. Changing auditors infrequently
    C. Significant off-balance-sheet financing
37. In credit analysis, capacity is *best* described as the:
    A. quality of management.
    B. ability of the borrower to make its debt payments on time.
    C. quality and value of the assets supporting an issuer's indebtedness.
38. Among the Four Cs of credit analysis, the recognition of revenue prematurely *most likely* reflects a company's:
    A. character.
    B. covenants.
    C. collateral.

Use the following Exhibit for Questions 39 and 40

EXHIBIT 4   Industrial Comparative Ratio Analysis, Year 20XX

	EBITDA Margin (%)	Return on Capital (%)	EBIT/Interest Expense (×)	EBITDA/ Interest Expense (×)	Debt/ EBITDA (×)	Debt/Capital (%)
Company A	25.1	25.0	15.9	19.6	1.6	35.2
Company B	29.6	36.3	58.2	62.4	0.5	15.9
Company C	21.8	16.6	8.9	12.4	2.5	46.3

39. Based on only the leverage ratios in Exhibit 4, the company with the *highest* credit risk is:
    A. Company A.
    B. Company B.
    C. Company C.
40. Based on only the coverage ratios in Exhibit 4, the company with the *highest* credit quality is:
    A. Company A.
    B. Company B.
    C. Company C.

Use the following Exhibits for Questions 41 and 42

EXHIBIT 5   Consolidated Income Statement (£ millions)

	Company X	Company Y
Net revenues	50.7	83.7
Operating expenses	49.6	70.4
Operating income	1.1	13.3
Interest income	0.0	0.0
Interest expense	0.6	0.8
Income before income taxes	0.5	12.5
Provision for income taxes	−0.2	−3.5
Net income	0.3	9.0

EXHIBIT 6   Consolidated Balance Sheets (£ millions)

	Company X	Company Y
ASSETS		
Current assets	10.3	21.9
Property, plant, and equipment, net	3.5	20.1
Goodwill	8.3	85.0
Other assets	0.9	5.1
Total assets	23.0	132.1
LIABILITIES AND SHAREHOLDERS' EQUITY		
Current liabilities		
Accounts payable and accrued expenses	8.4	16.2
Short-term debt	0.5	8.7
Total current liabilities	8.9	24.9
Long-term debt	11.7	21.1
Other non-current liabilities	1.1	22.1
Total liabilities	21.7	68.1
Total shareholders' equity	1.3	64.0
Total liabilities and shareholders' equity	23.0	132.1

EXHIBIT 7   Consolidated Statements of Cash Flow (£ millions)

	Company X	Company Y
CASH FLOWS FROM OPERATING ACTIVITIES		
Net income	0.3	9.0
Depreciation	1.0	3.8
Goodwill impairment	2.0	1.6
Changes in working capital	0.0	−0.4
Net cash provided by operating activities	3.3	14.0
CASH FLOWS FROM INVESTING ACTIVITIES		
Additions to property and equipment	−1.0	−4.0
Additions to marketable securities	−0.1	0.0
Proceeds from sale of property and equipment	0.2	2.9
Proceeds from sale of marketable securities	0.3	0.0
Net cash used in investing activities	−0.6	−1.1

EXHIBIT 7 (Continued)

	Company X	Company Y
CASH FLOWS FROM FINANCING ACTIVITIES		
Repurchase of common stock	−1.5	−4.0
Dividends to shareholders	−0.3	−6.1
Change in short-term debt	0.0	−3.4
Additions to long-term debt	3.9	3.9
Reductions in long-term debt	−3.4	−2.5
Net cash − financing activities	−1.3	−12.1
NET INCREASE IN CASH AND CASH EQUIVALENTS	1.4	0.8

41. Based on Exhibits 5–7, in comparison to Company X, Company Y has a higher:
    A. debt/capital ratio.
    B. debt/EBITDA ratio.
    C. free cash flow after dividends/debt ratio.
42. Based on Exhibits 5–7, in comparison to Company Y, Company X has greater:
    A. leverage.
    B. interest coverage.
    C. operating profit margin.

43. Credit yield spreads *most likely* widen in response to:
    A. high demand for bonds.
    B. weak performance of equities.
    C. strengthening economic conditions.
44. The factor that *most likely* results in corporate credit spreads widening is:
    A. an improving credit cycle.
    B. weakening economic conditions.
    C. a period of high demand for bonds.
45. Credit spreads are *most likely* to widen:
    A. in a strengthening economy.
    B. as the credit cycle improves.
    C. in periods of heavy new issue supply and low borrower demand.
46. Which of the following factors in credit analysis is more important for general obligation non-sovereign government debt than for sovereign debt?
    A. Per capita income
    B. Power to levy and collect taxes
    C. Requirement to balance an operating budget
47. In contrast to high-yield credit analysis, investment-grade analysis is *more likely* to rely on:
    A. spread risk.
    B. an assessment of bank credit facilities.
    C. matching of liquidity sources to upcoming debt maturities.
48. Which of the following factors would *best* justify a decision to avoid investing in a country's sovereign debt?
    A. Freely floating currency
    B. A population that is not growing
    C. Suitable checks and balances in policymaking

CHAPTER 7

THE TERM STRUCTURE AND INTEREST RATE DYNAMICS

LEARNING OUTCOMES

After completing this chapter, you will be able to do the following:

- describe relationships among spot rates, forward rates, yield to maturity, expected and realized returns on bonds, and the shape of the yield curve;
- describe the forward pricing and forward rate models and calculate forward and spot prices and rates using those models;
- describe how zero-coupon rates (spot rates) may be obtained from the par curve by bootstrapping;
- describe the assumptions concerning the evolution of spot rates in relation to forward rates implicit in active bond portfolio management;
- describe the strategy of riding the yield curve;
- explain the swap rate curve and why and how market participants use it in valuation;
- calculate and interpret the swap spread for a given maturity;
- describe the Z-spread;
- describe the TED and Libor–OIS spreads;
- explain traditional theories of the term structure of interest rates and describe the implications of each theory for forward rates and the shape of the yield curve;
- describe modern term structure models and how they are used;
- explain how a bond's exposure to each of the factors driving the yield curve can be measured and how these exposures can be used to manage yield curve risks;
- explain the maturity structure of yield volatilities and their effect on price volatility.

SUMMARY OVERVIEW

- The spot rate for a given maturity can be expressed as a geometric average of the short-term rate and a series of forward rates.
- Forward rates are above (below) spot rates when the spot curve is upward (downward) sloping, whereas forward rates are equal to spot rates when the spot curve is flat.
- If forward rates are realized, then all bonds, regardless of maturity, will have the same one-period realized return, which is the first-period spot rate.
- If the spot rate curve is upward sloping and is unchanged, then each bond "rolls down" the curve and earns the forward rate that rolls out of its pricing (i.e., a T^*-period zero-coupon bond earns the T^*-period forward rate as it rolls down to be a $T^* - 1$ period security). This implies an expected return in excess of short-maturity bonds (i.e., a term premium) for longer-maturity bonds if the yield curve is upward sloping.
- Active bond portfolio management is consistent with the expectation that today's forward curve does not accurately reflect future spot rates.
- The swap curve provides another measure of the time value of money.
- The swap markets are significant internationally because swaps are frequently used to hedge interest rate risk exposure.
- The swap spread, the I-spread, and the Z-spread are bond quoting conventions that can be used to determine a bond's price.
- Swap curves and Treasury curves can differ because of differences in their credit exposures, liquidity, and other supply/demand factors.
- The local expectations theory, liquidity preference theory, segmented markets theory, and preferred habitat theory provide traditional explanations for the shape of the yield curve.
- Modern finance seeks to provide models for the shape of the yield curve and the use of the yield curve to value bonds (including those with embedded options) and bond-related derivatives. General equilibrium and arbitrage-free models are the two major types of such models.
- Arbitrage-free models are frequently used to value bonds with embedded options. Unlike equilibrium models, arbitrage-free models begin with the observed market prices of a reference set of financial instruments, and the underlying assumption is that the reference set is correctly priced.
- Historical yield curve movements suggest that they can be explained by a linear combination of three principal movements: level, steepness, and curvature.
- The volatility term structure can be measured using historical data and depicts yield curve risk.
- The sensitivity of a bond value to yield curve changes may make use of effective duration, key rate durations, or sensitivities to parallel, steepness, and curvature movements. Using key rate durations or sensitivities to parallel, steepness, and curvature movements allows one to measure and manage shaping risk.

PROBLEMS

1. Given spot rates for one-, two-, and three-year zero coupon bonds, how many forward rates can be calculated?
2. Give two interpretations for the following forward rate: The two-year forward rate one year from now is 2%.

3. Describe the relationship between forward rates and spot rates if the yield curve is flat.
4. A. Define the yield to maturity for a coupon bond.
   B. Is it possible for a coupon bond to earn less than the yield to maturity if held to maturity?
5. If a bond trader believes that current forward rates overstate future spot rates, how might he or she profit from that conclusion?
6. Explain the strategy of riding the yield curve.
7. What are the advantages of using the swap curve as a benchmark of interest rates relative to a government bond yield curve?
8. Describe how the Z-spread can be used to price a bond.
9. What is the TED spread and what type of risk does it measure?
10. According to the local expectations theory, what would be the difference in the one-month total return if an investor purchased a five-year zero-coupon bond versus a two-year zero-coupon bond?
11. Compare the segmented market and the preferred habitat term structure theories.
12. A. List the three factors that have empirically been observed to affect Treasury security returns and explain how each of these factors affects returns on Treasury securities.
    B. What has been observed to be the most important factor in affecting Treasury returns?
    C. Which measures of yield curve risk can measure shaping risk?
13. Which forward rate cannot be computed from the one-, two-, three-, and four-year spot rates? The rate for a:
    A. one-year loan beginning in two years.
    B. two-year loan beginning in two years.
    C. three-year loan beginning in two years.
14. Consider spot rates for three zero-coupon bonds: $r(1) = 3\%$, $r(2) = 4\%$, and $r(3) = 5\%$. Which statement is correct? The forward rate for a one-year loan beginning in one year will be:
    A. less than the forward rate for a one-year loan beginning in two years.
    B. greater than the forward rate for a two-year loan beginning in one year.
    C. greater than the forward rate for a one-year loan beginning in two years.
15. If one-period forward rates are decreasing with maturity, the yield curve is *most likely*:
    A. flat.
    B. upward sloping.
    C. downward sloping.

The following information relates to Questions 16–29

A one-year zero-coupon bond yields 4.0%. The two- and three-year zero-coupon bonds yield 5.0% and 6.0%, respectively.

16. The rate for a one-year loan beginning in one year is *closest* to:
    A. 4.5%.
    B. 5.0%.
    C. 6.0%.
17. The forward rate for a two-year loan beginning in one year is *closest* to:
    A. 5.0%.
    B. 6.0%.
    C. 7.0%.

18. The forward rate for a one-year loan beginning in two years is *closest* to:
    A. 6.0%.
    B. 7.0%.
    C. 8.0%.
19. The five-year spot rate is not given above; however, the forward price for a two-year zero-coupon bond beginning in three years is known to be 0.8479. The price today of a five-year zero-coupon bond is *closest* to:
    A. 0.7119.
    B. 0.7835.
    C. 0.9524.
20. The one-year spot rate $r(1) = 4\%$, the forward rate for a one-year loan beginning in one year is 6%, and the forward rate for a one-year loan beginning in two years is 8%. Which of the following rates is *closest* to the three-year spot rate?
    A. 4.0%
    B. 6.0%
    C. 8.0%
21. The one-year spot rate $r(1) = 5\%$ and the forward price for a one-year zero-coupon bond beginning in one year is 0.9346. The spot price of a two-year zero-coupon bond is *closest* to:
    A. 0.87.
    B. 0.89.
    C. 0.93.
22. In a typical interest rate swap contract, the swap rate is *best* described as the interest rate for the:
    A. fixed-rate leg of the swap.
    B. floating-rate leg of the swap.
    C. difference between the fixed and floating legs of the swap.
23. A two-year fixed-for-floating Libor swap is 1.00% and the two-year US Treasury bond is yielding 0.63%. The swap spread is *closest* to:
    A. 37 bps.
    B. 100 bps.
    C. 163 bps.
24. The swap spread is quoted as 50 bps. If the five-year US Treasury bond is yielding 2%, the rate paid by the fixed payer in a five-year interest rate swap is *closest* to:
    A. 0.50%.
    B. 1.50%.
    C. 2.50%.
25. If the three-month T-bill rate drops and the Libor rate remains the same, the relevant TED spread:
    A. increases.
    B. decreases.
    C. does not change.
26. Given the yield curve for US Treasury zero-coupon bonds, which spread is *most* helpful pricing a corporate bond? The:
    A. Z-Spread.
    B. TED spread.
    C. Libor–OIS spread.

27. A four-year corporate bond with a 7% coupon has a Z-spread of 200 bps. Assume a flat yield curve with an interest rate for all maturities of 5% and annual compounding. The bond will *most likely* sell:
    A. close to par.
    B. at a premium to par.
    C. at a discount to par.

28. The Z-spread of Bond A is 1.05% and the Z-spread of Bond B is 1.53%. All else equal, which statement *best* describes the relationship between the two bonds?
    A. Bond B is safer and will sell at a lower price.
    B. Bond B is riskier and will sell at a lower price.
    C. Bond A is riskier and will sell at a higher price.

29. Which term structure model can be calibrated to closely fit an observed yield curve?
    A. The Ho–Lee Model
    B. The Vasicek Model
    C. The Cox–Ingersoll–Ross Model

The following information relates to Questions 30–36

Jane Nguyen is a senior bond trader and Christine Alexander is a junior bond trader for an investment bank. Nguyen is responsible for her own trading activities and also for providing assignments to Alexander that will develop her skills and create profitable trade ideas. Exhibit 1 presents the current par and spot rates.

EXHIBIT 1   Current Par and Spot Rates

Maturity	Par Rate	Spot Rate
One year	2.50%	2.50%
Two years	2.99%	3.00%
Three years	3.48%	3.50%
Four years	3.95%	4.00%
Five years	4.37%	

Note: Par and spot rates are based on annual-coupon sovereign bonds.

Nguyen gives Alexander two assignments that involve researching various questions:

Assignment 1:   What is the yield to maturity of the option-free, default risk–free bond presented in Exhibit 2? Assume that the bond is held to maturity, and use the rates shown in Exhibit 1.

EXHIBIT 2   Selected Data for $1,000 Par Bond

Bond Name	Maturity (T)	Coupon
Bond Z	Three years	6.00%

Note: Terms are today for a *T*-year loan.

Assignment 2:   Assuming that the projected spot curve two years from today will be below the current forward curve, is Bond Z fairly valued, undervalued, or overvalued?

After completing her assignments, Alexander asks about Nguyen's current trading activities. Nguyen states that she has a two-year investment horizon and will purchase Bond Z as part of a strategy to ride the yield curve. Exhibit 1 shows Nguyen's yield curve assumptions implied by the spot rates.

30. Based on Exhibit 1, the five-year spot rate is *closest to*:
    A. 4.40%.
    B. 4.45%.
    C. 4.50%.

31. Based on Exhibit 1, the market is *most likely* expecting:
    A. deflation.
    B. inflation.
    C. no risk premiums.

32. Based on Exhibit 1, the forward rate of a one-year loan beginning in three years is *closest to*:
    A. 4.17%.
    B. 4.50%.
    C. 5.51%.

33. Based on Exhibit 1, which of the following forward rates can be computed?
    A. A one-year loan beginning in five years
    B. A three-year loan beginning in three years
    C. A four-year loan beginning in one year

34. For Assignment 1, the yield to maturity for Bond Z is *closest* to the:
    A. one-year spot rate.
    B. two-year spot rate.
    C. three-year spot rate.

35. For Assignment 2, Alexander should conclude that Bond Z is currently:
    A. undervalued.
    B. fairly valued.
    C. overvalued.

36. By choosing to buy Bond Z, Nguyen is *most likely* making which of the following assumptions?
    A. Bond Z will be held to maturity.
    B. The three-year forward curve is above the spot curve.
    C. Future spot rates do not accurately reflect future inflation.

The following information relates to Questions 37–41

Laura Mathews recently hired Robert Smith, an investment adviser at Shire Gate Advisers, to assist her in investing. Mathews states that her investment time horizon is short, approximately two years or less. Smith gathers information on spot rates for on-the-run annual-coupon government securities and swap spreads, as presented in Exhibit 1. Shire Gate Advisers recently published a report for its clients stating its belief that, based on the weakness in the financial markets, interest rates will remain stable, the yield curve will not change its level or shape for the next two years, and swap spreads will also remain unchanged.

EXHIBIT 1   Government Spot Rates and Swap Spreads

	Maturity (years)			
	1	2	3	4
Government spot rate	2.25%	2.70%	3.30%	4.05%
Swap spread	0.25%	0.30%	0.45%	0.70%

Smith decides to examine the following three investment options for Mathews:

Investment 1:   Buy a government security that would have an annualized return that is nearly risk free. Smith is considering two possible implementations: a two-year investment or a combination of two one-year investments.

Investment 2:   Buy a four-year, zero-coupon corporate bond and then sell it after two years. Smith illustrates the returns from this strategy using the swap rate as a proxy for corporate yields.

Investment 3:   Buy a lower-quality, two-year corporate bond with a coupon rate of 4.15% and a Z-spread of 65 bps.

When Smith meets with Mathews to present these choices, Mathews tells him that she is somewhat confused by the various spread measures. She is curious to know whether there is one spread measure that could be used as a good indicator of the risk and liquidity of money market securities during the recent past.

37. In his presentation of Investment 1, Smith could show that under the no-arbitrage principle, the forward price of a one-year government bond to be issued in one year is *closest* to:
    A. 0.9662.
    B. 0.9694.
    C. 0.9780.

38. In presenting Investment 1, using Shire Gate Advisers' interest rate outlook, Smith could show that riding the yield curve provides a total return that is *most likely*:
    A. lower than the return on a maturity-matching strategy.
    B. equal to the return on a maturity-matching strategy.
    C. higher than the return on a maturity-matching strategy.

39. In presenting Investment 2, Smith should show a total return *closest* to:
    A. 4.31%.
    B. 5.42%.
    C. 6.53%.

40. The bond in Investment 3 is *most likely* trading at a price of:
    A. 100.97.
    B. 101.54.
    C. 104.09.

41. The *most* appropriate response to Mathews question regarding a spread measure is the:
    A. Z-spread.
    B. Treasury–Eurodollar (TED) spread.
    C. Libor–OIS (overnight indexed swap) spread.

The following information relates to Questions 42–48

Rowan Madison is a junior analyst at Cardinal Capital. Sage Winter, a senior portfolio manager and Madison's supervisor, meets with Madison to discuss interest rates and review two bond positions in the firm's fixed-income portfolio.

Winter begins the meeting by asking Madison to state her views on the term structure of interest rates. Madison responds:

> "Yields are a reflection of expected spot rates and risk premiums. Investors demand risk premiums for holding long-term bonds, and these risk premiums increase with maturity."

Winter next asks Madison to describe features of equilibrium and arbitrage-free term structure models. Madison responds by making the following statements:

Statement 1:   "Equilibrium term structure models are factor models that use the observed market prices of a reference set of financial instruments, assumed to be correctly priced, to model the market yield curve."

Statement 2:   "In contrast, arbitrage-free term structure models seek to describe the dynamics of the term structure by using fundamental economic variables that are assumed to affect interest rates."

Winter asks Madison about her preferences concerning term structure models. Madison states:

> "I prefer arbitrage-free models. Even though equilibrium models require fewer parameters to be estimated relative to arbitrage-free models, arbitrage-free models allow for time-varying parameters. In general, this allowance leads to arbitrage-free models being able to model the market yield curve more precisely than equilibrium models."

Winter tells Madison that, based on recent changes in spreads, she is concerned about a perceived increase in counterparty risk in the economy and its effect on the portfolio. Madison asks Winter:

> "Which spread measure should we use to assess changes in counterparty risk in the economy?"

Winter is also worried about the effect of yield volatility on the portfolio. She asks Madison to identify the economic factors that affect short-term and long-term rate volatility. Madison responds:

> "Short-term rate volatility is mostly linked to uncertainty regarding monetary policy, whereas long-term rate volatility is mostly linked to uncertainty regarding the real economy and inflation."

Finally, Winter asks Madison to analyze the interest rate risk portfolio positions in a 5-year and a 20-year bond. Winter requests that the analysis be based on level, slope, and curvature as term structure factors. Madison presents her analysis in Exhibit 1.

EXHIBIT 1   Three-Factor Model of Term Structure

	Time to Maturity (years)	
Factor	5	20
Level	−0.4352%	−0.5128%
Steepness	−0.0515%	−0.3015%
Curvature	0.3963%	0.5227%

Note: Entries indicate how yields would change for a one standard deviation increase in a factor.

Winter asks Madison to perform two analyses:

Analysis 1:   Calculate the expected change in yield on the 20-year bond resulting from a two standard deviation increase in the steepness factor.

Analysis 2:   Calculate the expected change in yield on the five-year bond resulting from a one standard deviation decrease in the level factor and a one standard deviation decrease in the curvature factor.

42. Madison's views on the term structure of interest rates are *most* consistent with the:
  A. local expectations theory.
  B. segmented markets theory.
  C. liquidity preference theory.
43. Which of Madison's statement(s) regarding equilibrium and arbitrage-free term structure models is *incorrect*?
  A. Statement 1 only
  B. Statement 2 only
  C. Both Statement 1 and Statement 2
44. Is Madison correct in describing key differences in equilibrium and arbitrage-free models as they relate to the number of parameters and model accuracy?
  A. Yes.
  B. No, she is incorrect about which type of model requires fewer parameter estimates.
  C. No, she is incorrect about which type of model is more precise at modeling market yield curves.
45. The *most appropriate* response to Madison's question regarding the spread measure is the:
  A. Z-spread.
  B. Treasury–Eurodollar (TED) spread.
  C. Libor–OIS (overnight indexed swap) spread.
46. Is Madison's response regarding the factors that affect short-term and long-term rate volatility correct?
  A. Yes.
  B. No, she is incorrect regarding factors linked to long-term rate volatility.
  C. No, she is incorrect regarding factors linked to short-term rate volatility.
47. Based on Exhibit 1, the results of Analysis 1 should show the yield on the 20-year bond decreasing by:
  A. 0.3015%.
  B. 0.6030%.
  C. 0.8946%.

48. Based on Exhibit 1, the results of Analysis 2 should show the yield on the five-year bond:
    A. decreasing by 0.8315%.
    B. decreasing by 0.0389%.
    C. increasing by 0.0389%.

The following information relates to Questions 49–57

Liz Tyo is a fund manager for an actively managed global fixed-income fund that buys bonds issued in Countries A, B, and C. She and her assistant are preparing the quarterly markets update. Tyo begins the meeting by distributing the daily rates sheet, which includes the current government spot rates for Countries A, B, and C as shown in Exhibit 1.

EXHIBIT 1　　Today's Government Spot Rates

Maturity	Country A	Country B	Country C
One year	0.40%	−0.22%	14.00%
Two years	0.70	−0.20	12.40
Three years	1.00	−0.12	11.80
Four years	1.30	−0.02	11.00
Five years	1.50	0.13	10.70

Tyo asks her assistant how these spot rates were obtained. The assistant replies, "Spot rates are determined through the process of bootstrapping. It entails backward substitution using par yields to solve for zero-coupon rates one by one, in order from latest to earliest maturities."

Tyo then provides a review of the fund's performance during the last year and comments, "The choice of an appropriate benchmark depends on the country's characteristics. For example, although Countries A and B have both an active government bond market and a swap market, Country C's private sector is much bigger than its public sector, and its government bond market lacks liquidity."

Tyo further points out, "The fund's results were mixed; returns did not benefit from taking on additional risk. We are especially monitoring the riskiness of the corporate bond holdings. For example, our largest holdings consist of three four-year corporate bonds (Bonds 1, 2, and 3) with identical maturities, coupon rates, and other contract terms. These bonds have Z-spreads of 0.55%, 1.52%, and 1.76%, respectively."

Tyo continues, "We also look at risk in terms of the swap spread. We considered historical three-year swap spreads for Country B, which reflect that market's credit and liquidity risks, at three different points in time." Tyo provides the information in Exhibit 2.

EXHIBIT 2　　Selected Historical Three-Year Rates for Country B

Period	Government Bond Yield (%)	Fixed-for-Floating Libor Swap (%)
1 Month ago	−0.10	0.16
6 Months ago	−0.08	0.01
12 Months ago	−0.07	0.71

Tyo then suggests that the firm was able to add return by riding the yield curve. The fund plans to continue to use this strategy but only in markets with an attractive yield curve for this strategy.

She moves on to present her market views on the respective yield curves for a five-year investment horizon.

Country A: "The government yield curve has changed little in terms of its level and shape during the last few years, and I expect this trend to continue. We assume that future spot rates reflect the current forward curve for all maturities."

Country B: "Because of recent economic trends, I expect a reversal in the slope of the current yield curve. We assume that future spot rates will be higher than current forward rates for all maturities."

Country C: "To improve liquidity, Country C's central bank is expected to intervene, leading to a reversal in the slope of the existing yield curve. We assume that future spot rates will be lower than today's forward rates for all maturities."

Tyo's assistant asks, "Assuming investors require liquidity premiums, how can a yield curve slope downward? What does this imply about forward rates?"

Tyo answers, "Even if investors require compensation for holding longer-term bonds, the yield curve can slope downward—for example, if there is an expectation of severe deflation. Regarding forward rates, it can be helpful to understand yield curve dynamics by calculating implied forward rates. To see what I mean, we can use Exhibit 1 to calculate the forward rate for a two-year Country C loan beginning in three years."

49. Did Tyo's assistant accurately describe the process of bootstrapping?
    A. Yes.
    B. No, with respect to par yields.
    C. No, with respect to backward substitution.

50. The swap curve is a better benchmark than the government spot curve for:
    A. Country A.
    B. Country B.
    C. Country C.

51. Based on the given *Z*-spreads for Bonds 1, 2, and 3, which bond has the greatest credit and liquidity risk?
    A. Bond 1
    B. Bond 2
    C. Bond 3

52. Based on Exhibit 2, the implied credit and liquidity risks as indicated by the historical three-year swap spreads for Country B were the lowest:
    A. 1 month ago.
    B. 6 months ago.
    C. 12 months ago.

53. Based on Exhibit 1 and Tyo's expectations, which country's term structure is currently best for traders seeking to ride the yield curve?
    A. Country A
    B. Country B
    C. Country C

54. Based on Exhibit 1 and assuming Tyo's market views on yield curve changes are realized, the forward curve of which country will lie below its spot curve?
    A. Country A
    B. Country B
    C. Country C

55. Based on Exhibit 1 and Tyo's expectations for the yield curves, Tyo *most likely* perceives the bonds of which country to be fairly valued?
    A. Country A
    B. Country B
    C. Country C

56. With respect to their discussion of yield curves, Tyo and her assistant are *most likely* discussing which term structure theory?
    A. Pure expectations theory
    B. Local expectations theory
    C. Liquidity preference theory

57. Tyo's assistant should calculate a forward rate *closest* to:
    A. 9.07%.
    B. 9.58%.
    C. 9.97%.

CHAPTER 8

THE ARBITRAGE-FREE
VALUATION FRAMEWORK

LEARNING OUTCOMES

After completing this chapter, you will be able to do the following:

- explain what is meant by arbitrage-free valuation of a fixed-income instrument;
- calculate the arbitrage-free value of an option-free, fixed-rate coupon bond;
- describe a binomial interest rate tree framework;
- describe the backward induction valuation methodology and calculate the value of a fixed-income instrument given its cash flow at each node;
- describe the process of calibrating a binomial interest rate tree to match a specific term structure;
- compare pricing using the zero-coupon yield curve with pricing using an arbitrage-free binomial lattice;
- describe pathwise valuation in a binomial interest rate framework and calculate the value of a fixed-income instrument given its cash flows along each path;
- describe a Monte Carlo forward-rate simulation and its application.

SUMMARY OVERVIEW

This chapter presents the principles and tools for arbitrage valuation of fixed-income securities. Much of the discussion centers on the binomial interest rate tree, which can be used extensively to value both option-free bonds and bonds with embedded options. The following are the main points made in the chapter:

- A fundamental principle of valuation is that the value of any financial asset is equal to the present value of its expected future cash flows.
- A fixed-income security is a portfolio of zero-coupon bonds.

- Each zero-coupon bond has its own discount rate that depends on the shape of the yield curve and when the cash flow is delivered in time.
- In well-functioning markets, prices adjust until there are no opportunities for arbitrage.
- The law of one price states that two goods that are perfect substitutes must sell for the same current price in the absence of transaction costs.
- An arbitrage opportunity is a transaction that involves no cash outlay yet results in a riskless profit.
- Using the arbitrage-free approach, viewing a security as a package of zero-coupon bonds means that two bonds with the same maturity and different coupon rates are viewed as different packages of zero-coupon bonds and valued accordingly.
- For bonds that are option free, an arbitrage-free value is simply the present value of expected future values using the benchmark spot rates.
- A binomial interest rate tree permits the short interest rate to take on one of two possible values consistent with the volatility assumption and an interest rate model.
- An interest rate tree is a visual representation of the possible values of interest rates (forward rates) based on an interest rate model and an assumption about interest rate volatility.
- The possible interest rates for any following period are consistent with the following three assumptions: (1) an interest rate model that governs the random process of interest rates, (2) the assumed level of interest rate volatility, and (3) the current benchmark yield curve.
- From the lognormal distribution, adjacent interest rates on the tree are multiples of e raised to the 2σ power.
- One of the benefits of a lognormal distribution is that if interest rates get too close to zero, then the absolute change in interest rates becomes smaller and smaller.
- We use the backward induction valuation methodology that involves starting at maturity, filling in those values, and working back from right to left to find the bond's value at the desired node.
- The interest rate tree is fit to the current yield curve by choosing interest rates that result in the benchmark bond value. By doing this, the bond value is arbitrage free.
- An option-free bond that is valued by using the binomial interest rate tree should have the same value as discounting by the spot rates.
- Pathwise valuation calculates the present value of a bond for each possible interest rate path and takes the average of these values across paths.
- The Monte Carlo method is an alternative method for simulating a sufficiently large number of potential interest rate paths in an effort to discover how the value of a security is affected and involves randomly selecting paths in an effort to approximate the results of a complete pathwise valuation.

PROBLEMS

The following information relates to Questions 1–6

Katrina Black, portfolio manager at Coral Bond Management, Ltd., is conducting a training session with Alex Sun, a junior analyst in the fixed income department. Black wants to explain to Sun the arbitrage-free valuation framework used by the firm. Black presents Sun with

Exhibit 1, showing a fictitious bond being traded on three exchanges, and asks Sun to identify the arbitrage opportunity of the bond. Sun agrees to ignore transaction costs in his analysis.

EXHIBIT 1   Three-Year, €100 par, 3.00% Coupon, Annual-Pay Option-Free Bond

	Eurex	NYSE Euronext	Frankfurt
Price	€103.7956	€103.7815	€103.7565

Black shows Sun some exhibits that were part of a recent presentation. Exhibit 3 presents most of the data of a binomial lognormal interest rate tree fit to the yield curve shown in Exhibit 2. Exhibit 4 presents most of the data of the implied values for a four-year, option-free, annual-pay bond with a 2.5% coupon based on the information in Exhibit 3.

EXHIBIT 2   Yield to Maturity Par Rates for One-, Two-, and Three-Year Annual-Pay Option-Free Bonds

One-Year	Two-Year	Three-Year
1.25%	1.50%	1.70%

EXHIBIT 3   Binomial Interest Rate Tree Fit to the Yield Curve (Volatility = 10%)

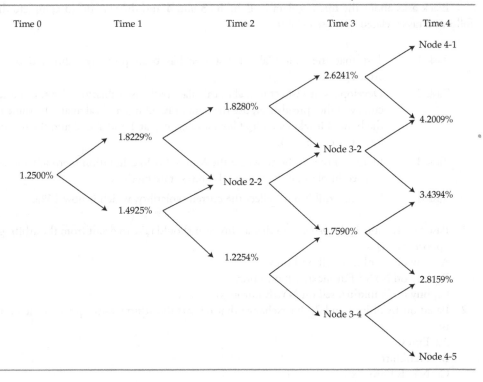

EXHIBIT 4   Implied Values (in Euros) for a 2.5%, Four-Year, Option-Free, Annual-Pay Bond Based on Exhibit 3

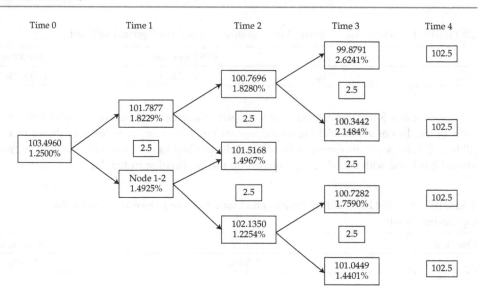

Black asks about the missing data in Exhibits 3 and 4 and directs Sun to complete the following tasks related to those exhibits:

Task 1   Test that the binomial interest tree has been properly calibrated to be arbitrage-free.

Task 2   Develop a spreadsheet model to calculate pathwise valuations. To test the accuracy of the spreadsheet, use the data in Exhibit 3 and calculate the value of the bond if it takes a path of lowest rates in Year 1 and Year 2 and the second lowest rate in Year 3.

Task 3   Identify a type of bond where the Monte Carlo calibration method should be used in place of the binomial interest rate method.

Task 4   Update Exhibit 3 to reflect the current volatility, which is now 15%.

1. Based on Exhibit 1, the *best* action that an investor should take to profit from the arbitrage opportunity is to:
   A. buy on Frankfurt, sell on Eurex.
   B. buy on NYSE Euronext, sell on Eurex.
   C. buy on Frankfurt, sell on NYSE Euronext.
2. Based on Exhibits 1 and 2, the exchange that reflects the arbitrage-free price of the bond is:
   A. Eurex.
   B. Frankfurt.
   C. NYSE Euronext.

3. Which of the following statements about the missing data in Exhibit 3 is correct?
    A. Node 3–2 can be derived from Node 2–2.
    B. Node 4–1 should be equal to Node 4–5 multiplied by $e^{0.4}$.
    C. Node 2–2 approximates the implied one-year forward rate two years from now.
4. Based on the information in Exhibits 3 and 4, the bond price in euros at Node 1–2 in Exhibit 4 is *closest* to:
    A. 102.7917.
    B. 104.8640.
    C. 105.2917.
5. A benefit of performing Task 1 is that it:
    A. enables the model to price bonds with embedded options.
    B. identifies benchmark bonds that have been mispriced by the market.
    C. allows investors to realize arbitrage profits through stripping and reconstitution.
6. If the assumed volatility is changed as Black requested in Task 4, the forward rates shown in Exhibit 3 will *most likely*:
    A. spread out.
    B. remain unchanged.
    C. converge to the spot rates.

The following information relates to Questions 7–10

Betty Tatton is a fixed income analyst with the hedge fund Sailboat Asset Management (SAM). SAM invests in a variety of global fixed-income strategies, including fixed-income arbitrage. Tatton is responsible for pricing individual investments and analyzing market data to assess the opportunity for arbitrage. She uses two methods to value bonds:

Method 1: Discount each year's cash flow separately using the appropriate interest rate curve.
Method 2: Build and use a binomial interest rate tree.

Tatton compiles pricing data for a list of annual pay bonds (Exhibit 1). Each of the bonds will mature in two years, and Tatton considers the bonds as being risk-free; both the one-year and two-year benchmark spot rates are 2%. Tatton calculates the arbitrage-free prices and identifies an arbitrage opportunity to recommend to her team.

EXHIBIT 1   Market Data for Selected Bonds

Asset	Coupon	Market Price
Bond A	1%	98.0584
Bond B	3%	100.9641
Bond C	5%	105.8247

Next, Tatton uses the benchmark yield curve provided in Exhibit 2 to consider arbitrage opportunities of both option-free corporate bonds and corporate bonds with embedded options. The benchmark bonds in Exhibit 2 pay coupons annually, and the bonds are priced at par.

EXHIBIT 2   Benchmark Par Curve

Maturity (years)	Yield to Maturity (YTM)
1	3.0%
2	4.0%
3	5.0%

Tatton then identifies three mispriced three-year annual-pay bonds and compiles data on the bonds (see Exhibit 3).

EXHIBIT 3   Market Data of Annual-Pay Corporate Bonds

Company	Coupon	Market Price	Yield	Embedded Option?
Hutto-Barkley Inc.	3%	94.9984	5.6%	No
Luna y Estrellas Intl.	0%	88.8996	4.0%	Yes
Peaton Scorpio Motors	0%	83.9619	6.0%	No

Last, Tatton identifies two mispriced Swiss bonds, Bond X, a three-year bond, and Bond Y, a five-year bond. Both are annual-pay bonds with a coupon rate of 6%. To calculate the bonds' values, Tatton devises the first three years of the interest rate lognormal tree presented in Exhibit 4 using historical interest rate volatility data. Tatton considers how these data would change if implied volatility, which is higher than historical volatility, were used instead.

EXHIBIT 4   Interest Rate Tree; Forward Rates Based on Swiss Market

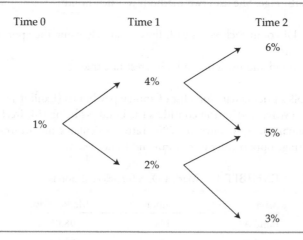

7. Based on Exhibit 1, which of the following bonds *most likely* includes an arbitrage opportunity?
   A. Bond A
   B. Bond B
   C. Bond C

8. Based on Exhibits 2 and 3 and using Method 1, the amount (in absolute terms) by which the Hutto-Barkley corporate bond is mispriced is *closest* to:
   A. 0.3368 per 100 of par value.
   B. 0.4682 per 100 of par value.
   C. 0.5156 per 100 of par value.
9. Method 1 would *most likely* **not** be an appropriate valuation technique for the bond issued by:
   A. Hutto-Barkley Inc.
   B. Luna y Estrellas Intl.
   C. Peaton Scorpio Motors.
10. Based on Exhibit 4 and using Method 2, the correct price for Bond X is *closest* to:
    A. 97.2998.
    B. 109.0085.
    C. 115.0085.

The following information relates to Questions 11–18

Meredith Alvarez is a junior fixed-income analyst with Canzim Asset Management. Her supervisor, Stephanie Hartson, asks Alvarez to review the asset price and payoff data shown in Exhibit 1 to determine whether an arbitrage opportunity exists.

EXHIBIT 1   Price and Payoffs for Two Risk-Free Assets

Asset	Price Today	Payoff in One Year
Asset A	$500	$525
Asset B	$1,000	$1,100

Hartson also shows Alvarez data for a bond that trades in three different markets in the same currency. These data appear in Exhibit 2.

EXHIBIT 2   2% Coupon, Five-Year Maturity, Annual-Pay Bond

	New York	Hong Kong	Mumbai
Yield to Maturity	1.9%	2.3%	2.0%

Hartson asks Alvarez to value two bonds (Bond C and Bond D) using the binomial tree in Exhibit 3. Exhibit 4 presents selected data for both bonds.

EXHIBIT 3   Binomial Interest Rate Tree with Volatility = 25%

Time 0	Time 1	Time 2
		2.7183%
	2.8853%	
1.500%		1.6487%
	1.7500%	
		1.0000%

EXHIBIT 4　Selected Data on Annual-Pay Bonds

Bond	Maturity	Coupon Rate
Bond C	2 years	2.5%
Bond D	3 years	3.0%

Hartson tells Alvarez that she and her peers have been debating various viewpoints regarding the conditions underlying binomial interest rate trees. The following statements were made in the course of the debate.

Statement 1:　The only requirements needed to create a binomial interest rate tree are current benchmark interest rates and an assumption about interest rate volatility.

Statement 2:　Potential interest rate volatility in a binomial interest rate tree can be estimated using historical interest rate volatility or observed market prices from interest rate derivatives.

Statement 3:　A bond value derived from a binomial interest rate tree with a relatively high volatility assumption will be different from the value calculated by discounting the bond's cash flows using current spot rates.

Based on data in Exhibit 5, Hartson asks Alvarez to calibrate a binomial interest rate tree starting with the calculation of implied forward rates shown in Exhibit 6.

EXHIBIT 5　Selected Data for a Binomial Interest Rate Tree

Maturity	Par Rate	Spot Rate
1	2.5000%	2.5000%
2	3.5000%	3.5177%

EXHIBIT 6　Calibration of Binomial Interest Rate Tree with Volatility = 25%

Time 0	Time 1
	5.8365%
2.500%	
	Lower one-period forward rate

Hartson mentions pathwise valuations as another method to value bonds using a binomial interest rate tree. Using the binomial interest rate tree in Exhibit 3, Alvarez calculates the possible interest rate paths for Bond D shown in Exhibit 7.

EXHIBIT 7　Interest Rate Paths for Bond D

Path	Time 0	Time 1	Time 2
1	1.500%	2.8853%	2.7183%
2	1.500	2.8853	1.6487
3	1.500	1.7500	1.6487
4	1.500	1.7500	1.0000

Before leaving for the day, Hartson asks Alvarez about the value of using the Monte Carlo method to simulate a large number of potential interest rate paths to value a bond. Alvarez makes the following statements.

Statement 4:   Increasing the number of paths increases the estimate's statistical accuracy.
Statement 5:   The bond value derived from a Monte Carlo simulation will be closer to the bond's true fundamental value.

11. Based on Exhibit 1, Alvarez finds that an arbitrage opportunity is:
    A. not available.
    B. available based on the dominance principle.
    C. available based on the value additivity principle.
12. Based on the data in Exhibit 2, the *most* profitable arbitrage opportunity would be to buy the bond in:
    A. Mumbai and sell it in Hong Kong.
    B. Hong Kong and sell it in New York.
    C. New York and sell it in Hong Kong.
13. Based on Exhibits 3 and 4, the value of Bond C at the upper node at Time 1 is *closest* to:
    A. 97.1957.
    B. 99.6255.
    C. 102.1255.
14. Based on Exhibits 3 and 4, the price for Bond D is *closest* to:
    A. 97.4785.
    B. 103.3230.
    C. 106.3230.
15. Which of the various statements regarding binomial interest rate trees is correct?
    A. Statement 1
    B. Statement 2
    C. Statement 3
16. Based on Exhibits 5 and 6, the value of the lower one-period forward rate is *closest to*:
    A. 3.5122%.
    B. 3.5400%.
    C. 4.8037%.
17. Based on Exhibits 4 and 7, the present value of Bond D's cash flows following Path 2 is *closest* to:
    A. 97.0322.
    B. 102.8607.
    C. 105.8607.
18. Which of the statements regarding Monte Carlo simulation is correct?
    A. Only Statement 4 is correct.
    B. Only Statement 5 is correct.
    C. Both Statement 4 and Statement 5 are correct.

CHAPTER 9

VALUATION AND ANALYSIS OF BONDS WITH EMBEDDED OPTIONS

LEARNING OUTCOMES

After completing this chapter, you will be able to do the following:

- describe fixed-income securities with embedded options;
- explain the relationships between the values of a callable or putable bond, the underlying option-free (straight) bond, and the embedded option;
- describe how the arbitrage-free framework can be used to value a bond with embedded options;
- explain how interest rate volatility affects the value of a callable or putable bond;
- explain how changes in the level and shape of the yield curve affect the value of a callable or putable bond;
- calculate the value of a callable or putable bond from an interest rate tree;
- explain the calculation and use of option-adjusted spreads;
- explain how interest rate volatility affects option-adjusted spreads;
- calculate and interpret effective duration of a callable or putable bond;
- compare effective durations of callable, putable, and straight bonds;
- describe the use of one-sided durations and key rate durations to evaluate the interest rate sensitivity of bonds with embedded options;
- compare effective convexities of callable, putable, and straight bonds;
- calculate the value of a capped or floored floating-rate bond;
- describe defining features of a convertible bond;
- calculate and interpret the components of a convertible bond's value;
- describe how a convertible bond is valued in an arbitrage-free framework;
- compare the risk–return characteristics of a convertible bond with the risk–return characteristics of a straight bond and of the underlying common stock.

SUMMARY OVERVIEW

This chapter covers the valuation and analysis of bonds with embedded options. The following are the main points made in this chapter:

- An embedded option represents a right that can be exercised by the issuer, by the bondholder, or automatically depending on the course of interest rates. It is attached to, or embedded in, an underlying option-free bond called a straight bond.
- Simple embedded option structures include call options, put options, and extension options. Callable and putable bonds can be redeemed prior to maturity, at the discretion of the issuer in the former case and of the bondholder in the latter case. An extendible bond gives the bondholder the right to keep the bond for a number of years after maturity. Putable and extendible bonds are equivalent, except that the underlying option-free bonds are different.
- Complex embedded option structures include bonds with other types of options or combinations of options. For example, a convertible bond includes a conversion option that allows the bondholders to convert their bonds into the issuer's common stock. A bond with an estate put can be put by the heirs of a deceased bondholder. Sinking fund bonds make the issuer set aside funds over time to retire the bond issue and are often callable, may have an acceleration provision, and may also contain a delivery option. Valuing and analyzing bonds with complex embedded option structures is challenging.
- According to the arbitrage-free framework, the value of a bond with an embedded option is equal to the arbitrage-free values of its parts—that is, the arbitrage-free value of the straight bond and the arbitrage-free values of each of the embedded options.
- Because the call option is an issuer option, the value of the call option decreases the value of the callable bond relative to an otherwise identical but non-callable bond. In contrast, because the put option is an investor option, the value of the put option increases the value of the putable bond relative to an otherwise identical but non-putable bond.
- In the absence of default and interest rate volatility, the bond's future cash flows are certain. Thus, the value of a callable or putable bond can be calculated by discounting the bond's future cash flows at the appropriate one-period forward rates, taking into consideration the decision to exercise the option. If a bond is callable, the decision to exercise the option is made by the issuer, which will exercise the call option when the value of the bond's future cash flows is higher than the call price. In contrast, if the bond is putable, the decision to exercise the option is made by the bondholder, who will exercise the put option when the value of the bond's future cash flows is lower than the put price.
- In practice, interest rates fluctuate, and interest rate volatility affects the value of embedded options. Thus, when valuing bonds with embedded options, it is important to consider the possible evolution of the yield curve over time.
- Interest rate volatility is modeled using a binomial interest rate tree. The higher the volatility, the lower the value of the callable bond and the higher the value of the putable bond.
- Valuing a bond with embedded options assuming an interest rate volatility requires three steps: (1) Generate a tree of interest rates based on the given yield curve and volatility assumptions; (2) at each node of the tree, determine whether the embedded options will be exercised; and (3) apply the backward induction valuation methodology to calculate the present value of the bond.
- The most commonly used approach to valuing risky bonds is to add a spread to the one-period forward rates used to discount the bond's future cash flows.

- The option-adjusted spread is the single spread added uniformly to the one-period forward rates on the tree to produce a value or price for a bond. OAS is sensitive to interest rate volatility: The higher the volatility, the lower the OAS for a callable bond.
- For bonds with embedded options, the best measure to assess the sensitivity of the bond's price to a parallel shift of the benchmark yield curve is effective duration. The effective duration of a callable or putable bond cannot exceed that of the straight bond.
- The effective convexity of a straight bond is negligible, but that of bonds with embedded options is not. When the option is near the money, the convexity of a callable bond is negative, indicating that the upside for a callable bond is much smaller than the downside, whereas the convexity of a putable bond is positive, indicating that the upside for a putable bond is much larger than the downside.
- Because the prices of callable and putable bonds respond asymmetrically to upward and downward interest rate changes of the same magnitude, one-sided durations provide a better indication regarding the interest rate sensitivity of bonds with embedded options than (two-sided) effective duration.
- Key rate durations show the effect of shifting only key points, one at a time, rather than the entire yield curve.
- The arbitrage-free framework can be used to value capped and floored floaters. The cap provision in a floater is an issuer option that prevents the coupon rate from increasing above a specified maximum rate. Thus, the value of a capped floater is equal to or less than the value of the straight bond. In contrast, the floor provision in a floater is an investor option that prevents the coupon from decreasing below a specified minimum rate. Thus, the value of a floored floater is equal to or higher than the value of the straight bond.
- The characteristics of a convertible bond include the conversion price, which is the applicable share price at which the bondholders can convert their bonds into common shares, and the conversion ratio, which reflects the number of shares of common stock that the bondholders receive from converting their bonds into shares. The conversion price is adjusted in case of corporate actions, such as stock splits, bonus share issuances, and rights and warrants issuances. Convertible bondholders may receive compensation when the issuer pays dividends to its common shareholders, and they may be given the opportunity to either put their bonds or convert their bonds into shares earlier and at more advantageous terms in the case of a change of control.
- There are a number of investment metrics and ratios that help analyze and value convertible bonds. The conversion value indicates the value of the bond if it is converted at the market price of the shares. The minimum value of a convertible bond sets a floor value for the convertible bond at the greater of the conversion value or the straight value. This floor is moving, however, because the straight value is not fixed. The market conversion premium represents the price investors effectively pay for the underlying shares if they buy the convertible bond and then convert it into shares. Scaled by the market price of the shares, it represents the premium payable when buying the convertible bond rather than the underlying common stock.
- Because convertible bonds combine characteristics of bonds, stocks, and options, as well as potentially other features, their valuation and analysis is challenging. Convertible bond investors should consider the factors that affect not only bond prices but also the underlying share price.
- The arbitrage-free framework can be used to value convertible bonds, including callable and putable ones. Each component (straight bond, call option of the stock, and call and/or put option on the bond) can be valued separately.

- The risk–return characteristics of a convertible bond depend on the underlying share price relative to the conversion price. When the underlying share price is well below the conversion price, the convertible bond is "busted" and exhibits mostly bond risk–return characteristics. Thus, it is mainly sensitive to interest rate movements. In contrast, when the underlying share price is well above the conversion price, the convertible bond exhibits mostly stock risk–return characteristics. Thus, its price follows similar movements to the price of the underlying stock. In between these two extremes, the convertible bond trades like a hybrid instrument.

PROBLEMS

The following information relates to Questions 1–10

Samuel & Sons is a fixed-income specialty firm that offers advisory services to investment management companies. On 1 October 20X0, Steele Ferguson, a senior analyst at Samuel, is reviewing three fixed-rate bonds issued by a local firm, Pro Star, Inc. The three bonds, whose characteristics are given in Exhibit 1, carry the highest credit rating.

EXHIBIT 1   Fixed-Rate Bonds Issued by Pro Star, Inc.

Bond	Maturity	Coupon	Type of Bond
Bond 1	1 October 20X3	4.40% annual	Option-free
Bond 2	1 October 20X3	4.40% annual	Callable at par on 1 October 20X1 and on 1 October 20X2
Bond 3	1 October 20X3	4.40% annual	Putable at par on 1 October 20X1 and on 1 October 20X2

The one-year, two-year, and three-year par rates are 2.250%, 2.750%, and 3.100%, respectively. Based on an estimated interest rate volatility of 10%, Ferguson constructs the binomial interest rate tree shown in Exhibit 2.

EXHIBIT 2   Binomial Interest Rate Tree

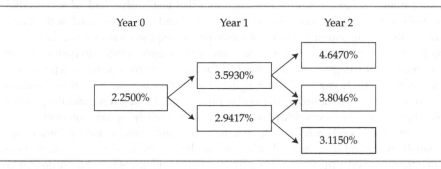

On 19 October 20X0, Ferguson analyzes the convertible bond issued by Pro Star given in Exhibit 3. That day, the option-free value of Pro Star's convertible bond is $1,060 and Pro Star's stock price is $37.50.

EXHIBIT 3   Convertible Bond Issued by Pro Star, Inc.

Issue Date:	6 December 20X0
Maturity Date:	6 December 20X4
Coupon Rate:	2%
Issue Price:	$1,000
Conversion Ratio:	31

1. The call feature of Bond 2 is *best* described as:
   A. European style.
   B. American style.
   C. Bermudan style.
2. The bond that would *most likely* protect investors against a significant increase in interest rates is:
   A. Bond 1.
   B. Bond 2.
   C. Bond 3.
3. A fall in interest rates would *most likely* result in:
   A. a decrease in the effective duration of Bond 3.
   B. Bond 3 having more upside potential than Bond 2.
   C. a change in the effective convexity of Bond 3 from positive to negative.
4. The value of Bond 2 is *closest* to:
   A. 102.103% of par.
   B. 103.121% of par.
   C. 103.744% of par.
5. The value of Bond 3 is *closest* to:
   A. 102.103% of par.
   B. 103.688% of par.
   C. 103.744% of par.
6. All else being equal, a rise in interest rates will *most likely* result in the value of the option embedded in Bond 3:
   A. decreasing.
   B. remaining unchanged.
   C. increasing.
7. All else being equal, if Ferguson assumes an interest rate volatility of 15% instead of 10%, the bond that would *most likely* increase in value is:
   A. Bond 1.
   B. Bond 2.
   C. Bond 3.

8. All else being equal, if the shape of the yield curve changes from upward sloping to flattening, the value of the option embedded in Bond 2 will *most likely*:
   A. decrease.
   B. remain unchanged.
   C. increase.
9. The conversion price of the bond in Exhibit 3 is *closest* to:
   A. $26.67.
   B. $32.26.
   C. $34.19.
10. If the market price of Pro Star's common stock falls from its level on 19 October 20X0, the price of the convertible bond will *most likely*:
   A. fall at the same rate as Pro Star's stock price.
   B. fall but at a slightly lower rate than Pro Star's stock price.
   C. be unaffected until Pro Star's stock price reaches the conversion price.

The following information relates to Questions 11–19

Rayes Investment Advisers specializes in fixed-income portfolio management. Meg Rayes, the owner of the firm, would like to add bonds with embedded options to the firm's bond portfolio. Rayes has asked Mingfang Hsu, one of the firm's analysts, to assist her in selecting and analyzing bonds for possible inclusion in the firm's bond portfolio.

Hsu first selects two corporate bonds that are callable at par and have the same characteristics in terms of maturity, credit quality and call dates. Hsu uses the option-adjusted spread (OAS) approach to analyse the bonds, assuming an interest rate volatility of 10%. The results of his analysis are presented in Exhibit 1.

EXHIBIT 1   Summary Results of Hsu's
Analysis Using the OAS Approach

Bond	OAS (in bps)
Bond 1	25.5
Bond 2	30.3

Hsu then selects the four bonds issued by RW, Inc. given in Exhibit 2. These bonds all have a maturity of three years and the same credit rating. Bonds 4 and 5 are identical to Bond 3, an option-free bond, except that they each include an embedded option.

EXHIBIT 2   Bonds Issued by RW, Inc.

Bond	Coupon	Special Provision
Bond 3	4.00% annual	
Bond 4	4.00% annual	Callable at par at the end of years 1 and 2
Bond 5	4.00% annual	Putable at par at the end of years 1 and 2
Bond 6	One-year Libor annually, set in arrears	

To value and analyze RW's bonds, Hsu uses an estimated interest rate volatility of 15% and constructs the binomial interest rate tree provided in Exhibit 3.

EXHIBIT 3   Binomial Interest Rate Tree Used to Value RW's Bonds

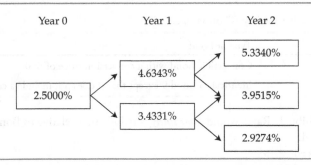

Rayes asks Hsu to determine the sensitivity of Bond 4's price to a 20 bps parallel shift of the benchmark yield curve. The results of Hsu's calculations are shown in Exhibit 4.

EXHIBIT 4   Summary Results of Hsu's Analysis about the Sensitivity of Bond 4's Price to a Parallel Shift of the Benchmark Yield Curve

Magnitude of the Parallel Shift in the Benchmark Yield Curve	+20 bps	−20 bps
Full Price of Bond 4 (% of par)	100.478	101.238

Hsu also selects the two floating-rate bonds issued by Varlep, plc given in Exhibit 5. These bonds have a maturity of three years and the same credit rating.

EXHIBIT 5   Floating-Rate Bonds Issued by Varlep, plc

Bond	Coupon
Bond 7	One-year Libor annually, set in arrears, capped at 5.00%
Bond 8	One-year Libor annually, set in arrears, floored at 3.50%

To value Varlep's bonds, Hsu constructs the binomial interest rate tree provided in Exhibit 6.

EXHIBIT 6   Binomial Interest Rate Tree Used to Value Varlep's Bonds

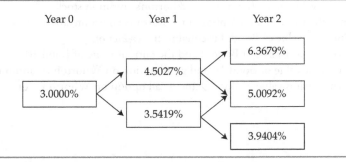

Last, Hsu selects the two bonds issued by Whorton, Inc. given in Exhibit 7. These bonds are close to their maturity date and are identical, except that Bond 9 includes a conversion option. Whorton's common stock is currently trading at $30 per share.

EXHIBIT 7   Bonds Issued by Whorton, Inc.

Bond	Type of Bond
Bond 9	Convertible bond with a conversion price of $50
Bond 10	Identical to Bond 9 except that it does not include a conversion option

11. Based on Exhibit 1, Rayes would *most likely* conclude that relative to Bond 1, Bond 2 is:
    A. overpriced.
    B. fairly priced.
    C. underpriced.
12. The effective duration of Bond 6 is:
    A. lower than or equal to 1.
    B. higher than 1 but lower than 3.
    C. higher than 3.
13. In Exhibit 2, the bond whose effective duration will lengthen if interest rates rise is:
    A. Bond 3.
    B. Bond 4.
    C. Bond 5.
14. The effective duration of Bond 4 is *closest* to:
    A. 0.76.
    B. 1.88.
    C. 3.77.
15. The value of Bond 7 is *closest* to:
    A. 99.697% of par.
    B. 99.936% of par.
    C. 101.153% of par.
16. The value of Bond 8 is *closest* to:
    A. 98.116% of par.
    B. 100.000% of par.
    C. 100.485% of par.
17. The value of Bond 9 is equal to the value of Bond 10:
    A. plus the value of a put option on Whorton's common stock.
    B. plus the value of a call option on Whorton's common stock.
    C. minus the value of a call option on Whorton's common stock.
18. The minimum value of Bond 9 is equal to the *greater* of:
    A. the conversion value of Bond 9 and the current value of Bond 10.
    B. the current value of Bond 10 and a call option on Whorton's common stock.
    C. the conversion value of Bond 9 and a call option on Whorton's common stock.

19. The factor that is currently *least likely* to affect the risk-return characteristics of Bond 9 is:
    A. Interest rate movements.
    B. Whorton's credit spreads.
    C. Whorton's common stock price movements.

The following information relates to Questions 20–27

John Smith, an investment adviser, meets with Lydia Carter to discuss her pending retirement and potential changes to her investment portfolio. Domestic economic activity has been weakening recently, and Smith's outlook is that equity market values will be lower during the next year. He would like Carter to consider reducing her equity exposure in favor of adding more fixed-income securities to the portfolio.

Government yields have remained low for an extended period, and Smith suggests considering investment-grade corporate bonds to provide additional yield above government debt issues. In light of recent poor employment figures and two consecutive quarters of negative GDP growth, the consensus forecast among economists is that the central bank, at its next meeting this month, will take actions that will lead to lower interest rates.

Smith and Carter review par, spot, and one-year forward rates (Exhibit 1) and four fixed-rate investment-grade bonds issued by Alpha Corporation that are being considered for investment (Exhibit 2).

EXHIBIT 1   Par, Spot, and One-Year Forward Rates (annual coupon payments)

Maturity (Years)	Par Rate (%)	Spot Rate (%)	One-Year Forward (%)
1	1.0000	1.0000	1.0000
2	1.2000	1.2012	1.4028
3	1.2500	1.2515	1.3522

EXHIBIT 2   Selected Fixed-Rate Bonds of Alpha Corporation

Bond	Annual Coupon	Type of Bond
Bond 1	1.5500%	Straight bond
Bond 2	1.5500%	Convertible bond: currently trading out of the money
Bond 3	1.5500%	Putable bond: putable at par one year and two years from now
Bond 4	1.5500%	Callable bond: callable at par without any lockout periods

Note: All bonds in Exhibit 2 have remaining maturities of exactly three years.

Carter tells Smith that the local news media have been reporting that housing starts, exports, and demand for consumer credit are all relatively strong, even in light of other poor macroeconomic indicators. Smith explains that the divergence in economic data leads him to believe that volatility in interest rates will increase. Smith also states that he recently read a report issued by Brown and Company forecasting that the yield curve could invert within the next six months.

Smith develops a binomial interest rate tree with a 15% interest rate volatility assumption to assess the value of Alpha Corporation's bonds. Exhibit 3 presents the interest rate tree.

EXHIBIT 3   Binomial Interest Rate Tree for Alpha Corporation 15% Interest Rate Volatility

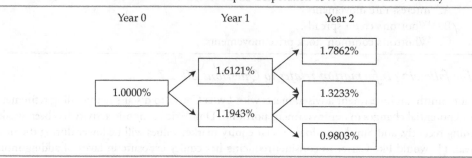

Carter asks Smith about the possibility of analyzing bonds that have lower credit ratings than the investment-grade Alpha bonds. Smith discusses four other corporate bonds with Carter. Exhibit 4 presents selected data on the four bonds.

EXHIBIT 4   Selected Information on Fixed-Rate Bonds for Beta, Gamma, Delta, and Rho Corporations

Bond	Issuer	Bond Features	Credit Rating
Bond 5	Beta Corporation	Coupon 1.70% Callable in Year 2 OAS of 45 bps	B
Bond 6	Gamma Corporation	Coupon 1.70% Callable in Year 2 OAS of 65 bps	B
Bond 7	Delta Corporation	Coupon 1.70% Callable in Year 2 OAS of 85 bps	B
Bond 8	Rho Corporation	Coupon 1.70% Callable in Year 2 OAS of 105 bps	CCC

Notes: All bonds have remaining maturities of three years. OAS stands for option-adjusted spread.

20. Based on Exhibit 2, and assuming that the forecast for interest rates and Smith's outlook for equity returns are validated, which bond's option is *most likely* to be exercised?
    A. Bond 2
    B. Bond 3
    C. Bond 4
21. Based on Exhibit 2, the current price of Bond 1 is *most likely* greater than the current price of:
    A. Bond 2.
    B. Bond 3.
    C. Bond 4.
22. Assuming the forecast for interest rates is proven accurate, which bond in Exhibit 2 will likely experience the smallest price increase?
    A. Bond 1
    B. Bond 3
    C. Bond 4

23. Based on the information in Exhibit 1 and Exhibit 2, the value of the embedded option in Bond 4 is *closest* to:
   A. nil.
   B. 0.1906.
   C. 0.3343.

24. If Smith's interest rate volatility forecast turns out to be true, which bond in Exhibit 2 is likely to experience the greatest price increase?
   A. Bond 2
   B. Bond 3
   C. Bond 4

25. If the Brown and Company forecast comes true, which of the following is *most* likely to occur? The value of the embedded option in:
   A. Bond 3 decreases.
   B. Bond 4 decreases.
   C. both Bond 3 and Bond 4 increase.

26. Based on Exhibit 2 and Exhibit 3, the market price of Bond 4 is *closest* to:
   A. 100.4578.
   B. 100.5123.
   C. 100.8790.

27. Which of the following conclusions regarding the bonds in Exhibit 4 is correct?
   A. Bond 5 is relatively cheaper than Bond 6.
   B. Bond 7 is relatively cheaper than Bond 6.
   C. Bond 8 is relatively cheaper than Bond 7.

The following information relates to Questions 28–36

Jules Bianchi is a bond analyst for Maneval Investments, Inc. Bianchi gathers data on three corporate bonds, as shown in Exhibit 1.

EXHIBIT 1   Selected Bond Data

Issuer	Coupon Rate	Price	Bond Description
Ayrault, Inc. (AI)	5.25%	100.200	Callable at par in one year and two years from today
Blum, Inc. (BI)	5.25%	101.300	Option-free
Cresson Enterprises (CE)	5.25%	102.100	Putable at par in one year from today

Note: Each bond has a remaining maturity of three years, annual coupon payments, and a credit rating of BBB.

To assess the interest rate risk of the three bonds, Bianchi constructs two binomial interest rate trees based on a 10% interest rate volatility assumption and a current one-year rate of 1%. Panel A of Exhibit 2 provides an interest rate tree assuming the benchmark yield curve shifts down by 30 bps, and Panel B provides an interest rate tree assuming the benchmark yield curve shifts up by 30 bps. Bianchi determines that the AI bond is currently trading at an option-adjusted spread (OAS) of 13.95 bps relative to the benchmark yield curve.

EXHIBIT 2 Binomial Interest Rate Trees

Panel A: Interest Rates Shift Down by 30 bps

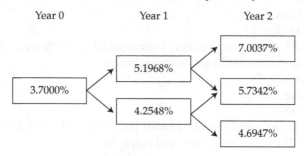

Year 0	Year 1	Year 2
3.7000%	5.1968%	7.0037%
	4.2548%	5.7342%
		4.6947%

Panel B: Interest Rates Shift Up by 30 bps

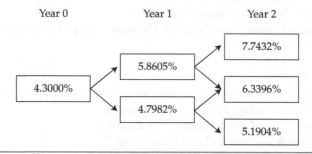

Year 0	Year 1	Year 2
4.3000%	5.8605%	7.7432%
	4.7982%	6.3396%
		5.1904%

Armand Gillette, a convertible bond analyst, stops by Bianchi's office to discuss two convertible bonds. One is issued by DeLille Enterprises (DE) and the other is issued by Raffarin Incorporated (RI). Selected data for the two bonds are presented in Exhibits 3 and 4.

EXHIBIT 3 Selected Data for DE Convertible Bond

Issue price	€1,000 at par
Conversion period	13 September 20X5 to 12 September 20X8
Initial conversion price	€10.00 per share
Threshold dividend	€0.50 per share
Change of control conversion price	€8.00 per share
Common stock share price on issue date	€8.70
Share price on 17 September 20X5	€9.10
Convertible bond price on 17 September 20X5	€1,123

EXHIBIT 4 Selected Data for RI Convertible Bond

Straight bond value	€978
Value of embedded issuer call option	€43
Value of embedded investor put option	€26
Value of embedded call option on issuer's stock	€147
Conversion price	€12.50
Current common stock share price	€11.75

Gillette makes the following comments to Bianchi:

- "The DE bond does not contain any call or put options but the RI bond contains both an embedded call option and a put option. I expect that DeLille Enterprises will soon announce a common stock dividend of €0.70 per share."
- "My belief is that, over the next year, Raffarin's share price will appreciate toward the conversion price but not exceed it."

28. Based on Exhibits 1 and 2, the effective duration for the AI bond is *closest to*:
    A. 1.98.
    B. 2.15.
    C. 2.73.
29. If benchmark yields were to fall, which bond in Exhibit 1 would *most likely* experience a decline in effective duration?
    A. AI bond
    B. BI bond
    C. CE bond
30. Based on Exhibit 1, for the BI bond, one-sided:
    A. up-duration will be greater than one-sided down-duration.
    B. down-duration will be greater than one-sided up-duration.
    C. up-duration and one-sided down-duration will be about equal.
31. Based on Exhibit 1, which key rate duration is the largest for the BI bond?
    A. One-year key rate duration
    B. Two-year key rate duration
    C. Three-year key rate duration
32. Which bond in Exhibit 1 *most likely* has the lowest effective convexity?
    A. AI bond
    B. BI bond
    C. CE bond
33. Based on Exhibit 3, if DeLille Enterprises pays the dividend expected by Gillette, the conversion price of the DE bond will:
    A. be adjusted downward.
    B. not be adjusted.
    C. be adjusted upward.
34. Based on Exhibit 3, the market conversion premium per share for the DE bond on 17 September 20X5 is *closest* to:
    A. €0.90.
    B. €2.13.
    C. €2.53.
35. Based on Exhibit 4, the arbitrage-free value of the RI bond is *closest* to:
    A. €814.
    B. €1,056.
    C. €1,108.
36. Based on Exhibit 4 and Gillette's forecast regarding Raffarin's share price, the return on the RI bond over the next year is *most likely* to be:
    A. lower than the return on Raffarin's common shares.
    B. the same as the return on Raffarin's common shares.
    C. higher than the return on Raffarin's common shares.

CHAPTER 10

CREDIT ANALYSIS MODELS

LEARNING OUTCOMES

After completing this chapter, you will be able to do the following:

- explain expected exposure, the loss given default, the probability of default, and the credit valuation adjustment;
- explain credit scores and credit ratings;
- calculate the expected return on a bond given transition in its credit rating;
- explain structural and reduced-form models of corporate credit risk, including assumptions, strengths, and weaknesses;
- calculate the value of a bond and its credit spread, given assumptions about the credit risk parameters;
- interpret changes in a credit spread;
- explain the determinants of the term structure of credit spreads and interpret a term structure of credit spreads;
- compare the credit analysis required for securitized debt to the credit analysis of corporate debt.

SUMMARY OVERVIEW

This chapter has covered several important topics in credit analysis. Among the points made are the following:
- Three factors important to modeling credit risk are the expected exposure to default, the recovery rate, and the loss given default.
- These factors permit the calculation of a credit valuation adjustment that is subtracted from the (hypothetical) value of the bond, if it were default risk free, to get the bond's fair value given its credit risk. The credit valuation adjustment is calculated as the sum of the present values of the expected loss for each period in the remaining life of the bond. Expected values are computed using risk-neutral probabilities, and discounting is done at the risk-free rates for the relevant maturities.
- The CVA captures investors' compensation for bearing default risk. The compensation can also be expressed in terms of a credit spread.
- Credit scores and credit ratings are third-party evaluations of creditworthiness used in distinct markets.

- Analysts may use credit ratings and a transition matrix of probabilities to adjust a bond's yield-to-maturity to reflect the probabilities of credit migration. Credit spread migration typically reduces expected return.
- Credit analysis models fall into two broad categories: structural models and reduced-form models.
- Structural models are based on an option perspective of the positions of the stakeholders of the company. Bondholders are viewed as owning the assets of the company; shareholders have call options on those assets.
- Reduced-form models seek to predict *when* a default may occur, but they do not explain the *why* as do structural models. Reduced-form models, unlike structural models, are based only on observable variables.
- When interest rates are assumed to be volatile, the credit risk of a bond can be estimated in an arbitrage-free valuation framework.
- The discount margin for floating-rate notes is similar to the credit spread for fixed-coupon bonds. The discount margin can also be calculated using an arbitrage-free valuation framework.
- Arbitrage-free valuation can be applied to judge the sensitivity of the credit spread to changes in credit risk parameters.
- The term structure of credit spreads depends on macro and micro factors.
- As it concerns macro factors, the credit spread curve tends to become steeper and widen in conditions of weak economic activity. Market supply and demand dynamics are important. The most frequently traded securities tend to determine the shape of this curve.
- Issuer- or industry-specific factors, such as the chance of a future leverage-decreasing event, can cause the credit spread curve to flatten or invert.
- When a bond is very likely to default, it often trades close to its recovery value at various maturities; moreover, the credit spread curve is less informative about the relationship between credit risk and maturity.
- For securitized debt, the characteristics of the asset portfolio themselves suggest the best approach for a credit analyst to take when deciding among investments. Important considerations include the relative concentration of assets and their similarity or heterogeneity as it concerns credit risk.

PROBLEMS

The following information relates to Questions 1–15

Daniela Ibarra is a senior analyst in the fixed-income department of a large wealth management firm. Marten Koning is a junior analyst in the same department, and David Lok is a member of the credit research team.

The firm invests in a variety of bonds. Ibarra is presently analyzing a set of bonds with some similar characteristics, such as four years until maturity and a par value of €1,000. Exhibit 1 includes details of these bonds.

EXHIBIT 1   A Brief Description of the Bonds Being Analyzed

Bond	Description
B1	A zero-coupon, four-year corporate bond with a par value of €1,000. The wealth management firm's research team has estimated that the risk-neutral probability of default (the hazard rate) for each date for the bond is 1.50%, and the recovery rate is 30%.

Bond	Description
B2	A bond similar to B1, except that it has a fixed annual coupon rate of 6% paid annually.
B3	A bond similar to B2 but rated AA.
B4	A bond similar to B2 but the coupon rate is the one-year benchmark rate plus 4%.

Ibarra asks Koning to assist her with analyzing the bonds. She wants him to perform the analysis with the assumptions that there is no interest rate volatility and that the government bond yield curve is flat at 3%.

Ibarra performs the analysis assuming an upward-sloping yield curve and volatile interest rates. Exhibit 2 provides the data on annual payment benchmark government bonds.[1] She uses these data to construct a binomial interest rate tree (shown in Exhibit 3) based on an assumption of future interest rate volatility of 20%.

EXHIBIT 2   Par Curve for Annual Payment Benchmark Government Bonds

Maturity	Coupon Rate	Price	Discount Factor	Spot Rate	Forward Rate
1	−0.25%	€100	1.002506	−0.2500%	
2	0.75%	€100	0.985093	0.7538%	1.7677%
3	1.50%	€100	0.955848	1.5166%	3.0596%
4	2.25%	€100	0.913225	2.2953%	4.6674%

EXHIBIT 3   One-Year Binomial Interest Rate Tree for 20% Volatility

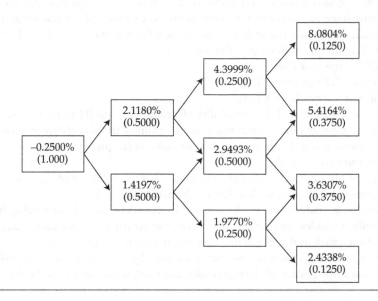

---

[1] For simplicity, this exhibit uses data for the first four years from Exhibit 9 of the reading.

Answer the first five questions (1–4) based on the assumptions made by Marten Koning, the junior analyst. Answer questions (8–12) based on the assumptions made by Daniela Ibarra, the senior analyst.

Note: All calculations in this problem set are carried out on spreadsheets to preserve precision. The rounded results are reported in the solutions.

1. The market price of bond B1 is €875. The bond is:
   A. fairly valued.
   B. overvalued.
   C. undervalued.
2. Koning realizes that an increase in the recovery rate would lead to an increase in the bond's fair value, whereas an increase in the probability of default would lead to a decrease in the bond's fair value. He is not sure which effect would be greater, however. So, he increases both the recovery rate and the probability of default by 25% of their existing estimates and recomputes the bond's fair value. The recomputed fair value is closest to:
   A. €843.14.
   B. €848.00.
   C. €855.91.
3. The fair value of bond B2 is closest to:
   A. €1,069.34.
   B. €1,111.51.
   C. €1,153.68.
4. The market price of bond B2 is €1,090. If the bond is purchased at this price and there is a default on Date 3, the rate of return to the bond buyer would be closest to:
   A. −28.38%.
   B. −41.72%.
   C. −69.49%.
5. Bond B3 will have a modified duration of 2.75 at the end of the year. Based on the representative one-year corporate transition matrix in Exhibit 7 of the reading and assuming no default, how should the analyst adjust the bond's yield to maturity (YTM) to assess the expected return on the bond over the next year?
   A. Add 7.7 bps to YTM.
   B. Subtract 7.7 bps from YTM.
   C. Subtract 9.0 bps from YTM.
6. David Lok has estimated the probability of default of bond B1 to be 1.50%. He is presenting the approach the research team used to estimate the probability of default. Which of the following statements is Lok likely to make in his presentation if the team used a reduced-form credit model?
   A. Option pricing methodologies were used, with the volatility of the underlying asset estimated based on historical data on the firm's stock price.
   B. Regression analysis was used, with the independent variables including both firm-specific variables, such as the debt ratio and return on assets, and macroeconomic variables, such as the rate of inflation and the unemployment rate.
   C. The default barrier was first estimated followed by the estimation of the probability of default as the portion of the probability distribution that lies below the default barrier.

7. In the presentation, Lok is asked why the research team chose to use a reduced-form credit model instead of a structural model. Which statement is he likely to make in reply?
   A. Structural models are outdated, having been developed in the 1970s; reduced-form models are more modern, having been developed in the 1990s.
   B. Structural models are overly complex because they require use of option pricing models, whereas reduced-form models use regression analysis.
   C. Structural models require "inside" information known to company management, whereas reduced-form models can use publicly available data on the firm.

8. As previously mentioned, Ibarra is considering a future interest rate volatility of 20% and an upward-sloping yield curve, as shown in Exhibit 2. Based on her analysis, the fair value of bond B2 is closest to:
   A. €1,101.24.
   B. €1,141.76.
   C. €1,144.63.

9. Ibarra wants to know the credit spread of bond B2 over a theoretical comparable-maturity government bond with the same coupon rate as this bond. The foregoing credit spread is closest to:
   A. 108 bps.
   B. 101 bps.
   C. 225 bps.

10. Ibarra is interested in analyzing how a simultaneous decrease in the recovery rate and the probability of default would affect the fair value of bond B2. She decreases both the recovery rate and the probability of default by 25% of their existing estimates and recomputes the bond's fair value. The recomputed fair value is closest to:
    A. €1,096.59.
    B. €1,108.40.
    C. €1,111.91.

11. The wealth management firm has an existing position in bond B4. The market price of B4, a floating-rate note, is €1,070. Senior management has asked Ibarra to make a recommendation regarding the existing position. Based on the assumptions used to calculate the estimated fair value only, her recommendation should be to:
    A. add to the existing position.
    B. hold the existing position.
    C. reduce the existing position.

12. The issuer of the floating-rate note B4 is in the energy industry. Ibarra personally believes that oil prices are likely to increase significantly within the next year, which will lead to an improvement in the firm's financial health and a decline in the probability of default from 1.50% in Year 1 to 0.50% in Years 2, 3, and 4. Based on these expectations, which of the following statements is correct?
    A. The CVA will decrease to €22.99.
    B. The note's fair value will increase to €1,177.26.
    C. The value of the FRN, assuming no default, will increase to €1,173.55.

13. Floating-rate note B4 is currently rated BBB by Standard & Poor's and Fitch Ratings (and Baa by Moody's Investors Service). Based on the research department assumption about the probability of default in Question 10 and her own assumption in Question 11, which action does Ibarra *most likely* expect from the credit rating agencies?
    A. Downgrade from BBB to BB
    B. Upgrade from BBB to AAA
    C. Place the issuer on watch with a positive outlook

14. During the presentation about how the research team estimates the probability of default for a particular bond issuer, Lok is asked for his thoughts on the shape of the term structure of credit spreads. Which statement is he most likely to include in his response?

   A. The term structure of credit spreads typically is flat or slightly upward sloping for high-quality investment-grade bonds. High-yield bonds are more sensitive to the credit cycle, however, and can have a more upwardly sloped term structure of credit spreads than investment-grade bonds or even an inverted curve.

   B. The term structure of credit spreads for corporate bonds is always upward sloping, the more so the weaker the credit quality because probabilities of default are positively correlated with the time to maturity.

   C. There is no consistent pattern to the term structure of credit spreads. The shape of the credit term structure depends entirely on industry factors.

15. The final question to Lok is about covered bonds. The person asking says, "I've heard about them but don't know what they are." Which statement is Lok most likely to make to describe a covered bond?

   A. A covered bond is issued in a non-domestic currency. The currency risk is then fully hedged using a currency swap or a package of foreign exchange forward contracts.

   B. A covered bond is issued with an attached credit default swap. It essentially is a "risk-free" government bond.

   C. A covered bond is a senior debt obligation giving recourse to the issuer as well as a predetermined underlying collateral pool, often commercial or residential mortgages.

The following information relates to Questions 16–22

Anna Lebedeva is a fixed-income portfolio manager. Paulina Kowalski, a junior analyst, and Lebedeva meet to review several positions in Lebedeva's portfolio.

Lebedeva begins the meeting by discussing credit rating migration. Kowalski asks Lebedeva about the typical impact of credit rating migration on the expected return on a bond. Lebedeva asks Kowalski to estimate the expected return over the next year on a bond issued by Entre Corp. The BBB rated bond has a yield to maturity of 5.50% and a modified duration of 7.54. Kowalski calculates the expected return on the bond over the next year given the partial credit transition and credit spread data in Exhibit 1. She assumes that market spreads and yields will remain stable over the year.

EXHIBIT 1   One-Year Transition Matrix for BBB Rated Bonds and Credit Spreads

	AAA	AA	A	BBB	BB	B	CCC, CC, C
Probability (%)	0.02	0.30	4.80	85.73	6.95	1.75	0.45
Credit spread	0.60%	0.90%	1.10%	1.50%	3.40%	6.50%	9.50%

Lebedeva next asks Kowalski to analyze a three-year bond, issued by VraiRive S.A., using an arbitrage-free framework. The bond's coupon rate is 5%, with interest paid annually and a par value of 100. In her analysis, she makes the following three assumptions:

• The annual interest rate volatility is 10%.
• The recovery rate is one-third of the exposure each period.
• The hazard rate, or conditional probability of default each year, is 2.00%.

Selected information on benchmark government bonds for the VraiRive bond is presented in Exhibit 2, and the relevant binomial interest rate tree is presented in Exhibit 3.

EXHIBIT 2   Par Curve Rates for Annual Payment Benchmark Government Bonds

Maturity	Coupon Rate	Price	Discount Factor	Spot Rate	Forward Rate
1	3.00%	100	0.970874	3.0000%	3.0000%
2	4.20%	100	0.920560	4.2255%	5.4656%
3	5.00%	100	0.862314	5.0618%	6.7547%

EXHIBIT 3   One-Year Binomial Interest Rate Tree for 10% Volatility (risk-neutral probabilities in parentheses)

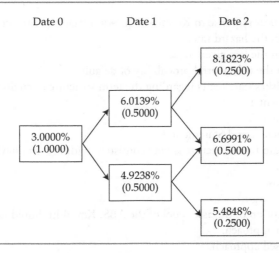

Kowalski estimates the value of the VraiRive bond assuming no default (VND) as well as the fair value of the bond. She then estimates the bond's yield to maturity and the bond's credit spread over the benchmark in Exhibit 2. Kowalski asks Lebedeva, "What might cause the bond's credit spread to decrease?"

Lebedeva and Kowalski next discuss the drivers of the term structure of credit spreads. Kowalski tells Lebedeva:

Statement 1:   The credit term structure for the most highly rated securities tends to be either flat or slightly upward sloping.

Statement 2:   The credit term structure for lower-rated securities is often steeper, and credit spreads widen with expectations of strong economic growth.

Next, Kowalski analyzes the outstanding bonds of DLL Corporation, a high-quality issuer with a strong, competitive position. Her focus is to determine the rationale for a positively sloped credit spread term structure.

Lebedeva ends the meeting by asking Kowalski to recommend a credit analysis approach for a securitized asset-backed security (ABS) held in the portfolio. This non-static asset pool is made up of many medium-term auto loans that are homogeneous, and each loan is small relative to the total value of the pool.

16. The *most appropriate* response to Kowalski's question regarding credit rating migration is that it has:
    A. a negative impact.
    B. no impact.
    C. a positive impact.
17. Based on Exhibit 1, the one-year expected return on the Entre Corp. bond is *closest* to:
    A. 3.73%.
    B. 5.50%.
    C. 7.27%.
18. Based on Kowalski's assumptions and Exhibits 2 and 3, the credit spread on the VraiRive bond is *closest* to:
    A. 0.6949%.
    B. 0.9388%.
    C. 1.4082%.
19. The *most appropriate* response to Kowalski's question relating to the credit spread is:
    A. an increase in the hazard rate.
    B. an increase in the loss given default.
    C. a decrease in the risk-neutral probability of default.
20. Which of Kowalski's statements regarding the term structure of credit spreads is correct?
    A. Only Statement 1
    B. Only Statement 2
    C. Both Statement 1 and Statement 2
21. DLL's credit spread term structure is *most* consistent with the firm having:
    A. low leverage.
    B. weak cash flow.
    C. a low profit margin.
22. Given the description of the asset pool of the ABS, Kowalski should recommend a:
    A. loan-by-loan approach.
    B. portfolio-based approach.
    C. statistics-based approach.

The following information relates to Questions 23–30

Lena Liecken is a senior bond analyst at Taurus Investment Management. Kristel Kreming, a junior analyst, works for Liecken in helping conduct fixed-income research for the firm's portfolio managers. Liecken and Kreming meet to discuss several bond positions held in the firm's portfolios.

Bonds I and II both have a maturity of one year, an annual coupon rate of 5%, and a market price equal to par value. The risk-free rate is 3%. Historical default experiences of bonds comparable to Bonds I and II are presented in Exhibit 1.

EXHIBIT 1   Credit Risk Information for Comparable Bonds

Bond	Recovery Rate	Percentage of Bonds That Survive and Make Full Payment
I	40%	98%
II	35%	99%

Bond III

Bond III is a zero-coupon bond with three years to maturity. Liecken evaluates similar bonds and estimates a recovery rate of 38% and a risk-neutral default probability of 2%, assuming conditional probabilities of default. Kreming creates Exhibit 2 to compute Bond III's credit valuation adjustment. She assumes a flat yield curve at 3%, with exposure, recovery, and loss given default values expressed per 100 of par value.

EXHIBIT 2   Analysis of Bond III

Date	Exposure	Recovery	Loss Given Default	Probability of Default	Probability of Survival	Expected Loss	Present Value of Expected Loss
0							
1	94.2596	35.8186	58.4410	2.0000%	98.0000%	1.1688	1.1348
2	97.0874	36.8932	60.1942	1.9600%	96.0400%	1.1798	1.1121
3	100.0000	38.0000	62.0000	1.9208%	94.1192%	1.1909	1.0898
Sum				5.8808%		3.5395	3.3367

Bond IV

Bond IV is an AA rated bond that matures in five years, has a coupon rate of 6%, and a modified duration of 4.2. Liecken is concerned about whether this bond will be downgraded to an A rating, but she does not expect the bond to default during the next year. Kreming constructs a partial transition matrix, which is presented in Exhibit 3, and suggests using a model to predict the rating change of Bond IV using leverage ratios, return on assets, and macroeconomic variables.

EXHIBIT 3   Partial One-Year Corporate Transition Matrix (entries in %)

From/To	AAA	AA	A
AAA	92.00	6.00	1.00
AA	2.00	89.00	8.00
A	0.05	1.00	85.00
Credit Spread (%)	0.50	1.00	1.75

Default Probabilities

Kreming calculates the risk-neutral probabilities, compares them with the actual default probabilities of bonds evaluated over the past 10 years, and observes that the actual and risk-neutral probabilities differ. She makes two observations regarding the comparison of these probabilities:

Observation 1:   Actual default probabilities include the default risk premium associated with the uncertainty in the timing of the possible default loss.

Observation 2:   The observed spread over the yield on a risk-free bond in practice includes liquidity and tax considerations, in addition to credit risk.

23. The expected exposure to default loss for Bond I is:
    A. less than the expected exposure for Bond II.
    B. the same as the expected exposure for Bond II.
    C. greater than the expected exposure for Bond II.
24. Based on Exhibit 1, the loss given default for Bond II is:
    A. less than that for Bond I.
    B. the same as that for Bond I.
    C. greater than that for Bond I.
25. Based on Exhibit 1, the expected future value of Bond I at maturity is *closest* to:
    A. 98.80.
    B. 103.74.
    C. 105.00.
26. Based on Exhibit 1, the risk-neutral default probability for Bond I is *closest* to:
    A. 2.000%.
    B. 3.175%.
    C. 4.762%.
27. Based on Exhibit 2, the credit valuation adjustment (CVA) for Bond III is *closest* to:
    A. 3.3367.
    B. 3.5395.
    C. 5.8808.
28. Based on Exhibit 3, if Bond IV's credit rating changes during the next year to an A rating, its expected price change would be *closest* to:
    A. −8.00%.
    B. −7.35%.
    C. −3.15%.
29. Kreming's suggested model for Bond IV is a:
    A. structural model.
    B. reduced-form model.
    C. term structure model.
30. Which of Kreming's observations regarding actual and risk-neutral default probabilities is correct?
    A. Only Observation 1
    B. Only Observation 2
    C. Both Observation 1 and Observation 2

CHAPTER **11**

CREDIT DEFAULT SWAPS

LEARNING OUTCOMES

After completing this chapter, you will be able to do the following:

- describe credit default swaps (CDS), single-name and index CDS, and the parameters that define a given CDS product;
- describe credit events and settlement protocols with respect to CDS;
- explain the principles underlying, and factors that influence, the market's pricing of CDS;
- describe the use of CDS to manage credit exposures and to express views regarding changes in shape and/or level of the credit curve;
- describe the use of CDS to take advantage of valuation disparities among separate markets, such as bonds, loans, equities, and equity-linked instruments.

SUMMARY OVERVIEW

This chapter on credit default swaps provides a basic introduction to these instruments and their markets. The following key points are covered:

- A credit default swap (CDS) is a contract between two parties in which one party purchases protection from another party against losses from the default of a borrower for a defined period of time.
- A CDS is written on the debt of a third party, called the reference entity, whose relevant debt is called the reference obligation, typically a senior unsecured bond.
- A CDS written on a particular reference obligation normally provides coverage for all obligations of the reference entity that have equal or higher seniority.
- The two parties to the CDS are the credit protection buyer, who is said to be short the reference entity's credit, and the credit protection seller, who is said to be long the reference entity's credit. The seller (buyer) is said to be long (short) because the seller is bullish (bearish) on the financial condition of the reference entity.
- The CDS pays off upon occurrence of a credit event, which includes bankruptcy, failure to pay, and, in some countries, restructuring.
- Settlement of a CDS can occur through a cash payment from the credit protection seller to the credit protection buyer as determined by the cheapest-to-deliver obligation of the

reference entity, or by physical delivery of the reference obligation from the protection buyer to the protection seller in exchange for the CDS notional.

- A cash settlement payoff is determined by an auction of the reference entity's debt, which gives the market's assessment of the likely recovery rate. The credit protection buyer must accept the outcome of the auction even though the ultimate recovery rate could differ.
- CDS can be constructed on a single entity or as indexes containing multiple entities.
- The fixed payments made from CDS buyer to CDS seller are customarily set at a fixed annual rate of 1% for investment-grade debt or 5% for high-yield debt.
- Valuation of a CDS is determined by estimating the present value of the protection leg, which is the payment from the protection seller to the protection buyer in event of default, and the present value of the payment leg, which is the series of payments made from the protection buyer to the protection seller. Any difference in the two series results in an upfront payment from the party having the claim on the greater present value to the counterparty.
- An important determinant of the value of the expected payments is the hazard rate, the probability of default given that default has not already occurred.
- CDS prices are often quoted in terms of credit spreads, the implied number of basis points that the credit protection seller receives from the credit protection buyer to justify providing the protection.
- Credit spreads are often expressed in terms of a credit curve, which expresses the relationship between the credit spreads on bonds of different maturities for the same borrower.
- CDS change in value over their lives as the credit quality of the reference entity changes, which leads to gains and losses for the counterparties, even though default may not have occurred or may never occur.
- Either party can monetize an accumulated gain or loss by entering into an offsetting position that matches the terms of the original CDS.
- CDS are used to increase or decrease credit exposures or to capitalize on different assessments of the cost of credit among different instruments tied to the reference entity, such as debt, equity, and derivatives of debt and equity.

PROBLEMS

The following information relates to Questions 1–6

UNAB Corporation

On 1 January 20X2, Deem Advisors purchased a $10 million six-year senior unsecured bond issued by UNAB Corporation. Six months later (1 July 20X2), concerned about the portfolio's credit exposure to UNAB, Doris Morrison, the chief investment officer at Deem Advisors, purchases a $10 million CDS with a standardized coupon rate of 5%. The reference obligation of the CDS is the UNAB bond owned by Deem Advisors.

On 1 January 20X3, Morrison asks Bill Watt, a derivatives analyst, to assess the current credit quality of UNAB bonds and the value of Deem Advisors' CDS on UNAB debt. Watt gathers the following information on UNAB's debt issues currently trading in the market:

Bond 1: A two-year senior unsecured bond trading at 40% of par
Bond 2: A six-year senior unsecured bond trading at 50% of par
Bond 3: A six-year subordinated unsecured bond trading at 20% of par

With respect to the credit quality of UNAB, Watt makes the following statement:

> "There is severe near-term stress in the financial markets and UNAB's credit curve clearly reflects the difficult environment."

On 1 July 20X3, UNAB fails to make a scheduled interest payment on the outstanding subordinated unsecured obligation after a grace period; however, the company does not file for bankruptcy. Morrison asks Watt to determine if UNAB experienced a credit event and, if so, to recommend a settlement preference.

Kand Corporation

Morrison is considering purchasing a 10-year CDS on Kand Corporation debt to hedge its current portfolio position. She instructs Watt to determine if an upfront payment would be required and, if so, the amount of the premium. Watt presents the information for the CDS in Exhibit 1.

EXHIBIT 1   Summary Data for 10-year CDS on Kand Corporation

Credit spread	700 basis points
Duration	7 years
Coupon rate	5%

Morrison purchases the 10-year CDS on Kand Corporation debt. Two months later the credit spread for Kand Corp. has increased by 200 basis points. Morrison asks Watt to close out the firm's CDS position on Kand Corporation by entering into new offsetting contracts.

Tollunt Corporation

Deem Advisors' chief credit analyst recently reported that Tollunt Corporation's five-year bond is currently yielding 7% and a comparable CDS contract has a credit spread of 4.25%. Since Libor is 2.5%, Watt has recommended executing a basis trade to take advantage of the pricing of Tollunt's bonds and CDS. The basis trade would consist of purchasing both the bond and the CDS contract.

1. If UNAB experienced a credit event on 1 July, Watt should recommend that Deem Advisors:
   A. prefer a cash settlement.
   B. prefer a physical settlement.
   C. be indifferent between a cash or a physical settlement.
2. According to Watt's statement, the shape of UNAB's credit curve is *most likely*:
   A. flat.
   B. upward-sloping.
   C. downward-sloping.
3. Should Watt conclude that UNAB experienced a credit event?
   A. Yes.
   B. No, because UNAB did not file for bankruptcy.
   C. No, because the failure to pay occurred on a subordinated unsecured bond.

4. Based on Exhibit 1, the upfront premium as a percent of the notional for the CDS protection on Kand Corp. would be *closest* to:
   A. 2.0%.
   B. 9.8%.
   C. 14.0%.
5. If Deem Advisors enters into a new offsetting contract two months after purchasing the CDS protection on Kand Corporation, this action will *most likely* result in:
   A. a loss on the CDS position.
   B. a gain on the CDS position.
   C. neither a loss or a gain on the CDS position.
6. Based on basis trade for Tollunt Corporation, if convergence occurs in the bond and CDS markets, the trade will capture a profit *closest* to:
   A. 0.25%.
   B. 1.75%.
   C. 2.75%.

The following information relates to Questions 7–15

John Smith, a fixed-income portfolio manager at a €10 billion sovereign wealth fund (SWF), meets with Sofia Chan, a derivatives strategist with Shire Gate Securities (SGS), to discuss investment opportunities for the fund. Chan notes that SGS adheres to ISDA (International Swaps and Derivatives Association) protocols for credit default swap (CDS) transactions and that any contract must conform to ISDA specifications. Before the fund can engage in trading CDS products with SGS, the fund must satisfy compliance requirements.

Smith explains to Chan that fixed-income derivatives strategies are being contemplated for both hedging and trading purposes. Given the size and diversified nature of the fund, Smith asks Chan to recommend a type of CDS that would allow the SWF to simultaneously fully hedge multiple fixed-income exposures.

Next, Smith asks Chan to assess the impact on derivative products of recent events affecting Maxx Corporation, a US company. The SWF holds an unsecured debt instrument issued by Maxx. Chan says she is very familiar with Maxx because many of its unsecured debt obligations are commonly included in broad baskets of bonds used for hedging purposes. SGS recently sold €400 million of protection on the on-the-run CDX high yield (HY) index that includes a Maxx bond; the index contains 100 entities. Chan reports that creditors met with company executives to impose a restructuring on Maxx bonds; as a result, all outstanding principal obligations will be reduced by 30%.

Smith and Chan discuss opportunities to add trading profits to the SWF. Smith asks Chan to determine the probability of default associated with a five-year investment-grade bond issued by Orion Industrial. Selected data on the Orion Industrial bond are presented in Exhibit 1.

EXHIBIT 1   Selected Data on Orion Industrial Five-Year Bond

Year	Hazard Rate
1	0.22%
2	0.35%
3	0.50%
4	0.65%
5	0.80%

Chan explains that a single-name CDS can also be used to add profit to the fund over time. Chan describes a hypothetical trade in which the fund sells £6 million of five-year CDS protection on Orion, where the CDS contract has a duration of 3.9 years. Chan assumes that the fund closes the position six months later, after Orion's credit spread narrowed from 150 bps to 100 bps.

Chan discusses the mechanics of a long/short trade. In order to structure a number of potential trades, Chan and Smith exchange their respective views on individual companies and global economies. Chan and Smith agree on the following outlooks.

Outlook 1: Italy's economy will weaken.

Outlook 2: The US economy will strengthen relative to that of Canada.

Outlook 3: The credit quality of electric car manufacturers will improve relative to that of traditional car manufacturers.

Chan believes US macroeconomic data are improving and that the general economy will strengthen in the short term. Chan suggests that a curve trade could be used by the fund to capitalize on her short-term view of a steepening of the US credit curve.

Another short-term trading opportunity that Smith and Chan discuss involves the merger and acquisition market. SGS believes that Delta Corporation may make an unsolicited bid at a premium to the market price for all publicly traded shares of Zega, Inc. Zega's market capitalization and capital structure are comparable to Delta's; both firms are highly levered. It is anticipated that Delta will issue new equity along with 5- and 10-year senior unsecured debt to fund the acquisition, which will significantly increase its debt ratio.

7. To satisfy the compliance requirements referenced by Chan, the fund is *most likely* required to:
   A. set a notional amount.
   B. post an upfront payment.
   C. sign an ISDA master agreement.
8. Which type of CDS should Chan recommend to Smith?
   A. CDS index
   B. Tranche CDS
   C. Single-name CDS
9. Following the Maxx restructuring, the CDX HY notional will be *closest* to:
   A. €396.0 million.
   B. €398.8 million.
   C. $400.0 million.
10. Based on Exhibit 1, the probability of Orion defaulting on the bond during the first three years is *closest* to:
    A. 1.07%.
    B. 2.50%.
    C. 3.85%.
11. To close the position on the hypothetical Orion trade, the fund:
    A. sells protection at a higher premium than it paid at the start of the trade.
    B. buys protection at a lower premium than it received at the start of the trade.
    C. buys protection at a higher premium than it received at the start of the trade.
12. The hypothetical Orion trade generated an approximate:
    A. loss of £117,000.
    B. gain of £117,000.
    C. gain of £234,000.

13. Based on the three economic outlook statements, a profitable long/short trade would be to:
    A. go long a Canadian CDX IG and short a US CDX IG.
    B. short an iTraxx Crossover and go long an iTraxx Main.
    C. short electric car CDS and go long traditional car CDS.
14. The curve trade that would *best* capitalize on Chan's view of the US credit curve is to:
    A. short a 20-year CDX and short a 2-year CDX.
    B. short a 20-year CDX and go long a 2-year CDX.
    C. go long a 20-year CDX and short a 2-year CDX.
15. A profitable equity-versus-credit trade involving Delta and Zega is to:
    A. short Zega shares and short Delta 10-year CDS.
    B. go long Zega shares and short Delta 5-year CDS.
    C. go long Delta shares and go long Delta 5-year CDS.

CHAPTER 12

OVERVIEW OF FIXED-INCOME PORTFOLIO MANAGEMENT

LEARNING OUTCOMES

After completing this chapter, you will be able to do the following:

- discuss roles of fixed-income securities in portfolios;
- describe how fixed-income mandates may be classified and compare features of the mandates;
- describe bond market liquidity, including the differences among market sub-sectors, and discuss the effect of liquidity on fixed-income portfolio management;
- describe and interpret a model for fixed-income returns;
- discuss the use of leverage, alternative methods for leveraging, and risks that leverage creates in fixed-income portfolios;
- discuss differences in managing fixed-income portfolios for taxable and tax-exempt investors.

SUMMARY OVERVIEW

This chapter describes the roles of fixed-income securities in an investment portfolio and introduces fixed-income portfolio management. Key points of the chapter include the following:

- Fixed-income investments provide diversification benefits in a portfolio context. These benefits arise from the generally low correlations of fixed-income investments with other major asset classes such as equities.
- Fixed-income investments have regular cash flows, which is beneficial for the purposes of funding future liabilities.
- Floating-rate and inflation-linked bonds can be used to hedge inflation risk.
- Liability-based fixed-income mandates are managed to match or cover expected liability payments with future projected cash inflows.

- For liability-based fixed-income mandates, portfolio construction follows two main approaches—cash flow matching and duration matching—to match fixed-income assets with future liabilities.
- Cash flow matching is an immunization approach based on matching bond cash flows with liability payments.
- Duration matching is an immunization approach based on matching the duration of assets and liabilities.
- Hybrid forms of duration and cash flow matching include contingent immunization and horizon matching.
- Total return mandates are generally structured to either track or outperform a benchmark.
- Total return mandates can be classified into different approaches based on their target active return and active risk levels. Approaches range from pure indexing to enhanced indexing to active management.
- Liquidity is an important consideration in fixed-income portfolio management. Bonds are generally less liquid than equities, and liquidity varies greatly across sectors.
- Liquidity affects pricing in fixed-income markets because many bonds either do not trade or trade infrequently.
- Liquidity affects portfolio construction because there is a trade-off between liquidity and yield. Less liquid bonds have higher yields, all else being equal, and may be more desirable for buy-and-hold investors. Investors anticipating liquidity needs may forgo higher yields for more-liquid bonds.
- Fixed-income derivatives, as well as fixed-income exchange-traded funds and pooled investment vehicles, are often more liquid than their underlying bonds and provide investment managers with an alternative to trading in illiquid underlying bonds.
- When evaluating fixed-income investment strategies, it is important to consider expected returns and to understand the different components of expected returns.
- Decomposing expected fixed-income returns allows investors to understand the different sources of returns given expected changes in bond market conditions.
- A model for expected fixed-income returns can decompose them into the following components: yield income, rolldown return, expected change in price based on investors' views of yields and yield spreads, expected credit losses, and expected currency gains or losses.
- Leverage is the use of borrowed capital to increase the magnitude of portfolio positions. By using leverage, fixed-income portfolio managers may be able to increase portfolio returns relative to what they can achieve in unleveraged portfolios. The potential for increased returns, however, comes with increased risk.
- Methods for leveraging fixed-income portfolios include the use of futures contracts, swap agreements, structured financial instruments, repurchase agreements, and securities lending.
- Taxes can complicate investment decisions in fixed-income portfolio management. Complications result from the difference in taxation across investor types, countries, and income sources (interest income or capital gains).

PROBLEMS

The following information relates to Questions 1–6

Cécile Perreaux is a junior analyst for an international wealth management firm. Her supervisor, Margit Daasvand, asks Perreaux to evaluate three fixed-income funds as part of the firm's global fixed-income offerings. Selected financial data for the funds Aschel, Permot, and Rosaiso are presented in Exhibit 1. In Perreaux's initial review, she assumes that there is no reinvestment income and that the yield curve remains unchanged.

EXHIBIT 1   Selected Data on Fixed-Income Funds

	Aschel	Permot	Rosaiso
Current average bond price	$117.00	$91.50	$94.60
Expected average bond price in one year (end of Year 1)	$114.00	$96.00	$97.00
Average modified duration	7.07	7.38	6.99
Average annual coupon payment	$3.63	$6.07	$6.36
Present value of portfolio's assets (millions)	$136.33	$68.50	$74.38
Bond type*			
Fixed-coupon bonds	95%	38%	62%
Floating-coupon bonds	2%	34%	17%
Inflation-linked bonds	3%	28%	21%
Quality*			
AAA	65%	15%	20%
BBB	35%	65%	50%
B	0%	20%	20%
Not rated	0%	0%	10%
Value of portfolio's equity (millions)	$94.33		
Value of borrowed funds (millions)	$42.00		
Borrowing rate	2.80%		
Return on invested funds	6.20%		

* Bond type and Quality are shown as a percentage of total for each fund.

After further review of the composition of each of the funds, Perreaux notes the following.

Note 1:   Aschel is the only fund of the three that uses leverage.

Note 2:   Rosaiso is the only fund of the three that holds a significant number of bonds with embedded options.

Daasvand asks Perreaux to analyze immunization approaches to liability-based mandates for a meeting with Villash Foundation. Villash Foundation is a tax-exempt client. Prior to the meeting, Perreaux identifies what she considers to be two key features of a cash flow–matching approach.

Feature 1:   It requires no yield curve assumptions.

Feature 2:   Cash flows come from coupons and liquidating bond portfolio positions.

Two years later, Daasvand learns that Villash Foundation needs $5,000,000 in cash to meet liabilities. She asks Perreaux to analyze two bonds for possible liquidation. Selected data on the two bonds are presented in Exhibit 2.

EXHIBIT 2   Selected Data for Bonds 1 and 2

	Bond 1	Bond 2
Current market value	$5,000,000	$5,000,000
Capital gain/loss	400,000	−400,000
Coupon rate	2.05%	2.05%
Remaining maturity	8 years	8 years
Investment view	Overvalued	Undervalued
Income tax rate	39%	
Capital gains tax rate	30%	

1. Based on Exhibit 1, which fund provides the highest level of protection against inflation for coupon payments?
   A. Aschel
   B. Permot
   C. Rosaiso
2. Based on Exhibit 1, the rolling yield of Aschel over a one-year investment horizon is *closest* to:
   A. −2.56%.
   B. 0.54%.
   C. 5.66%.
3. The levered portfolio return for Aschel is *closest* to:
   A. 7.25%.
   B. 7.71%.
   C. 8.96%.
4. Based on Note 2, Rosaiso is the only fund for which the expected change in price based on the investor's views of yields and yield spreads should be calculated using:
   A. convexity.
   B. modified duration.
   C. effective duration.
5. Is Perreaux correct with respect to key features of cash flow matching?
   A. Yes.
   B. No, only Feature 1 is correct.
   C. No, only Feature 2 is correct.
6. Based on Exhibit 2, the optimal strategy to meet Villash Foundation's cash needs is the sale of:
   A. 100% of Bond 1.
   B. 100% of Bond 2.
   C. 50% of Bond 1 and 50% of Bond 2.

The following information relates to Questions 7–12

Celia Deveraux is chief investment officer for the Topanga Investors Fund, which invests in equities and fixed income. The clients in the fund are all taxable investors. The fixed-income allocation includes a domestic (US) bond portfolio and an externally managed global bond portfolio.

The domestic bond portfolio has a total return mandate, which specifies a long-term return objective of 25 basis points (bps) over the benchmark index. Relative to the benchmark, small deviations in sector weightings are permitted, such risk factors as duration must closely match, and tracking error is expected to be less than 50 bps per year.

The objectives for the domestic bond portfolio include the ability to fund future liabilities, protect interest income from short-term inflation, and minimize the correlation with the fund's equity portfolio. The correlation between the fund's domestic bond portfolio and equity portfolio is currently 0.14. Deveraux plans to reduce the fund's equity allocation and increase the allocation to the domestic bond portfolio. She reviews two possible investment strategies.

Strategy 1:   Purchase AAA rated fixed-coupon corporate bonds with a modified duration of two years and a correlation coefficient with the equity portfolio of −0.15.

Strategy 2:   Purchase US government agency floating-coupon bonds with a modified duration of one month and a correlation coefficient with the equity portfolio of −0.10.

Deveraux realizes that the fund's return may decrease if the equity allocation of the fund is reduced. Deveraux decides to liquidate $20 million of US Treasuries that are currently owned and to invest the proceeds in the US corporate bond sector. To fulfill this strategy, Deveraux asks Dan Foster, a newly hired analyst for the fund, to recommend Treasuries to sell and corporate bonds to purchase.

Foster recommends Treasuries from the existing portfolio that he believes are overvalued and will generate capital gains. Deveraux asks Foster why he chose only overvalued bonds with capital gains and did not include any bonds with capital losses. Foster responds with two statements.

Statement 1:   Taxable investors should prioritize selling overvalued bonds and always sell them before selling bonds that are viewed as fairly valued or undervalued.

Statement 2:   Taxable investors should never intentionally realize capital losses.

Regarding the purchase of corporate bonds, Foster collects relevant data, which are presented in Exhibit 1.

EXHIBIT 1   Selected Data on Three US Corporate Bonds

Bond Characteristics	Bond 1	Bond 2	Bond 3
Credit quality	AA	AA	A
Issue size ($ millions)	100	75	75
Maturity (years)	5	7	7
Total issuance outstanding ($ millions)	1,000	1,500	1,000
Months since issuance	New issue	3	6

Deveraux and Foster review the total expected 12-month return (assuming no reinvestment income) for the global bond portfolio. Selected financial data are presented in Exhibit 2.

EXHIBIT 2   Selected Data on Global Bond Portfolio

Notional principal of portfolio (in millions)	€200
Average bond coupon payment (per €100 par value)	€2.25
Coupon frequency	Annual
Current average bond price	€98.45
Expected average bond price in one year (assuming an unchanged yield curve)	€98.62
Average bond convexity	22
Average bond modified duration	5.19
Expected average yield and yield spread change	0.15%
Expected credit losses	0.13%
Expected currency gains (€ appreciation vs. $)	0.65%

Deveraux contemplates adding a new manager to the global bond portfolio. She reviews three proposals and determines that each manager uses the same index as its benchmark but pursues a different total return approach, as presented in Exhibit 3.

EXHIBIT 3   New Manager Proposals Fixed-Income Portfolio Characteristics

Sector Weights (%)	Manager A	Manager B	Manager C	Index
Government	53.5	52.5	47.8	54.1
Agency/quasi-agency	16.2	16.4	13.4	16.0
Corporate	20.0	22.2	25.1	19.8
MBS	10.3	8.9	13.7	10.1
Risk and Return Characteristics	Manager A	Manager B	Manager C	Index
Average maturity (years)	7.63	7.84	8.55	7.56
Modified duration (years)	5.23	5.25	6.16	5.22
Average yield (%)	1.98	2.08	2.12	1.99
Turnover (%)	207	220	290	205

7. Which approach to its total return mandate is the fund's domestic bond portfolio *most likely* to use?
   A. Pure indexing
   B. Enhanced indexing
   C. Active management
8. Strategy 2 is *most likely* preferred to Strategy 1 for meeting the objective of:
   A. protecting inflation.
   B. funding future liabilities.
   C. minimizing the correlation of the fund's domestic bond portfolio and equity portfolio.
9. Are Foster's statements to Deveraux supporting Foster's choice of bonds to sell correct?
   A. Only Statement 1 is correct.
   B. Only Statement 2 is correct.
   C. Neither Statement 1 nor Statement 2 is correct.

10. Based on Exhibit 1, which bond *most likely* has the highest liquidity premium?
    A. Bond 1
    B. Bond 2
    C. Bond 3
11. Based on Exhibit 2, the total expected return of the fund's global bond portfolio is *closest* to:
    A. 0.90%.
    B. 2.20%.
    C. 3.76%.
12. Based on Exhibit 3, which manager is *most likely* to have an active management total return mandate?
    A. Manager A
    B. Manager B
    C. Manager C

CHAPTER 13

LIABILITY-DRIVEN AND INDEX-BASED STRATEGIES

LEARNING OUTCOMES

After completing this chapter, you will be able to do the following:

- describe liability-driven investing;
- evaluate strategies for managing a single liability;
- compare strategies for a single liability and for multiple liabilities, including alternative means of implementation;
- evaluate liability-based strategies under various interest rate scenarios and select a strategy to achieve a portfolio's objectives;
- explain risks associated with managing a portfolio against a liability structure;
- discuss bond indexes and the challenges of managing a fixed-income portfolio to mimic the characteristics of a bond index;
- compare alternative methods for establishing bond market exposure passively;
- discuss criteria for selecting a benchmark and justify the selection of a benchmark;
- describe construction, benefits, limitations, and risk–return characteristics of a laddered bond portfolio.

SUMMARY OVERVIEW

This chapter covers structured and passive total return fixed-income strategies: immunization of single and multiple liabilities, indexation, and laddering. The chapter makes the following main points:

- Passive fixed-income investing requires a frame of reference, such as a balance sheet, to structure the bond portfolio. This frame of reference can be as simple as the time to retirement for an individual or as complex as a balance sheet of rate-sensitive assets and liabilities for a company.
- Asset–liability management strategies consider both assets and liabilities.

- Liability-driven investing takes the liabilities as given and builds the asset portfolio in accordance with the interest rate risk characteristics of the liabilities.
- Asset-driven liabilities take the assets as given and structure debt liabilities in accordance with the interest rate characteristics of the assets.
- Assets and liabilities can be categorized by the degree of certainty surrounding the amount and timing of cash flows. Type I assets and liabilities, such as traditional fixed-rate bonds with no embedded options, have known amounts and payment dates. For Type I assets and liabilities, yield duration statistics such as Macaulay, modified, and money duration apply. Type II, III, and IV assets and liabilities have uncertain amounts and/or uncertain timing of payment. For Type II, III, and IV assets and liabilities, curve duration statistics such as effective duration are needed. A model is used to obtain the estimated values when the yield curve shifts up and down by the same amount.
- Immunization is the process of structuring and managing a fixed-income portfolio to minimize the variance in the realized rate of return over a known investment horizon.
- In the case of a single liability, immunization is achieved by matching the Macaulay duration of the bond portfolio to the horizon date. As time passes and bond yields change, the duration of the bonds changes and the portfolio needs to be rebalanced. This rebalancing can be accomplished by buying and selling bonds or using interest rate derivatives such as futures contracts and interest rate swaps.
- An immunization strategy aims to lock in the cash flow yield on the portfolio, which is the internal rate of return on the cash flows. It is not the weighted average of the yields to maturity on the bonds that constitute the portfolio.
- Immunization can be interpreted as "zero replication" in that the performance of the bond portfolio over the investment horizon replicates the zero-coupon bond that provides for perfect immunization. This zero-coupon bond has a maturity that matches the date of the single liability—there is no coupon reinvestment risk nor price risk as the bond is held to maturity (assuming no default).
- The risk to immunization is that as the yield curve shifts and twists, the cash flow yield on the bond portfolio does not match the change in the yield on the zero-coupon bond that would provide for perfect immunization.
- A sufficient, but not necessary, condition for immunization is a parallel (or shape-preserving) shift whereby all yields change by the same amount in the same direction. If the change in the cash flow yield is the same as that on the zero-coupon bond being replicated, immunization can be achieved even with a non-parallel shift to the yield curve.
- Structural risk to immunization arises from some non-parallel shifts and twists to the yield curve. This risk is reduced by minimizing the dispersion of cash flows in the portfolio, which can be accomplished by minimizing the convexity statistic for the portfolio. Concentrating the cash flows around the horizon date makes the immunizing portfolio closely track the zero-coupon bond that provides for perfect immunization.
- For multiple liabilities, one method of immunization is cash flow matching. A portfolio of high-quality zero-coupon or fixed-income bonds is purchased to match as closely as possible the amount and timing of the liabilities.
- A motive for cash flow matching can be accounting defeasance, whereby both the assets and liabilities are removed from the balance sheet.
- Immunization of multiple liabilities can be achieved by structuring and managing a portfolio of fixed income bonds. Because the market values of the assets and liabilities differ, the strategy is to match the money durations. The money duration is the modified duration

multiplied by the market value. The basis point value is a measure of money duration calculated by multiplying the money duration by 0.0001.

- The conditions to immunize multiple liabilities are that (1) the market value of assets is greater than or equal to the market value of the liabilities, (2) the asset basis point value (BPV) equals the liability BPV, and (3) the dispersion of cash flows and the convexity of assets are greater than those of the liabilities.

- A derivatives overlay—for example, interest rate futures contracts—can be used to immunize single or multiple liabilities.

- The number of futures contracts needed to immunize is the liability BPV minus the asset BPV, divided by the futures BPV. If the result is a positive number, the entity buys, or goes long, futures contracts. If the result is a negative number, the entity sells, or goes short, futures contracts. The futures BPV can be approximated by the BPV for the cheapest-to-deliver security divided by the conversion factor for the cheapest-to-deliver security.

- Contingent immunization adds active management of the surplus, which is the difference between the asset and liability market values, with the intent to reduce the overall cost of retiring the liabilities. In principle, any asset classes can be used for the active investment. The entity can choose to over-hedge or under-hedge the number of futures contracts needed for passive immunization.

- Liability-driven investing (LDI) often is used for complex rate-sensitive liabilities, such as those for a defined benefit pension plan. The retirement benefits for covered employees depend on many variables, such as years of employment, age at retirement, wage level at retirement, and expected lifetime. There are different measures for the liabilities: for instance, the accumulated benefit obligation (ABO) that is based on current wages and the projected benefit obligation (PBO) that is based on expected future wages. For each liability measure (ABO or PBO), a model is used to extract the effective duration and BPV.

- Interest rate swap overlays can be used to reduce the duration gap as measured by the asset and liability BPVs. There often is a large gap because pension funds hold sizable asset positions in equities that have low or zero effective durations and their liability durations are high.

- The hedging ratio is the percentage of the duration gap that is closed with the derivatives. A hedging ratio of zero implies no hedging. A hedging ratio of 100% implies immunization—that is, complete removal of interest rate risk.

- Strategic hedging is the active management of the hedging ratio. Because asset BPVs are less than liability BPVs in typical pension funds, the derivatives overlay requires the use of receive-fixed interest rate swaps. Because receive-fixed swaps gain value as current swap market rates fall, the fund manager could choose to raise the hedging ratio when lower rates are anticipated. If rates are expected to go up, the manager could strategically reduce the hedging ratio.

- An alternative to the receive-fixed interest rate swap is a purchased receiver swaption. This swaption confers to the buyer the right to enter the swap as the fixed-rate receiver. Because of its negative duration gap (asset BPV is less than liability BPV), the typical pension plan suffers when interest rates fall and could become underfunded. The gain on the receiver swaption as rates decline offsets the losses on the balance sheet.

- Another alternative is a swaption collar, the combination of buying the receiver swaption and writing a payer swaption. The premium received on the payer swaption that is written offsets the premium needed to buy the receiver swaption.

- The choice among hedging with the receive-fixed swap, the purchased receiver swaption, and the swaption collar depends in part on the pension fund manager's view on future interest rates. If rates are expected to be low, the receive-fixed swap typically is the preferred derivative. If rates are expected to go up, the swaption collar can become attractive. And if rates are projected to reach a certain threshold that depends on the option costs and the strike rates, the purchased receiver swaption can become the favored choice.
- Model risks arise in LDI strategies because of the many assumptions in the models and approximations used to measure key parameters. For example, the liability BPV for the defined benefit pension plan depends on the choice of measure (ABO or PBO) and the assumptions that go into the model regarding future events (e.g., wage levels, time of retirement, and time of death).
- Spread risk in LDI strategies arises because it is common to assume equal changes in asset, liability, and hedging instrument yields when calculating the number of futures contracts, or the notional principal on an interest rate swap, to attain a particular hedging ratio. The assets and liabilities are often on corporate securities, however, and their spreads to benchmark yields can vary over time.
- The Credit Support Annex to the standard ISDA swap agreement often calls for collateralization by one or both counterparties to the contract. This requirement introduces the risk of exhausting available securities or cash assets to serve as collateral.
- Investing in a fund that tracks a bond market index offers the benefits of both diversification and low administrative costs. The deviation of the returns between the index and the fund is called tracking risk, or tracking error. Tracking risk arises when the fund manager chooses to buy only a subset of the index, a strategy called enhanced indexing, because fully replicating the index can be impractical as a result of the large number of bonds in the fixed-income universe.
- Corporate bonds are often illiquid. Capital requirements have reduced the incentive for broker/dealers to maintain inventory in thinly traded securities. The lack of active trading is a challenge for valuation. Matrix pricing uses available data on comparable securities to estimate the fair value of the illiquid bonds.
- The primary risk factors encountered by an investor tracking a bond index include decisions regarding duration (option-adjusted duration for callable bonds, convexity for possible large yield shifts, and key rate durations for non-parallel shifts) and portfolio weights (assigned by sector, credit quality, maturity, coupon rate, and issuer).
- Index replication is one method to establish a passive exposure to the bond market. The manager buys or sells bonds only when there are changes to the index. Full replication can be expensive, however, as well as infeasible for broad-based fixed-income indexes that include many illiquid bonds.
- Several enhancement strategies can reduce the costs to track a bond index: lowering trading costs, using models to identify undervalued bonds and to gauge relative value at varying points along the yield curve, over/under weighting specific credit sectors over the business cycle, and evaluating specific call features to identify value given large yield changes.
- Investors can obtain passive exposure to the bond market using mutual funds and exchange-traded funds that track a bond index. Shares in mutual funds are redeemable at the net asset value with a one-day time lag. Exchange-traded fund (ETF) shares have the advantage of trading on an exchange.
- A total return swap, an over-the-counter derivative, allows an institutional investor to transform an asset or liability from one asset category to another—for instance, from variable-rate cash flows referencing Libor to the total return on a particular bond index.

- A total return swap (TRS) can have some advantages over a direct investment in a bond mutual fund or ETF. As a derivative, it requires less initial cash outlay than direct investment in the bond portfolio for similar performance. A TRS also carries counterparty credit risk, however. As a customized over-the-counter product, a TRS can offer exposure to assets that are difficult to access directly, such as some high-yield and commercial loan investments.
- Selecting a particular bond index is a major decision for a fixed-income investment manager. Selection is guided by the specified goals and objectives for the investment. The decision should recognize several features of bond indexes: (1) Given that bonds have finite maturities, the duration of the index drifts down over time; (2) the composition of the index changes over time with the business cycle and maturity preferences of issuers; and (3) value-weighted indexes assign larger shares to borrowers having more debt, leading to the "bums problem" that bond index investors can become overly exposed to leveraged firms.
- A laddered bond portfolio is a common investment strategy in the wealth management industry. The laddered portfolio offers "diversification" over the yield curve compared with "bullet" or "barbell" portfolios. This structure is especially attractive in stable, upwardly sloped yield curve environments as maturing short-term debt is replaced with higher-yielding long-term debt at the back of the ladder.
- A laddered portfolio offers an increase in convexity because the cash flows have greater dispersions than a more concentrated (bullet) portfolio.
- A laddered portfolio provides liquidity in that it always contains a soon-to-mature bond that could provide high-quality, low-duration collateral on a repo contract if needed.
- A laddered portfolio can be constructed with fixed-maturity corporate bond ETFs that have a designated maturity and credit risk profile.

PROBLEMS

The following information relates to Questions 1–8

Serena Soto is a risk management specialist with Liability Protection Advisors. Trey Hudgens, CFO of Kiest Manufacturing, enlists Soto's help with three projects. The first project is to defease some of Kiest's existing fixed-rate bonds that are maturing in each of the next three years. The bonds have no call or put provisions and pay interest annually. Exhibit 1 presents the payment schedule for the bonds.

EXHIBIT 1   Kiest Manufacturing Bond
Payment Schedule as of 1 October 2017

Maturity Date	Payment Amount
1 October 2018	$9,572,000
1 October 2019	$8,392,000
1 October 2020	$8,200,000

The second project for Soto is to help Hudgens immunize a $20 million portfolio of liabilities. The liabilities range from 3.00 years to 8.50 years with a Macaulay duration of 5.34 years, cash flow yield of 3.25%, portfolio convexity of 33.05, and basis point value (BPV) of

$10,505. Soto suggested employing a duration-matching strategy using one of the three AAA rated bond portfolios presented in Exhibit 2.

EXHIBIT 2   Possible AAA Rated Duration-Matching Portfolios

	Portfolio A	Portfolio B	Portfolio C
Bonds (term, coupon)	4.5 years, 2.63%	3.0 years, 2.00%	1.5 years, 1.25%
	7.0 years, 3.50%	6.0 years, 3.25%	11.5 years, 4.38%
		8.5 years, 3.88%	
Macaulay duration	5.35	5.34	5.36
Cash flow yield	3.16%	3.33%	3.88%
Convexity	31.98	34.51	50.21
BPV	$10,524	$10,506	$10,516

Soto explains to Hudgens that the underlying duration-matching strategy is based on the following three assumptions.

1. Yield curve shifts in the future will be parallel.
2. Bond types and quality will closely match those of the liabilities.
3. The portfolio will be rebalanced by buying or selling bonds rather than using derivatives.

The third project for Soto is to make a significant direct investment in broadly diversified global bonds for Kiest's pension plan. Kiest has a young workforce, and thus, the plan has a long-term investment horizon. Hudgens needs Soto's help to select a benchmark index that is appropriate for Kiest's young workforce and avoids the "bums" problem. Soto discusses three benchmark candidates, presented in Exhibit 3.

EXHIBIT 3   Global Bond Index Benchmark Candidates

Index Name	Effective Duration	Index Characteristics
Global Aggregate	7.73	Market cap weighted; Treasuries, corporates, agency, securitized debt
Global Aggregate GDP Weighted	7.71	Same as Global Aggregate, except GDP weighted
Global High Yield	4.18	GDP weighted; sovereign, agency, corporate debt

With the benchmark selected, Hudgens provides guidelines to Soto directing her to (1) use the most cost-effective method to track the benchmark and (2) provide low tracking error.

After providing Hudgens with advice on direct investment, Soto offered him additional information on alternative indirect investment strategies using (1) bond mutual funds, (2) exchange-traded funds (ETFs), and (3) total return swaps. Hudgens expresses interest in using bond mutual funds rather than the other strategies for the following reasons.

Reason 1   Total return swaps have much higher transaction costs and initial cash outlay than bond mutual funds.

Reason 2   Unlike bond mutual funds, bond ETFs can trade at discounts to their underlying indexes, and those discounts can persist.

Reason 3   Bond mutual funds can be traded throughout the day at the net asset value of the underlying bonds.

1. Based on Exhibit 1, Kiest's liabilities would be classified as:
   A. Type I.
   B. Type II.
   C. Type III.

2. Based on Exhibit 2, the portfolio with the greatest structural risk is:
   A. Portfolio A.
   B. Portfolio B.
   C. Portfolio C.

3. Which portfolio in Exhibit 2 fails to meet the requirements to achieve immunization for multiple liabilities?
   A. Portfolio A
   B. Portfolio B
   C. Portfolio C

4. Based on Exhibit 2, relative to Portfolio C, Portfolio B:
   A. has higher cash flow reinvestment risk.
   B. is a more desirable portfolio for liquidity management.
   C. provides less protection from yield curve shifts and twists.

5. Soto's three assumptions regarding the duration-matching strategy indicate the presence of:
   A. model risk.
   B. spread risk.
   C. counterparty credit risk.

6. The global bond benchmark in Exhibit 3 that is *most* appropriate for Kiest to use is the:
   A. Global Aggregate Index.
   B. Global High Yield Index.
   C. Global Aggregate GDP Weighted Index.

7. To meet both of Hudgens's guidelines for the pension's bond fund investment, Soto should recommend:
   A. full replication.
   B. stratified sampling.
   C. active management.

8. Which of Hudgens's reasons for choosing bond mutual funds as an investment vehicle is correct?
   A. Reason 1
   B. Reason 2
   C. Reason 3

The following information relates to Questions 9–17

SD&R Capital (SD&R), a global asset management company, specializes in fixed-income investments. Molly Compton, chief investment officer, is meeting with a prospective client, Leah Mowery of DePuy Financial Company (DFC).

Mowery informs Compton that DFC's previous fixed income manager focused on the interest rate sensitivities of assets and liabilities when making asset allocation decisions. Compton explains that, in contrast, SD&R's investment process first analyzes the size and timing of client liabilities, then builds an asset portfolio based on the interest rate sensitivity of those liabilities.

Compton notes that SD&R generally uses actively managed portfolios designed to earn a return in excess of the benchmark portfolio. For clients interested in passive exposure to fixed-income instruments, SD&R offers two additional approaches.

Approach 1   Seeks to fully replicate the Bloomberg Barclays US Aggregate Bond Index.

Approach 2   Follows a stratified sampling or cell approach to indexing for a subset of the bonds included in the Bloomberg Barclays US Aggregate Bond Index. Approach 2 may also be customized to reflect client preferences.

To illustrate SD&R's immunization approach for controlling portfolio interest rate risk, Compton discusses a hypothetical portfolio composed of two non-callable, investment-grade bonds. The portfolio has a weighted average yield-to-maturity of 9.55%, a weighted average coupon rate of 10.25%, and a cash flow yield of 9.85%.

Mowery informs Compton that DFC has a single $500 million liability due in nine years, and she wants SD&R to construct a bond portfolio that earns a rate of return sufficient to pay off the obligation. Mowery expresses concern about the risks associated with an immunization strategy for this obligation. In response, Compton makes the following statements about liability-driven investing:

Statement 1   Although the amount and date of SD&R's liability is known with certainty, measurement errors associated with key parameters relative to interest rate changes may adversely affect the bond portfolios.

Statement 2   A cash flow matching strategy will mitigate the risk from non-parallel shifts in the yield curve.

Compton provides the four US dollar–denominated bond portfolios in Exhibit 1 for consideration. Compton explains that the portfolios consist of non-callable, investment-grade corporate and government bonds of various maturities because zero-coupon bonds are unavailable.

EXHIBIT 1   Proposed Bond Portfolios to Immunize SD&R Single Liability

	Portfolio 1	Portfolio 2	Portfolio 3	Portfolio 4
Cash flow yield	7.48%	7.50%	7.53%	7.51%
Average time to maturity	11.2 years	9.8 years	9.0 years	10.1 years
Macaulay duration	9.8	8.9	8.0	9.1
Market value weighted duration	9.1	8.5	7.8	8.6
Convexity	154.11	131.75	130.00	109.32

The discussion turns to benchmark selection. DFC's previous fixed-income manager used a custom benchmark with the following characteristics:

Characteristic 1   The benchmark portfolio invests only in investment-grade bonds of US corporations with a minimum issuance size of $250 million.

Characteristic 2   Valuation occurs on a weekly basis, because many of the bonds in the index are valued weekly.

Characteristic 3   Historical prices and portfolio turnover are available for review.

Compton explains that, in order to evaluate the asset allocation process, fixed-income portfolios should have an appropriate benchmark. Mowery asks for benchmark advice regarding

DFC's portfolio of short-term and intermediate-term bonds, all denominated in US dollars. Compton presents three possible benchmarks in Exhibit 2.

EXHIBIT 2   Proposed Benchmark Portfolios

Benchmark	Index	Composition	Duration
1	Bloomberg Barclays US Bond Index	80% US government bonds 20% US corporate bonds	8.7
2 Index Blend	50% Bloomberg Barclays US Corporate Bond Index	100% US corporate bonds	7.5
	50% Bloomberg Barclays Short-Term Treasury Index	100% short-term US government debt	0.5
3	Bloomberg Barclays Global Aggregate Bond Index	60% EUR-denominated corporate bonds 40% US-denominated corporate debt	12.3

9. The investment process followed by DFC's previous fixed-income manager is *best* described as:
   A. asset-driven liabilities.
   B. liability-driven investing.
   C. asset–liability management.
10. Relative to Approach 2 of gaining passive exposure, an advantage of Approach 1 is that it:
   A. reduces the need for frequent rebalancing.
   B. limits the need to purchase bonds that are thinly traded.
   C. provides a higher degree of portfolio risk diversification.
11. Relative to Approach 1 of gaining passive exposure, an advantage of Approach 2 is that it:
   A. minimizes tracking error.
   B. requires less risk analysis.
   C. is more appropriate for socially responsible investors.
12. The two-bond hypothetical portfolio's immunization goal is to lock in a rate of return equal to:
   A. 9.55%.
   B. 9.85%.
   C. 10.25%.
13. Which of Compton's statements about liability-driven investing is (are) correct?
   A. Statement 1 only.
   B. Statement 2 only.
   C. Both Statement 1 and Statement 2.
14. Based on Exhibit 1, which of the portfolios will *best* immunize SD&R's single liability?
   A. Portfolio 1
   B. Portfolio 2
   C. Portfolio 3
15. Which of the portfolios in Exhibit 1 *best* minimizes the structural risk to a single-liability immunization strategy?
   A. Portfolio 1
   B. Portfolio 3
   C. Portfolio 4

16. Which of the custom benchmark's characteristics violates the requirements for an appropriate benchmark portfolio?
    A. Characteristic 1
    B. Characteristic 2
    C. Characteristic 3
17. Based on DFC's bond holdings and Exhibit 2, Compton should recommend:
    A. Benchmark 1.
    B. Benchmark 2.
    C. Benchmark 3.

The following information relates to Questions 18–23

Doug Kepler, the newly hired chief financial officer for the City of Radford, asks the deputy financial manager, Hui Ng, to prepare an analysis of the current investment portfolio and the city's current and future obligations. The city has multiple liabilities of different amounts and maturities relating to the pension fund, infrastructure repairs, and various other obligations.

Ng observes that the current fixed-income portfolio is structured to match the duration of each liability. Previously, this structure caused the city to access a line of credit for temporary mismatches resulting from changes in the term structure of interest rates.

Kepler asks Ng for different strategies to manage the interest rate risk of the city's fixed-income investment portfolio against one-time shifts in the yield curve. Ng considers two different strategies:

Strategy 1: Immunization of the single liabilities using zero-coupon bonds held to maturity.
Strategy 2: Immunization of the single liabilities using coupon-bearing bonds while continuously matching duration.

The city also manages a separate, smaller bond portfolio for the Radford School District. During the next five years, the school district has obligations for school expansions and renovations. The funds needed for those obligations are invested in the Bloomberg Barclays US Aggregate Index. Kepler asks Ng which portfolio management strategy would be most efficient in mimicking this index.

A Radford School Board member has stated that she prefers a bond portfolio structure that provides diversification over time, as well as liquidity. In addressing the board member's inquiry, Ng examines a bullet portfolio, a barbell portfolio, and a laddered portfolio.

18. A disadvantage of Strategy 1 is that:
    A. price risk still exists.
    B. interest rate volatility introduces risk to effective matching.
    C. there may not be enough bonds available to match all liabilities.
19. Which duration measure should be matched when implementing Strategy 2?
    A. Key rate
    B. Modified
    C. Macaulay

20. An upward shift in the yield curve on Strategy 2 will *most likely* result in the:
    A. price effect canceling the coupon reinvestment effect.
    B. price effect being greater than the coupon reinvestment effect.
    C. coupon reinvestment effect being greater than the price effect.
21. The effects of a non-parallel shift in the yield curve on Strategy 2 can be reduced by:
    A. minimizing the convexity of the bond portfolio.
    B. maximizing the cash flow yield of the bond portfolio.
    C. minimizing the difference between liability duration and bond-portfolio duration.
22. Ng's response to Kepler's question about the most efficient portfolio management strategy should be:
    A. full replication.
    B. active management.
    C. a stratified sampling approach to indexing.
23. Which portfolio structure should Ng recommend that would satisfy the school board member's preference?
    A. Bullet portfolio
    B. Barbell portfolio
    C. Laddered portfolio

The following information relates to Questions 24–26

Chaopraya Av is an investment advisor for high-net-worth individuals. One of her clients, Schuylkill Cy, plans to fund her grandson's college education and considers two options:

Option 1   Contribute a lump sum of $300,000 in 10 years.
Option 2   Contribute four level annual payments of $76,500 starting in 10 years.

The grandson will start college in 10 years. Cy seeks to immunize the contribution today.
For Option 1, Av calculates the present value of the $300,000 as $234,535. To immunize the future single outflow, Av considers three bond portfolios given that no zero-coupon government bonds are available. The three portfolios consist of non-callable, fixed-rate, coupon-bearing government bonds considered free of default risk. Av prepares a comparative analysis of the three portfolios, presented in Exhibit 1.

EXHIBIT 1   Results of Comparative Analysis of Potential Portfolios

	Portfolio A	Portfolio B	Portfolio C
Market value	$235,727	$233,428	$235,306
Cash flow yield	2.504%	2.506%	2.502%
Macaulay duration	9.998	10.002	9.503
Convexity	119.055	121.498	108.091

Av evaluates the three bond portfolios and selects one to recommend to Cy.

24. **Recommend** the portfolio in Exhibit 1 that would *best* achieve the immunization. **Justify** your response.

Template for Question 24

Recommend the portfolio in Exhibit 1 that would *best* achieve the immunization. (circle one)	**Justify** your response.
Portfolio A	
Portfolio B	
Portfolio C	

Cy and Av now discuss Option 2.

Av estimates the present value of the four future cash flows as $230,372, with a money duration of $2,609,700 and convexity of 135.142. She considers three possible portfolios to immunize the future payments, as presented in Exhibit 2.

EXHIBIT 2   Data for Bond Portfolios to Immunize Four Annual Contributions

	Portfolio 1	Portfolio 2	Portfolio 3
Market value	$245,178	$248,230	$251,337
Cash flow yield	2.521%	2.520%	2.516%
Money duration	2,609,981	2,609,442	2,609,707
Convexity	147.640	139.851	132.865

25. **Determine** the *most appropriate* immunization portfolio in Exhibit 2. **Justify** your decision.

Template for Question 25

Determine the *most appropriate* immunization portfolio in Exhibit 2. (circle one)	**Justify** your decision.
Portfolio 1	
Portfolio 2	
Portfolio 3	

After selecting a portfolio to immunize Cy's multiple future outflows, Av prepares a report on how this immunization strategy would respond to various interest rate scenarios. The scenario analysis is presented in Exhibit 3.

EXHIBIT 3   Projected Portfolio Response to Interest Rate Scenarios

	Immunizing Portfolio	Outflow Portfolio	Difference
Upward parallel shift			
Δ Market value	−6,410	−6,427	18
Δ Cash flow yield	0.250%	0.250%	0.000%
Δ Portfolio BPV	−9	−8	−1

	Immunizing Portfolio	Outflow Portfolio	Difference
Downward parallel shift			
Δ Market value	6,626	6,622	4
Δ Cash flow yield	−0.250%	−0.250%	0.000%
Δ Portfolio BPV	9	8	1
Steepening twist			
Δ Market value	−1,912	347	−2,259
Δ Cash flow yield	0.074%	−0.013%	0.087%
Δ Portfolio BPV	−3	0	−3
Flattening twist			
Δ Market value	1,966	−343	2,309
Δ Cash flow yield	−0.075%	0.013%	−0.088%
Δ Portfolio BPV	3	0	3

26. **Discuss** the effectiveness of Av's immunization strategy in terms of duration gaps.

CHAPTER 14

YIELD CURVE STRATEGIES

LEARNING OUTCOMES

After completing this chapter, you will be able to do the following:

- describe major types of yield curve strategies;
- explain how to execute a carry trade;
- explain why and how a fixed-income portfolio manager might choose to alter portfolio convexity;
- formulate a portfolio positioning strategy given forward interest rates and an interest rate view;
- explain how derivatives may be used to implement yield curve strategies;
- evaluate a portfolio's sensitivity to a change in curve slope using key rate durations of the portfolio and its benchmark;
- discuss inter-market curve strategies;
- construct a duration-neutral government bond portfolio to profit from a change in yield curve curvature;
- evaluate the expected return and risks of a yield curve strategy.

SUMMARY OVERVIEW

This chapter focused on the strategies a fixed-income portfolio manager may use to position his portfolio in anticipation of the future state of yield curves.

- Macaulay duration is a weighted average of time to receive the bond's cash flows.
- Modified duration is the Macaulay duration statistic divided by one plus the yield to maturity per period. It provides an estimate of the percentage price change for a bond given a 100 bps change in its yield to maturity.
- Effective duration is the sensitivity of the bond's price to a change in a benchmark yield curve, as opposed to the price response to a change in the bond's own yield. It is similar to modified duration, but its calculation is flexible to allow for its use in cases when the bond has an embedded option.

- Key rate duration is a measure of a bond's sensitivity to a change in the benchmark yield curve at a specific maturity point or segment. Key rate durations help identify a portfolio's sensitivity to changes in the shape of the benchmark yield curve.
- The money duration of a bond is a measure of the bond's price change in units of the currency in which the bond is denominated.
- The price value of a basis point scales money duration so that it can be interpreted as money gained or lost for each basis point change in the reference interest rate.
- The three primary yield curve movements of importance to the fixed-income manager are changes in level, slope, and curvature of the yield curve.
- Curvature of the yield curve can be measured using the butterfly spread, which describes the relationship between yields at short, intermediate, and long maturities.
- Duration management is the primary tool used by fixed-income portfolio managers.
- Convexity supplements duration as a measure of a bond's price sensitivity for larger movements in interest rates. Adjusting convexity can be an important portfolio management tool.
- Adding convexity to a portfolio using physical bonds typically requires a give-up in yield.
- For two portfolios with the same duration, the portfolio with higher convexity has higher sensitivity to large declines in yields and lower sensitivity to large increases in yields.
- Interest rate derivatives can be used effectively to add convexity to a portfolio.
- The four major strategies used when the yield curve is expected to remain stable are buy and hold; ride the yield curve; sell convexity; and the carry trade.
- A carry trade involves buying a security and financing it at a rate that is lower than the yield on that security.
- There are three basic ways to implement a carry trade to exploit a stable, upward-sloping yield curve: (a) Buy a bond and finance it in the repo market, (b) receive fixed and pay floating on an interest rate swap, and (c) take a long position in a bond (or note) futures contract.
- Inter-market carry trades may or may not involve a duration mismatch.
- Among the ways to implement an inter-market carry trade subject to currency exposure are the following: (a) Borrow from a bank in the lower interest rate currency, convert the proceeds to the higher interest rate currency, and invest in a bond denominated in that currency; (b) borrow in the higher rate currency, invest the proceeds in an instrument denominated in that currency, and convert the financing to the lower rate currency via the FX forward market; and (c) enter into a currency swap, receiving payments in the higher rate currency and making payments in the lower rate currency.
- Inter-market carry trades can be implemented without currency risk by (a) receiving fixed/paying floating in the steeper market and paying fixed/receiving floating in the flatter market or (b) taking a long position in bond (or note) futures in the steeper market and a short futures position in the flatter market.
- The major strategies used when changes are expected in the level, slope, or curvature of the yield curve are duration management; buying convexity; and bullet and barbell structures.
- Selling convexity can be accomplished by selling calls on bonds owned, selling puts on bonds one would be willing to own, or buying securities with negative convexity, such as callable bonds or mortgage-backed securities.
- Duration should not be extended or shortened without considering the manner in which the changed duration will be distributed throughout the portfolio. The same duration change can be effected with any number of trades, each of which has its own sensitivity to changes in the curve.

- Portfolio duration can be modified using futures, options, or leverage.
- A bullet portfolio holds securities targeting a single segment of the curve, with the bonds clustered around the portfolio's duration target. A bullet is typically used to take advantage of a steepening yield curve.
- A barbell portfolio combines securities with short and long maturities (and fewer intermediate maturities) compared with the duration target. A barbell is typically used to take advantage of a flattening yield curve.
- A barbell portfolio structure has higher convexity than a bullet portfolio structure.
- Key rate durations can be used to estimate a bond or portfolio's sensitivity to changes in the shape of the yield curve as well as to identify bullets and barbells.
- A butterfly trade combines a bullet and a barbell in a duration-neutral long–short structure. (This trade is distinct from the butterfly spread measure used to determine curvature.)
- A butterfly long in the wings and short in the body is long (has positive) convexity and benefits from volatile interest rates. This butterfly also benefits from a yield curve flattening (unrelated to its convexity).
- A butterfly short in the wings and long in the body is short convexity and benefits from stable interest rates. This butterfly also benefits from a yield curve steepening (unrelated to its convexity).
- Comparing forward yields (implied yield change) with a manager's yield forecast (forecast yield change) can help determine which bonds are likely to perform the best over the forecast horizon.
- Options can be used to add or reduce convexity in a portfolio.
- Inter-market trades involve more than one yield curve and require the investor to either accept or somehow hedge currency risk.
- In addition to carry, the primary driver of inter-market trades is a view on the narrowing or widening of yield spreads between markets.
- The lack of credibly fixed exchange rates allows (default-free) yield curves, and hence bond returns, to be less than perfectly correlated across markets.
- Currency hedging does not eliminate the opportunity to add value via inter-market trades.
- Inter-market asset decisions should be made on the basis of prospective currency-hedged returns. Currency exposure decisions should be based on projected appreciation or depreciation relative to forward FX rates rather than on projected spot FX appreciation/depreciation alone.
- The expected return of a fixed income portfolio can be estimated using the following formula:

$$E(R) \approx \text{Yield income} + \text{Rolldown return}$$
$$+ E(\text{Change in price}) - E(\text{Credit losses}) + E(\text{Currency gains or losses})$$

- Changes in the level and shape of the yield curve can be decomposed into three types of movements that explain nearly all of the variation in yields: (1) a non-parallel increase/decrease in all yields ("shift"), (2) a steepening/flattening ("twist"), and (3) a change in curvature in which the long and short ends of the curve move in the direction opposite to that of the intermediate maturities ("butterfly").
- The risk of a yield curve trade or, more generally, portfolio positioning on the curve, can be described and measured based on exposures to combinations of the three basic components: shift, twist, and butterfly.

Relative Performance of Bullets and Barbells under Different Yield Curve Scenarios

Yield Curve Scenario		Barbell	Bullet
Level change	Parallel shift	Outperforms	Underperforms
Slope change	Flattening	Outperforms	Underperforms
	Steepening	Underperforms	Outperforms
Curvature change	Less curvature	Underperforms	Outperforms
	More curvature	Outperforms	Underperforms
Rate volatility change	Decreased rate volatility	Underperforms	Outperforms
	Increased rate volatility	Outperforms	Underperforms

PROBLEMS

The following information relates to Questions 1–6

Amy McLaughlin is a fixed-income portfolio manager at UK-based Delphi Investments. One year ago, given her expectations of a stable yield curve over the coming 12 months and noting that the yield curve was upward sloping, McLaughlin elected to position her portfolio solely in 20-year US Treasury bonds with a coupon rate of 4% and a price of 101.7593, with the expectation of selling the bonds in one year at a price of 109.0629. McLaughlin expected the US dollar to depreciate relative to the British pound by 1.50% during the year. McLaughlin chose the 20-year Treasury bonds because they were on the steepest part of the yield curve.

    McLaughlin and Michaela Donaldson, a junior analyst at Delphi, are now discussing how to reposition the portfolio in light of McLaughlin's expectations about interest rates over the next 12 months. She expects interest rate volatility to be high and the yield curve to experience an increase in the 2s/10s/30s butterfly spread, with the 30-year yield remaining unchanged. Selected yields on the Treasury yield curve, and McLaughlin's expected changes in yields over the next 12 months, are presented in Exhibit 1.

EXHIBIT 1   Current Treasury Yield Curve and Forecasted Yields

Maturity (years)	Starting Yield (Current)	Forecasted Change in Yield	Ending Yield
2	1.01%	+0.04%	1.05%
5	1.55%	+0.40%	1.95%
10	2.75%	+0.50%	3.25%
30	3.50%	+0.00%	3.50%

    Based on these interest rate expectations, McLaughlin asks Donaldson to recommend a portfolio strategy. Donaldson considers the following three options.

Bullet portfolio:	Invest solely in 10-year Treasury government bonds
Barbell portfolio:	Invest solely in 2-year and 30-year Treasury government bonds
Laddered portfolio:	Invest equally in 2-year, 5-year, 10-year, and 30-year Treasury government bonds

After recommending a portfolio strategy, McLaughlin tells Donaldson that using a duration-neutral, long/short structure may be a better strategy for attempting to enhance portfolio return. McLaughlin suggests that Donaldson consider a butterfly trade or a condor trade using some combination of 2-year, 5-year, 10-year, and 30-year bonds.

Donaldson suggests they also consider altering the portfolio's convexity to enhance expected return given McLaughlin's interest rate expectations. Donaldson tells McLaughlin the following.

Statement 1:   Portfolios with larger convexities often have higher yields.

Statement 2:   If yields rise, a portfolio of a given duration with higher convexity will experience less of a price decrease than a similar-duration, lower-convexity portfolio.

1. The portfolio strategy implemented by McLaughlin last year is *mostly likely* to be described as:
   A. a carry trade.
   B. a barbell structure.
   C. riding the yield curve.
2. At the start of last year, the expected return on the portfolio strategy implemented by McLaughlin was *closest* to:
   A. 9.61%.
   B. 9.68%.
   C. 12.61%.
3. Using the yield curve forecast shown in Exhibit 1, which portfolio strategy should Donaldson recommend for the year ahead?
   A. The bullet portfolio
   B. The barbell portfolio
   C. The laddered portfolio
4. Given McLaughlin's interest rate expectations over the next 12 months, which long/short structure would be most appropriate?
   A. Condor: short wings, long body
   B. Butterfly: short barbell, long bullet
   C. Butterfly: long barbell, short bullet
5. Given McLaughlin's interest rate expectations over the next 12 months, one way that Donaldson and McLaughlin could alter convexity to enhance expected return would be to:
   A. sell call options on bonds held in the portfolio.
   B. buy call options on long-maturity government bond futures.
   C. sell put options on bonds they would be willing to own in the portfolio.
6. Which of Donaldson's statements is correct?
   A. Only Statement 1
   B. Only Statement 2
   C. Both Statements 1 and 2

The following information relates to Questions 7–14

Sanober Hirji is a junior analyst with Northco Securities, which is based in Canada. The institutional clients of Northco are active investors in Canadian coupon-bearing government bonds. Client portfolios are benchmarked to a Canadian government bond index, which is a diverse maturity index portfolio. After reviewing the portfolio of a French institutional client, Hirji evaluates yield curve strategies for Canadian government bond portfolios under various interest rate scenarios. Hirji's supervisor, Éliane Prégent, forecasts that Canadian long-term rates will rise and short-term rates will fall over the next 12 months.

Northco's chief economist forecasts that Canadian interest rates will increase or decrease by 100 basis points over the next 12 months. Based on the chief economist's forecast, Hirji suggests increasing the convexity of the French institutional client's portfolio by selling 10-year bonds and investing the proceeds in a duration-matched barbell position of Canadian government 3-year and long-term bonds. She notes that the duration of the 10-year bonds, along with the durations of the other portfolio bonds, aligns the portfolio's effective duration with that of the benchmark. Selected data on Canadian government bonds are presented in Exhibit 1.

EXHIBIT 1   Canadian Government Bonds as of 1 January

Security	Effective Duration	Effective Convexity
1-year	0.99	0.007
3-year	2.88	0.118
10-year	9.51	0.701
Long-term	21.30	2.912

* There is no single convention for how convexity numbers are presented; for example, Bloomberg has historically followed a convention of dividing the "raw" convexity number by 100 (as presented here). However, it is important to use the raw convexity number when estimating returns.

Hirji then considers a strategy to sell some long-term bonds from the French institutional client's portfolio and purchase short maturity at-the-money options on long-term bond futures. The portfolio's duration would remain unchanged. Prégent asks:

"How would portfolio performance be affected by this strategy if the yield curve were to remain stable?"

Hirji also proposes the following duration-neutral trades for the French institutional client:

• Long/short trade on 1-year and 3-year Canadian government bonds
• Short/long trade on 10-year and long-term Canadian government bonds

Six months later, Hirji reviews Canadian government bonds for a Malaysian institutional client. Prégent and Hirji expect changes in the curvature of the yield curve but are not sure whether curvature will increase or decrease. Hirji first analyzes positions that would profit from an increase in the curvature of the yield curve. The positions must be duration neutral, and the maximum position that the Malaysian client can take in long-term bonds is C$150 million. Hirji notes that interest rates have increased by 100 basis points over the past six months. Selected data for on-the-run Canadian government bonds are shown in Exhibit 2.

EXHIBIT 2   On-the-Run Canadian Government Bonds as of 1 July

Maturity	YTM (%)	Duration	PVBP (C$ million)
2-year	1.73	1.97	197
5-year	2.01	4.78	478
10-year	2.55	8.89	889
Long-term	3.16	19.60	1,960

Hirji then considers the scenario where the yield curve will lose curvature for the Malaysian institutional client. She notes that a 7-year Canadian government bond is also available in the market. Hirji proposes a duration-neutral portfolio comprised of 47% in 5-year bonds and 53% in 7-year bonds.

Finally, Hirji uses the components of expected returns to compare the performance of a bullet portfolio and a barbell portfolio for a British institutional client. Characteristics of these portfolios are shown in Exhibit 3.

EXHIBIT 3   Characteristics of Bullet and Barbell Portfolios

	Bullet Portfolio	Barbell Portfolio
Investment horizon (years)	1.0	1.0
Average annual coupon rate for portfolio	1.86%	1.84%
Average beginning bond price for portfolio	C$100.00	C$100.00
Average ending bond price for portfolio (assuming rolldown and stable yield curve)	C$100.38	C$100.46
Current modified duration for portfolio	4.96	4.92
Expected effective duration for portfolio (at the horizon)	4.12	4.12
Expected convexity for portfolio (at the horizon)	14.68	24.98
Expected change in government yield curve	−0.55%	−0.55%

7. Based on Prégent's interest rate forecast over the next 12 months, the yield curve strategy that would *most likely* realize the highest profit is:
   A. a carry trade.
   B. a bullet structure.
   C. duration management by buying long-term Canadian bonds.
8. Based on Exhibit 1, the gain in convexity from Hirji's suggestion is *closest* to:
   A. 0.423.
   B. 1.124.
   C. 1.205.
9. The answer to Prégent's question is that the portfolio would *most likely* experience:
   A. a loss.
   B. no change.
   C. a gain.

10. Which yield curve forecast will *most likely* result in the highest profit for Hirji's proposed duration-neutral trades?
    A. Increase in curvature
    B. Decrease in curvature
    C. Parallel downward shift
11. Based on Exhibit 2, the amount that Hirji should allocate to the 2-year bond position is *closest* to:
    A. C$331 million.
    B. C$615 million.
    C. C$1,492 million.
12. Relative to the Canadian government bond index, the portfolio that Hirji proposes for the Malaysian client will *most likely*:
    A. underperform.
    B. remain stable.
    C. outperform.
13. Based on Exhibit 3, the difference in the rolling yield between Hirji's bullet portfolio and barbell portfolio is:
    A. −8 basis points.
    B. −6 basis points.
    C. 2 basis points.
14. Based on Exhibit 3, the total expected return of Hirji's barbell portfolio is *closest* to:
    A. −2.30%.
    B. 0.07%.
    C. 4.60%.

The following information relates to Questions 15–22

Silvia Abram and Walter Edgarton are analysts with Cefrino Investments, which sponsors the Cefrino Sovereign Bond Fund (the Fund). Abram and Edgarton recently attended an investment committee meeting where interest rate expectations for the next 12 months were discussed. The Fund's mandate allows its duration to fluctuate ±0.30 per year from the benchmark duration. The Fund's duration is currently equal to its benchmark. Although the Fund is presently invested entirely in annual coupon sovereign bonds, its investment policy also allows investments in mortgage-backed securities (MBS) and call options on government bond futures. The Fund's current holdings of on-the-run bonds are presented in Exhibit 1.

EXHIBIT 1   Cefrino Sovereign Bond Fund Current Fund Holdings of On-the-Run Bonds

Maturity	Coupon/YTM	Market Value	Modified Duration
1-year	0.78%	$10,000,000	0.99
3-year	1.40%	$10,000,000	2.92
5-year	1.80%	$10,000,000	4.74
10-year	2.34%	$10,000,000	8.82
30-year	2.95%	$10,000,000	19.69
Portfolio	1.85%	$50,000,000	7.43

Over the next 12 months, Abram expects a stable yield curve; however, Edgarton expects a steepening yield curve, with short-term yields rising by 1.00% and long-term yields rising by more than 1.00%.

Based on her yield curve forecast, Abram recommends to her supervisor changes to the Fund's holdings using the following three strategies:

Strategy 1   Sell the 3-year bonds, and use the proceeds to buy 10-year bonds.

Strategy 2   Sell the 5-year bonds, and use the proceeds to buy 30-year MBS with an effective duration of 4.75.

Strategy 3   Sell the 10-year bonds, and buy call options on 10-year government bond futures.

Abram's supervisor disagrees with Abram's yield curve outlook. The supervisor develops two alternative portfolio scenarios based on her own yield curve outlook:

Scenario 1   Sell all bonds in the Fund except the 2-year and 30-year bonds, and increase positions in these two bonds while keeping duration neutral to the benchmark.

Scenario 2   Construct a condor to benefit from less curvature in the 5-year to 10-year area of the yield curve. The condor will utilize the same 1-year, 5-year, 10-year, and 30-year bonds held in the Fund. The maximum allowable position in the 30-year bond in the condor is $17 million, and the bonds must have equal (absolute value) money duration.

Edgarton evaluates the Fund's positions from Exhibit 1 along with two of his pro forma portfolios, which are summarized in Exhibit 2:

EXHIBIT 2   Selected Partial Durations

Maturity	Beginning Yield Curve	Curve Shift	Current Portfolio Partial PVBP	Pro Forma Portfolio 1 Partial PVBP	Pro Forma Portfolio 2 Partial PVBP
1-year	0.78%	1.00%	0.0020	0.0018	0.0021
3-year	1.40%	1.00%	0.0058	0.0044	0.0061
5-year	1.80%	1.25%	0.0095	0.0114	0.0095
10-year	2.34%	1.60%	0.0177	0.0212	0.0159
30-year	2.95%	1.75%	0.0394	0.0374	0.0394

Last, Edgarton reviews a separate account for Cefrino's US clients that invest in Australian government bonds. He expects a stable Australian yield curve over the next 12 months. He evaluates the return from buying and holding a 1-year Australian government bond versus buying the 2-year Australian government bond and selling it in one year.

EXHIBIT 3   Cefrino Australian Government Bond Portfolio Assumptions for Stable Yield Curve

	Portfolio Strategies	
	Buy and Hold Portfolio	Ride the Yield Curve Portfolio
Investment horizon (years)	1.0	1.0
Bonds maturity at purchase (years)	1.0	2.0
Coupon rate	1.40%	1.75%
Yield to maturity	1.65%	1.80%

EXHIBIT 3   (Continued)

	Portfolio Strategies	
	Buy and Hold Portfolio	Ride the Yield Curve Portfolio
Current average portfolio bond price	A$99.75	A$99.90
Expected average bond price in one year for portfolio	A$100.00	A$100.10
Expected currency gains or losses	−0.57%	−0.57%

15. Based on Exhibit 1 and Abram's expectation for the yield curve over the next 12 months, the strategy *most likely* to improve the Fund's return relative to the benchmark is to:
    A. buy and hold.
    B. increase convexity.
    C. ride the yield curve.

16. Based on Edgarton's expectation for the yield curve over the next 12 months, the Fund's return relative to the benchmark would *most likely* increase by:
    A. riding the yield curve.
    B. implementing a barbell structure.
    C. shortening the portfolio duration relative to the benchmark.

17. Based on Exhibit 1 and Abram's interest rate expectations, which of the following strategies is expected to perform *best* over the next 12 months?
    A. Strategy 1
    B. Strategy 2
    C. Strategy 3

18. The yield curve expectation that Abram's supervisor targets with Scenario 1 is *most likely* a:
    A. flattening yield curve.
    B. reduction in yield curve curvature.
    C. 100 bps parallel shift downward of the yield curve.

19. Based on Exhibit 1, which short position is *most likely* to be included in the condor outlined in Scenario 2?
    A. 1-year $338 million
    B. 5-year $71 million
    C. 10-year $38 million

20. Based on Exhibits 1 and 2, which of the following portfolios is *most likely* to have the *best* performance given Edgarton's yield curve expectations?
    A. Current Portfolio
    B. Pro Forma Portfolio 1
    C. Pro Forma Portfolio 2

21. Based on Exhibit 3, the 1-year expected return of the Buy and Hold Portfolio for the Cefrino Australian government bond portfolio is *closest* to:
    A. 0.83%.
    B. 1.08%.
    C. 2.22%.

22. Based on Exhibit 3, the implied Australian dollar (A$) 1-year rate, 1-year forward is *closest* to:
    A. 0.15%.
    B. 1.95%.
    C. 2.10%.

The following information relates to Questions 23–32

Susan Winslow manages bond funds denominated in US dollars, euros, and British pounds. Each fund invests in sovereign bonds and related derivatives. Each fund can invest a portion of its assets outside its base currency market with or without hedging the currency exposure, but to date Winslow has not utilized this capacity. She believes she can also hedge bonds into currencies other than a portfolio's base currency when she expects doing so will add value. However, the legal department has not yet confirmed this interpretation. If the lawyers disagree, Winslow will be limited to either unhedged positions or hedging into each portfolio's base currency.

Given the historically low rates available in the US, Euro, and UK markets, Winslow has decided to look for inter-market opportunities. With that in mind, she gathered observations about such trades from various sources. Winslow's notes with respect to carry trades include these statements:

I. Carry trades may or may not involve a maturity mismatch.
II. Carry trades require two yield curves with substantially different slopes.
III. Inter-market carry trades just break even if both yield curves move to the forward rates.

Regarding inter-market trades in general her notes indicate:

IV. Inter-market trades should be assessed based on currency-hedged returns.
V. Anticipated changes in yield spreads are the primary driver of inter-market trades.
VI. Whether a bond offers a relatively attractive return depends on both the portfolio's base currency and the currency in which the bond is denominated.

Winslow thinks the Mexican and Greek markets may offer attractive opportunities to enhance returns. Yields in these markets are given in Exhibit 1, along with those for the base currencies of her portfolios. The Greek rates are for euro-denominated government bonds priced at par. In the other markets, the yields apply to par sovereign bonds as well as to the fixed side of swaps versus six-month Libor (i.e., swap spreads are zero in each market). The six-month Libor rates also represent the rates at which investors can borrow or lend in each currency. Winslow observes that the five-year Treasury-note and the five-year German government note are the cheapest to deliver against their respective futures contracts expiring in six months.

EXHIBIT 1   Sovereign Yields in Five Markets

	Floating	Fixed Rate with Semi-annual Payments				
	6 Mo Libor	1 Yr	2 Yr	3 Yr	4 Yr	5 Yr
Mexico	7.10%	7.15%	7.20%	7.25%	7.25%	7.25%
Greece	—	3.30%	5.20%	5.65%	5.70%	5.70%
Euro	0.15%	0.25%	0.30%	0.40%	0.50%	0.60%
UK	0.50%	0.70%	0.80%	0.95%	1.00%	1.10%
US	1.40%	1.55%	1.70%	1.80%	1.90%	1.95%

Winslow expects yields in the US, Euro, UK, and Greek markets to remain stable over the next six months. She expects Mexican yields to decline to 7.0% at all maturities. Meanwhile, she projects that the Mexican peso will depreciate by 2% against the euro, the US dollar will depreciate by 1% against the euro, and the British pound will remain stable versus the euro.

Winslow believes bonds of the same maturity may be viewed as having the same duration for purposes of identifying the most attractive positions.

Based on these views, Winslow is considering three types of trades. First, she is looking at carry trades, with or without taking currency exposure, among her three base currency markets. Each such trade will involve extending duration (e.g., lend long/borrow short) in no more than one market. Second, assuming the legal department confirms her interpretation of permissible currency hedging, she wants to identify the most attractive five-year bond and currency exposure for each of her three portfolios from among the five markets shown in Exhibit 1. Third, she wants to identify the most attractive five-year bond and hedging decision for each portfolio if she is only allowed to hedge into the portfolio's base currency.

23. Which of Winslow's statements about carry trades is correct?
    A. Statement I
    B. Statement II
    C. Statement III
24. Which of Winslow's statements about inter-market trades is *incorrect*?
    A. Statement IV
    B. Statement V
    C. Statement VI
25. Among the carry trades available in the US, Euro, and UK markets, the highest expected return for the USD-denominated portfolio over the next 6 months is *closest to*:
    A. 0.275%.
    B. 0.85%.
    C. 0.90%.
26. Considering only the US, UK, and Euro markets, the most attractive duration-neutral, currency-neutral carry trade could be implemented as:
    A. Buy 3-year UK gilts, Sell 3-year German notes, and enter a 6-month FX forward contract to pay EUR/receive GBP.
    B. Receive fixed/pay floating on a 3-year GBP interest rate swap and receive floating/pay fixed on a 3-year EUR interest rate swap.
    C. Buy the T-note futures contract and sell the German note futures contract for delivery in six months.
27. If Winslow is limited to unhedged positions or hedging into each portfolio's base currency, she can obtain the highest expected returns by
    A. buying the Mexican 5-year in each of the portfolios and hedging it into the base currency of the portfolio.
    B. buying the Greek 5-year in each of the portfolios, hedging the currency in the GBP-based portfolio, and leaving the currency unhedged in the dollar-based portfolio.
    C. buying the Greek 5-year in the euro-denominated portfolio, buying the Mexican 5-year in the GBP- and USD-denominated portfolios, and leaving the currency unhedged in each case.
28. If Winslow is allowed to hedge into any of the currencies, she can obtain the highest expected returns by
    A. buying the Greek 5-year in each portfolio and hedging it into pesos.
    B. buying the Greek 5-year in each portfolio and hedging it into USD.
    C. buying the Mexican 5-year in each portfolio and not hedging the currency.

The following information relates to Questions 29–32

Katsuko Zhao and Johan Flander are portfolio managers with Cowiler Investments, a US-based company. They are assessing the effect of their yield curve forecasts on their bond portfolios. The yield curve is currently upward sloping.

Zhao's portfolio is currently invested in US Treasury securities. Zhao forecasts an instantaneous parallel downward shift in the yield curve. Zhao considers two alternatives to reposition her current portfolio given her yield curve forecast and assesses the trade-off between convexity and yield. Exhibit 1 presents allocations for the current and two alternative portfolios. The durations of the current and alternative portfolios are closely matched.

EXHIBIT 1   Allocations for Current and Alternative Portfolios

Remaining Term	Current	Alternative 1	Alternative 2
2 years	33.33%	0.00%	50.00%
10 years	33.33%	100.00%	0.00%
20 years	33.33%	0.00%	50.00%

29. **Determine** which alternative portfolio in Exhibit 1 would be *most appropriate* for Zhao given her yield curve forecast. **Justify** your selection.

Template for Question 29

Determine which alternative portfolio in Exhibit 1 would be *most appropriate* for Zhao, given her yield curve forecast. (circle one)

Alternative 1	Alternative 2
Justify your selection.	

Based on Zhao's forecast of an instantaneous parallel downward shift in the yield curve, she also considers selling a portion of the US Treasury securities in her portfolio and buying one of the following two investments:

Investment 1   A mortgage-backed security (MBS)
Investment 2   A near-the-money call option on 20-year Treasury bond futures

The effective duration of the resulting portfolio will be closely matched to Zhao's current portfolio.

30. **Determine** which investment would be *most appropriate* for Zhao given her yield curve forecast. **Justify** your response.

Template for Question 30

Determine which investment would be *most appropriate* for Zhao given her yield curve forecast. (circle one)

Investment 1	Investment 2

Justify your response.

Flander forecasts that the yield curve will steepen over the next 12 months, with long rates remaining the same and short and intermediate rates falling. Flander evaluates the effect of these interest rate changes on his three bond portfolios. The partial or key rate price value of a basis point (PVBP) data for Flander's three portfolios is presented in Exhibit 2.

EXHIBIT 2   Partial or Key Rate PVBPs for Short, Intermediate, and Long-Term Maturities

	Total	Short	Intermediate	Long
Portfolio A	0.0374	0.0056	0.0127	0.0191
Portfolio B	0.0374	0.0102	0.0079	0.0193
Portfolio C	0.0374	0.0103	0.0169	0.0102

31. **Determine** which portfolio in Exhibit 2 will *most likely* have the *best* performance over the next 12 months given Flander's yield curve forecast. **Justify** your response.

Template for Question 31

Determine which portfolio in Exhibit 2 will *most likely* have the *best* performance over the next 12 months given Flander's yield curve forecast. (circle one)

Portfolio A	Portfolio B	Portfolio C

Justify your response.

Flander evaluates a new bullet portfolio and a new barbell portfolio, each with a 12-month time horizon, using zero-coupon notes issued by the Australian government. Flander projects that over the next 12 months, the Australian zero-coupon yield curve will experience a downward parallel shift of 60 bps. The Australian dollar is projected to remain stable relative to the US dollar. Exhibit 3 presents the data for the two portfolios.

EXHIBIT 3   Selected Data for Australian Bullet and Barbell Portfolios

	Bullet	Barbell
Investment horizon (years)	1.0	1.0
Average bond price for portfolio currently	98.00	98.00
Average bond price for portfolio in one year (assuming stable yield curve)	99.75	100.00
Expected effective duration for portfolio (at the horizon)	3.95	3.95
Expected convexity for portfolio (at the horizon)	19.50	34.00
Expected change in government bond yield curve	−0.60%	−0.60%

32. **Calculate** the total expected return for the bullet and barbell portfolios presented in Exhibit 3. **Show** your calculations. **Identify** the component factor that contributes most of the outperformance of the higher-performing portfolio.

Template for Question 32

Calculate the total expected return for the bullet and barbell portfolios presented in Exhibit 3. **Show** your calculations.

Identify the component factor that contributes most of the outperformance of the higher-performing portfolio.

CHAPTER 15

FIXED-INCOME ACTIVE MANAGEMENT: CREDIT STRATEGIES

LEARNING OUTCOMES

After completing this chapter, you will be able to do the following:

- describe risk considerations in investment-grade and high-yield corporate bond portfolios;
- compare the use of credit spread measures in portfolio construction;
- discuss bottom-up approaches to credit strategies;
- discuss top-down approaches to credit strategies;
- discuss liquidity risk in credit markets and how liquidity risk can be managed in a credit portfolio;
- describe how to assess and manage tail risk in credit portfolios;
- discuss considerations in constructing and managing portfolios across international credit markets;
- describe the use of structured financial instruments as an alternative to corporate bonds in credit portfolios.

SUMMARY OVERVIEW

This chapter covers strategies and risk considerations in the construction and management of credit portfolios. Key points include the following:
- Credit risk is usually the most important consideration for high-yield portfolio managers. For investment-grade portfolio managers, interest rate risk, spread risk, and credit migration (or credit downgrade) risk are typically the most relevant considerations.
- The risk in a portfolio of investment-grade bonds is typically measured in terms of spread duration.

- Credit spreads tend to be negatively correlated with risk-free interest rates.
- When default losses are low and credit spreads are relatively tight, high-yield bonds tend to behave more like investment-grade bonds; that is, with greater interest rate sensitivity.
- High-yield bonds tend to be less liquid than investment-grade bonds because of higher return volatility in the high-yield bond market; smaller inventories of high-yield bonds than of investment-grade bonds held by broker/dealers; and smaller size of the high-yield market compared with the investment-grade market.
- Reflecting differences in liquidity between high-yield and investment-grade bonds, bid–offer spreads are larger for high-yield bonds.
- Credit spread measures include spread over the benchmark, the G-spread, the I-spread, the Z-spread, and option-adjusted spread. Each measure has advantages and disadvantages in use.
- Excess return is the compensation that a bond investor receives for assuming credit risk. When considering excess return, credit portfolio managers typically manage interest rate risk separately.
- A bottom-up approach to credit strategy involves selecting the individual bonds or issuers that the investor views as having the best relative value from among a set of bonds or issuers with similar characteristics (usually the same industry and often the same country of domicile).
- A spread curve is the fitted curve of credit spreads for each bond of an issuer plotted against either the maturity or duration of each of those bonds. A spread curve may be useful in conducting bottom-up relative value analysis.
- A top-down approach to credit strategy involves the investor formulating a view on major macroeconomic trends, such as economic growth and corporate default rates, and then selecting the bonds that she expects to perform best in the expected environment.
- Top-down portfolio managers commonly use several measures to gauge the credit quality of their portfolios: (1) average credit quality; (2) average OAS; (3) average spread duration; (4) duration multiplied by spread.
- In practice, investors often employ a combination of a top-down and bottom-up approach to credit strategy.
- Some fixed-income mandates include a requirement that the portfolio consider environmental, social, and governance factors in the investment process. ESG factors are particularly relevant to the credit component of fixed-income portfolio mandates.
- Liquidity risk is prominent in the credit markets, particularly following the global financial crisis. Measures of secondary market liquidity include trading volume, spread sensitivity to fund outflows, and bid–ask spreads.
- Liquidity management tools used by credit portfolio managers include cash, position sizing, credit default swap index derivatives, exchange-traded funds, and liquid bonds outside the benchmark.
- Scenario analysis is a common tool for assessing tail risk in credit portfolios. Two principal tools that investors use to manage tail risk include portfolio diversification and tail risk hedges.
- Many investors manage bonds that are issued in multiple countries and currencies and therefore need to consider international (global) implications.
- Credit portfolio managers can improve returns through geographic diversification (investing across various countries and regions). Risks of geographic diversification include geopolitical risk, elevated liquidity risk, currency risk, and legal risk.

- Credit investors sometimes use structured financial instruments as alternatives to corporate bonds. Common types of structured financial instruments include mortgage-backed securities, asset-backed securities, collateralized debt obligations, and covered bonds.

PROBLEMS

The following information relates to Questions 1–9

Emma Gerber and Juliette Petit are senior and junior credit portfolio managers, respectively, for a European money management firm. They are discussing credit management strategies and preparing for an annual meeting with a major client.

One of their high-yield bond holdings is a 10-year bond issued by EKN Corporation (EKN). The bond has a price of 91.82, a modified duration of 8.47, and a spread duration of 8.47. For this bond, Petit speculates on the effects of an interest rate increase of 20 bps and, because of a change in its credit risk, an increase in the EKN bond's credit spread of 20 bps. Petit comments that because the modified duration and credit spread duration of the EKN bond are equal, the bond's price will not change (all else being equal) in response to the interest rate and credit spread changes.

Gerber explains the concept of empirical duration to Petit and makes the following points.

Point 1:   A common way to calculate a bond's empirical duration is to run a regression of its price returns on changes in a benchmark interest rate.

Point 2:   A bond's empirical duration tends to be larger than its effective duration.

Point 3:   The price sensitivity of high-yield bonds to interest rate changes is typically higher than that of investment-grade bonds.

Exhibit 1 shows information for three BBB rated bonds issued by a large automotive company. Gerber asks Petit to interpret the data in the table and notes that the current interest rate environment is characterized by a positively sloped yield curve.

EXHIBIT 1   Selected Data for Three BBB Rated Bonds

	Bond 1	Bond 2	Bond 3
Price	99.350	130.054	101.135
Coupon (%)	3.100	7.500	4.300
G-spread (bps)	162.3	228.3	148.6
I-spread (bps)	176.9	242.8	103.3
Z-spread (bps)	178.4	246.9	102.4
OAS (bps)	70.2	234.9	78.8

Petit makes three observations about these bonds.

Observation 1:   We should buy Bond 1 because the difference between its Z-spread and OAS is the largest.

Observation 2:   We prefer Bond 1 to Bond 3 because Bond 1 has a greater Z-spread.

Observation 3:   Bond 2 is a non-callable bond because its option-adjusted spread (OAS) is similar to the bond's other three spread levels.

Petit observes that credit spread levels for bonds are currently higher than normal, and she recommends that the firm increase its investment in high-yield bonds. She mentions three reasons for increasing high-yield bond exposure.

- Reason 1: The portfolio's liquidity will improve.
- Reason 2: Defaults on high-yield bonds will be relatively low.
- Reason 3: The firm's view is that economic growth will be greater than the consensus forecast.

Petit develops investment recommendations for a currency-hedged portfolio of US and European corporate bonds. She expects US interest rates to decline relative to European interest rates. Furthermore, the spread curve for US corporate bonds indicates that the average spread of five-year BB bonds exceeds the average spread of two-year BB bonds by +90 bps. Petit expects the difference between average credit spreads for these two sectors to narrow to +50 bps.

Gerber is looking at the high-yield portfolio and investigates secondary market characteristics that would increase the portfolio's liquidity.

On another topic, Gerber is concerned that the scenario analysis models for the credit portfolio underestimate tail risk, and she asks Petit how to address this issue. Petit responds, "We can change the expected correlations between prices in our models to generate more extremely unusual outcomes."

Gerber is preparing for the annual meeting with one of the firm's largest clients. The client wants to explore more international credit investing. Gerber anticipates that the client will ask about differences between investing in emerging markets (EM) credits and developed markets credits. To address this potential inquiry, Gerber plans to emphasize the following differences.

Difference 1:   Commodity producers and banks represent a higher proportion of EM indexes than of developed market indexes.

Difference 2:   Total or partial government ownership of EM issuers is common, which results in a higher average recovery rate for defaulted senior unsecured bonds for EM markets than for developed markets.

Difference 3:   Compared with developed markets, the credit quality of EM issuers tends to be more concentrated at the very high and very low portions of the credit spectrum.

Gerber also is preparing a more general discussion about domestic versus international portfolio management. In Gerber's written report, Petit identifies three statements that she wants to check for accuracy.

Statement 1:   Currency risk in global credit portfolios can be mitigated by using currency swaps or by investing in credits denominated in currencies that are pegged or tightly managed by the government.

Statement 2:   Liquidity concerns for EM credits are mitigated by their frequency of trading and modest legal risk.

Statement 3:   Sectors tend to perform similarly across regions.

1. Is Petit's prediction correct that the EKN bond price will not change in response to the interest rate and credit spread changes, all else being equal?
   A. Yes
   B. No, the bond price should decrease.
   C. No, the bond price should increase.
2. Which of Gerber's points about empirical duration is correct?
   A. Point 1
   B. Point 2
   C. Point 3
3. Which of Petit's observations about the three BBB rated bonds is *most likely* correct?
   A. Observation 1
   B. Observation 2
   C. Observation 3
4. Which reason *best* supports Petit's recommendation to increase the firm's investment in high-yield bonds?
   A. Reason 1
   B. Reason 2
   C. Reason 3
5. Based on Petit's expectations for US and European corporate bonds, which of the following positions relative to the portfolio's benchmark should she recommend?

	US Bonds	European Bonds	US Two-Year BB	US Five-Year BB
A	Overweight	Underweight	Overweight	Underweight
B	Overweight	Underweight	Underweight	Overweight
C	Underweight	Overweight	Underweight	Overweight

6. What secondary market characteristics would *most likely* have Gerber's desired effect on portfolio liquidity?
   A. Decreased trading volume
   B. Less spread sensitivity to fund outflows
   C. A decrease in broker/dealer holdings
7. To address Gerber's tail risk concern, Petit should recommend that expected correlations with their models:
   A. decrease.
   B. do not change.
   C. increase.
8. Which of Gerber's three differences about investing in EM credits compared with developed market credits is most correct?
   A. Difference 1
   B. Difference 2
   C. Difference 3
9. Which of Gerber's statements about international credit management is correct?
   A. Statement 1
   B. Statement 2
   C. Statement 3

The following information relates to Questions 10–15

Megan Easton is a portfolio manager with Dynamo Investment Partners (Dynamo) and manages a bond portfolio that invests primarily in investment-grade corporate bonds with a limited amount of US government bonds. Easton meets with John Avelyn, a newly hired analyst, to discuss the structure and management of this investment portfolio, as well as some possible changes to the portfolio composition.

Easton begins the meeting by stating her belief that the credit spread is the single most important measure that investors use when selecting bonds. Among the various credit spread measures, including the G-spread, I-spread, and Z-spread, Easton prefers the G-spread.

Easton and Avelyn next discuss credit strategy approaches. Dynamo uses a bottom-up approach that selects bonds with the best relative value from the universe of bonds with similar characteristics. Avelyn comments on the following considerations in a bottom-up approach.

Comment 1:   Callable debt has a smaller option-adjusted spread than comparable non-callable debt.

Comment 2:   Benchmark corporate bond issues normally have wider spreads than older bonds of the same issuer.

Comment 3:   The announcement of a new corporate bond issue often leads to an increase in the credit spread on the existing bonds.

Dynamo is changing the bond portfolio's investment constraints so that it can invest up to 20% of the assets in high-yield corporate bonds and 20% in structured financial instruments. Easton makes the following statement about these changes:

> Liquidity and trading issues for high-yield bonds, such as investment-grade bonds, will be a key consideration in our security selection. Although both high-yield and investment-grade bonds are quoted as spreads over benchmark government bonds, we must be aware that dealers are likely to hold larger inventories of high-yield bonds and their bid–offer spreads will be larger.

Avelyn makes the following statements about the differences between investment-grade and high-yield bonds.

Statement 1:   When default losses are low and credit spreads are relatively tight, high-yield bonds tend to perform more like investment-grade bonds.

Statement 2:   Investment-grade bonds have greater exposure to credit risk than high-yield bonds.

Statement 3:   High-yield bonds have more exposure to interest rate risk than investment-grade bonds.

Two of the structured financial instruments that Easton and Avelyn are considering for Dynamo's portfolio are collateralized debt obligations (CDOs) and covered bonds. Easton and Avelyn make the following comments about the securities.

Easton: If the correlation of the expected defaults on the CDO collateral of the senior and subordinated tranches is positive, the relative value of the mezzanine tranche compared with the senior and equity tranches will increase.

Avelyn: Replacing a portion of the corporate bonds with CDOs will provide meaningful diversification to the investment portfolio.

Avelyn: Investing in covered bonds will give us the yield increase we are seeking compared with investing in corporate bonds or asset-backed securities.

10. A benefit of Easton's preferred credit spread measure is that it:
    A. provides a good measure of credit spread for bonds with optionality.
    B. uses swap rates denominated in the same currency as the credit security.
    C. reduces the potential for maturity mismatch.

11. Which of the following is *most likely* to be used when selecting securities based on Dynamo's credit strategy approach?
    A. Macro factors
    B. Expected excess returns
    C. Average option-adjusted spread

12. Which of Avelyn's comments regarding considerations in the bottom-up approach is *most* accurate?
    A. Comment 1
    B. Comment 2
    C. Comment 3

13. Which of Easton's statements about the liquidity and trading characteristics of high-yield and investment-grade bonds is *most* correct?
    A. Dealers generally hold larger inventories of high-yield bonds than investment-grade bonds.
    B. Both high-yield and investment-grade bonds are quoted as spreads over benchmark government bonds.
    C. The bid–offer spread of high-yield bonds is normally larger than that of investment-grade bonds with similar maturities.

14. Which of Avelyn's statements about the differences between investment-grade and high-yield bonds is accurate?
    A. Statement 1
    B. Statement 2
    C. Statement 3

15. Which comment regarding CDOs and covered bonds is accurate?
    A. Easton's comment
    B. Avelyn's first comment
    C. Avelyn's second comment

SOLUTIONS

CHAPTER 1

FIXED-INCOME SECURITIES: DEFINING ELEMENTS

SOLUTIONS

1. A is correct. The tenor of the bond is the time remaining until the bond's maturity date. Although the bond had a maturity of 10 years at issuance (original maturity), it was issued four years ago. Thus, there are six years remaining until the maturity date.

   B is incorrect because the nominal rate is the coupon rate, i.e., the interest rate that the issuer agrees to pay each year until the maturity date. Although interest is paid semi-annually, the nominal rate is 10%, not 5%. C is incorrect because it is the bond's price, not its redemption value (also called principal amount, principal value, par value, face value, nominal value, or maturity value), that is equal to 102% of the par value.

2. C is correct. A capital market security has an original maturity longer than one year.

   A is incorrect because a perpetual bond does not have a stated maturity date. Thus, the sovereign bond, which has a maturity of 15 years, cannot be a perpetual bond. B is incorrect because a pure discount bond is a bond issued at a discount to par value and redeemed at par. Some sovereign bonds (e.g., Treasury bills) are pure discount bonds, but others are not.

3. C is correct. The coupon rate that applies to the interest payment due on 30 June is based on the three-month Libor rate prevailing on 31 March. Thus, the coupon rate is 1.55% + 0.65% = 2.20%.

4. B is correct. The indenture, also referred to as trust deed, is the legal contract that describes the form of the bond, the obligations of the issuer, and the rights of the bondholders.

   A is incorrect because covenants are only one element of a bond's indenture. Covenants are clauses that specify the rights of the bondholders and any actions that the issuer is obligated to perform or prohibited from performing. C is incorrect because a debenture is a type of bond.

5. B is correct. A surety bond is an external credit enhancement, i.e., a guarantee received from a third party. If the issuer defaults, the guarantor who provided the surety bond

will reimburse investors for any losses, usually up to a maximum amount called the penal sum.

A is incorrect because covenants are legally enforceable rules that borrowers and lenders agree upon when the bond is issued. C is incorrect because overcollateralization is an internal, not external, credit enhancement. Collateral is a guarantee underlying the debt above and beyond the issuer's promise to pay, and overcollateralization refers to the process of posting more collateral than is needed to obtain or secure financing. Collateral, such as assets or securities pledged to ensure debt payments, is not provided by a third party. Thus, overcollateralization is not an external credit enhancement.

6. B is correct. Affirmative (or positive) covenants enumerate what issuers are required to do and are typically administrative in nature. A common affirmative covenant describes what the issuer intends to do with the proceeds from the bond issue.

   A and C are incorrect because imposing a limit on the issuer's leverage ratio or on the percentage of the issuer's gross assets that can be sold are negative covenants. Negative covenants prevent the issuer from taking actions that could reduce its ability to make interest payments and repay the principal.

7. B is correct. Prohibiting the issuer from investing in risky projects restricts the issuer's potential business decisions. These restrictions are referred to as negative bond covenants.

   A and C are incorrect because paying taxes as they come due and maintaining the current lines of business are positive covenants.

8. C is correct. Bonds sold in a country and denominated in that country's currency by an entity from another country are referred to as foreign bonds.

   A is incorrect because Eurobonds are bonds issued outside the jurisdiction of any single country. B is incorrect because global bonds are bonds issued in the Eurobond market and at least one domestic country simultaneously.

9. A is correct. Eurobonds are typically issued as bearer bonds, i.e., bonds for which the trustee does not keep records of ownership. In contrast, domestic and foreign bonds are typically registered bonds for which ownership is recorded by either name or serial number.

   B is incorrect because Eurobonds are typically issued as bearer bonds, not registered bonds. C is incorrect because Eurobonds are typically subject to lower, not greater, regulation than domestic and foreign bonds.

10. C is correct. The original issue discount tax provision requires the investor to include a prorated portion of the original issue discount in his taxable income every tax year until maturity. The original issue discount is equal to the difference between the bond's par value and its original issue price.

    A is incorrect because the original issue discount tax provision allows the investor to increase his cost basis in the bond so that when the bond matures, he faces no capital gain or loss. B is incorrect because the original issue discount tax provision does not require any tax deduction in the year the bond is purchased or afterward.

11. C is correct. A fully amortized bond calls for equal cash payments by the bond's issuer prior to maturity. Each fixed payment includes both an interest payment component and a principal repayment component such that the bond's outstanding principal amount is reduced to zero by the maturity date.

    A and B are incorrect because a bullet bond or plain vanilla bond only make interest payments prior to maturity. The entire principal repayment occurs at maturity.

12. C is correct. A cap in a floating-rate note (capped FRN) prevents the coupon rate from increasing above a specified maximum rate. This feature benefits the issuer in a rising interest rate environment because it sets a limit to the interest rate paid on the debt.

A is incorrect because a bond with a step-up coupon is one in which the coupon, which may be fixed or floating, increases by specified margins at specified dates. This feature benefits the bondholders, not the issuer, in a rising interest rate environment because it allows bondholders to receive a higher coupon in line with the higher market interest rates. B is incorrect because inflation-linked bonds have their coupon payments and/or principal repayment linked to an index of consumer prices. If interest rates increase as a result of inflation, this feature is a benefit for the bondholders, not the issuer.

13. C is correct. In contrast to fixed-rate bonds that decline in value in a rising interest rate environment, floating-rate notes (FRNs) are less affected when interest rates increase because their coupon rates vary with market interest rates and are reset at regular, short-term intervals. Consequently, FRNs are favored by investors who believe that interest rates will rise.

    A is incorrect because an inverse floater is a bond whose coupon rate has an inverse relationship to the reference rate, so when interest rates rise, the coupon rate on an inverse floater decreases. Thus, inverse floaters are favored by investors who believe that interest rates will decline, not rise. B is incorrect because fixed-rate bonds decline in value in a rising interest rate environment. Consequently, investors who expect interest rates to rise will likely avoid investing in fixed-rate bonds.

14. C is correct. Capital-indexed bonds pay a fixed coupon rate that is applied to a principal amount that increases in line with increases in the index during the bond's life. If the consumer price index increases by 2%, the coupon rate remains unchanged at 6%, but the principal amount increases by 2% and the coupon payment is based on the inflation-adjusted principal amount. On the first coupon payment date, the inflation-adjusted principal amount is $1,000 \times (1 + 0.02) = 1,020$ and the semi-annual coupon payment is equal to $(0.06 \times 1,020) \div 2 = 30.60$.

15. A is correct. A put provision provides bondholders the right to sell the bond back to the issuer at a predetermined price prior to the bond's maturity date.

    B is incorrect because a make-whole call provision is a form of call provision; i.e., a provision that provides the issuer the right to redeem all or part of the bond before its maturity date. A make-whole call provision requires the issuer to make a lump-sum payment to the bondholders based on the present value of the future coupon payments and principal repayments not paid because of the bond being redeemed early by the issuer. C is incorrect because an original issue discount provision is a tax provision relating to bonds issued at a discount to par value. The original issue discount tax provision typically requires the bondholders to include a prorated portion of the original issue discount (i.e., the difference between the par value and the original issue price) in their taxable income every tax year until the bond's maturity date.

16. B is correct. A call provision (callable bond) gives the issuer the right to redeem all or part of the bond before the specified maturity date. If market interest rates decline or the issuer's credit quality improves, the issuer of a callable bond can redeem it and replace it by a cheaper bond. Thus, the call provision is beneficial to the issuer.

    A is incorrect because a put provision (putable bond) is beneficial to the bondholders. If interest rates rise, thus lowering the bond's price, the bondholders have the right to sell the bond back to the issuer at a predetermined price on specified dates. C is incorrect because a conversion provision (convertible bond) is beneficial to the bondholders. If the issuing company's share price increases, the bondholders have the right to exchange the bond for a specified number of common shares in the issuing company.

17. A is correct. A put feature is beneficial to the bondholders. Thus, the price of a putable bond will typically be higher than the price of an otherwise similar non-putable bond.

    B is incorrect because a call feature is beneficial to the issuer. Thus, the price of a callable bond will typically be lower, not higher, than the price of an otherwise similar non-callable bond. C is incorrect because a conversion feature is beneficial to the bondholders. Thus, the price of a convertible bond will typically be higher, not lower, than the price of an otherwise similar non-convertible bond.

18. C is correct. A zero-coupon, or pure discount, bond pays no interest; instead, it is issued at a discount to par value and redeemed at par. As a result, the interest earned is implied and equal to the difference between the par value and the purchase price.

19. A is correct. Covenants specify the rights of the bondholders and any actions that the issuer is obligated to perform or is prohibited from performing.

20. A is correct. A covered bond is a debt obligation backed by a segregated pool of assets called a "cover pool." When the assets that are included in the cover pool become non-performing (i.e., the assets are not generating the promised cash flows), the issuer must replace them with performing assets.

21. C is correct. Negative covenants enumerate what issuers are prohibited from doing. Restrictions on debt, including maintaining a minimum interest coverage ratio or a maximum debt usage ratio, are typical examples of negative covenants.

22. A is correct. Affirmative covenants typically do not impose additional costs to the issuer, while negative covenants are frequently costly. B is incorrect because all bond covenants are legally enforceable rules, so there is no difference in this regard between positive and negative bond covenants. C is incorrect because borrowers and lenders agree on all bond covenants at the time of a new bond issue, so there is no difference in this regard between positive and negative bond covenants.

23. B is correct. A bond that is fully amortized is characterized by a fixed periodic payment schedule that reduces the bond's outstanding principal amount to zero by the maturity date. The stream of £230.97 payments reflects the cash flows of a fully amortized bond with a coupon rate of 5% and annual interest payments.

24. B is correct. A credit-linked coupon bond has a coupon that changes when the bond's credit rating changes. Because credit ratings tend to decline the most during recessions, credit-linked coupon bonds may thus provide some general protection against a poor economy by offering increased coupon payments when credit ratings decline.

25. B is correct. Deferred coupon bonds pay no coupon for their first few years but then pay higher coupons than they otherwise normally would for the remainder of their life. Deferred coupon bonds are common in project financing when the assets being developed may not generate any income during the development phase, thus not providing cash flows to make interest payments. A deferred coupon bond allows the issuer to delay interest payments until the project is completed and the cash flows generated by the assets can be used to service the debt.

26. C is correct. A putable bond is beneficial for the bondholder by guaranteeing a pre-specified selling price at the redemption date, thus offering protection when interest rates rise and bond prices decline. Relative to a one-time put bond that incorporates a single sellback opportunity, a multiple put bond offers more frequent sellback opportunities, thus providing the most benefit to bondholders.

27. C is correct. An American call option gives the issuer the right to call the bond at any time starting on the first call date.

28. A is correct. The conversion premium is the difference between the convertible bond's price and its conversion value.

CHAPTER 2

FIXED-INCOME MARKETS: ISSUANCE, TRADING, AND FUNDING

SOLUTIONS

1. C is correct. In most countries, the largest issuers of bonds are the national and local governments as well as financial institutions. Thus, the bond market sector with the smallest amount of bonds outstanding is the non-financial corporate sector.

2. B is correct. The distinction between investment grade and non-investment grade debt relates to differences in credit quality, not tax status or maturity dates. Debt markets are classified based on the issuer's creditworthiness as judged by the credit rating agencies. Ratings of Baa3 or above by Moody's Investors Service or BBB– or above by Standard & Poor's and Fitch Ratings are considered investment grade, whereas ratings below these levels are referred to as non-investment grade (also called high yield, speculative, or junk).

3. A is correct. Eurobonds are issued internationally, outside the jurisdiction of any single country. B is incorrect because foreign bonds are considered international bonds, but they are issued in a specific country, in the currency of that country, by an issuer domiciled in another country. C is incorrect because municipal bonds are US domestic bonds issued by a state or local government.

4. B is correct. Asset-backed securities (ABS) are securitized debt instruments created by securitization, a process that involves transferring ownership of assets from the original owners to a special legal entity. The special legal entity then issues securities backed by the transferred assets. The assets' cash flows are used to pay interest and repay the principal owed to the holders of the securities. Assets that are typically used to create securitized debt instruments include loans (such as mortgage loans) and receivables (such as credit card receivables). The structured finance sector includes such securitized debt instruments (also called asset-backed securities).

5. B is correct. Many emerging countries lag developed countries in the areas of political stability, property rights, and contract enforcement. Consequently, emerging market bonds usually exhibit higher risk than developed markets bonds. A is incorrect because emerging markets bonds typically offer higher (not lower) yields than developed markets bonds to compensate investors for the higher risk. C is incorrect because emerging markets bonds usually benefit from higher (not lower) growth prospects than developed markets bonds.

6. B is correct. The coupon rate of a floating-rate bond is expressed as a reference rate plus a spread. Different reference rates are used depending on where the bond is issued and its currency denomination, but one of the most widely used set of reference rates is Libor. A and C are incorrect because a bond's spread and frequency of coupon payments are typically set when the bond is issued and do not change during the bond's life.

7. A is correct. Changes in the coupon rate of interest on a floating-rate bond that uses a Libor reference rate are due to changes in the reference rate (for example, 90-day Libor), which resets periodically. "Therefore, the coupon rate adjusts to the level of market interest rates (plus the spread) each time the reference rate is reset."

8. C is correct. Interbank offered rates are used as reference rates not only for floating-rate bonds, but also for other debt instruments including mortgages, derivatives such as interest rate and currency swaps, and many other financial contracts and products. A and B are incorrect because an interbank offered rate such as Libor or Euribor is a set of reference rates (not a single reference rate) for different borrowing periods of up to one year (not 10 years).

9. A is correct. In an underwritten offering (also called firm commitment offering), the investment bank (called the underwriter) guarantees the sale of the bond issue at an offering price that is negotiated with the issuer. Thus, the underwriter takes the risk of buying the newly issued bonds from the issuer, and then reselling them to investors or to dealers who then sell them to investors. B and C are incorrect because the bond issuing mechanism where an investment bank acts as a broker and receives a commission for selling the bonds to investors, and incurs less risk associated with selling the bonds, is a best effort offering (not an underwritten offering).

10. A is correct. In major developed bond markets, newly issued sovereign bonds are sold to the public via an auction. B and C are incorrect because sovereign bonds are rarely issued via private placements or best effort offerings.

11. A is correct. Private placements are typically non-underwritten, unregistered bond offerings that are sold only to a single investor or a small group of investors.

12. B is correct. A shelf registration allows certain authorized issuers to offer additional bonds to the general public without having to prepare a new and separate offering circular. The issuer can offer multiple bond issuances under the same master prospectus, and only has to prepare a short document when additional bonds are issued. A is incorrect because the grey market is a forward market for bonds about to be issued. C is incorrect because a private placement is a non-underwritten, unregistered offering of bonds that are not sold to the general public but directly to an investor or a small group of investors.

13. B is correct. Secondary bond markets are where bonds are traded between investors. A is incorrect because newly issued bonds (whether from corporate issuers or other types of issuers) are issued in primary (not secondary) bond markets. C is incorrect because the major participants in secondary bond markets globally are large institutional investors and central banks (not retail investors).

14. C is correct. In over-the-counter (OTC) markets, buy and sell orders are initiated from various locations and then matched through a communications network. Most bonds

are traded in OTC markets. A is incorrect because on organized exchanges, buy and sell orders may come from anywhere, but the transactions must take place at the exchange according to the rules imposed by the exchange. B is incorrect because open market operations refer to central bank activities in secondary bond markets. Central banks buy and sell bonds, usually sovereign bonds issued by the national government, as a means to implement monetary policy.

15. C is correct. Liquidity in secondary bond markets refers to the ability to buy or sell bonds quickly at prices close to their fair market value. A and B are incorrect because a liquid secondary bond market does not guarantee that a bond will sell at the price sought by the investor, or that the investor will not face a loss on his or her investment.

16. A is correct. The vast majority of corporate bonds are traded in over-the-counter (OTC) markets that use electronic trading platforms through which users submit buy and sell orders. Settlement of trades in the OTC markets occurs by means of a simultaneous exchange of bonds for cash on the books of the clearing system "on a paperless, computerized book-entry basis."

17. C is correct. Sovereign bonds are usually unsecured obligations of the national government issuing the bonds; they are not backed by collateral, but by the taxing authority of the national government. A is incorrect because bonds issued by local governments are non-sovereign (not sovereign) bonds. B is incorrect because sovereign bonds are typically unsecured (not secured) obligations of a national government.

18. C is correct. Bonds issued in the sovereign's currency and a strong domestic savings base are both favorable sovereign rating factors. It is common to observe a higher credit rating for sovereign bonds issued in local currency because of the sovereign's ability to tax its citizens and print its own currency. Although there are practical limits to the sovereign's taxing and currency-printing capacities, each tends to support a sovereign's ability to repay debt. A strong domestic savings base is advantageous because it supports the sovereign's ability to issue debt in local currency to domestic investors.

19. A is correct. Floaters are bonds with a floating rate of interest that resets periodically based on changes in the level of a reference rate, such as Libor. Because changes in the reference rate reflect changes in market interest rates, price changes of floaters are far less pronounced than those of fixed-rate bonds, such as coupon bonds and discount bonds. Thus, investors holding floaters are less exposed to interest rate risk than investors holding fixed-rate discount or coupon bonds.

20. C is correct. Agency bonds are issued by quasi-government entities. These entities are agencies and organizations usually established by national governments to perform various functions for them. A and B are incorrect because local and national governments issue non-sovereign and sovereign bonds, respectively.

21. B is correct. The IMF is a multilateral agency that issues supranational bonds. A and C are incorrect because sovereign bonds and quasi-government bonds are issued by national governments and by entities that perform various functions for national governments, respectively.

22. C is correct. Bonds issued by levels of government below the national level—such as provinces, regions, states, cities, and local government authorities—are classified as non-sovereign government bonds. These bonds are typically not guaranteed by the national government.

23. C is correct. Companies use commercial paper not only as a source of funding working capital and seasonal demand for cash, but also as a source of interim financing for long-term projects until permanent financing can be arranged. A is incorrect because there is a

secondary market for trading commercial paper, although trading is limited except for the largest issues. B is incorrect because commercial paper is issued by companies across the risk spectrum, although only the strongest, highly rated companies issue *low-cost* commercial paper.

24. A is correct. Commercial paper, whether US commercial paper or Eurocommercial paper, is negotiable—that is, investors can buy and sell commercial paper on secondary markets. B is incorrect because Eurocommercial paper can be denominated in any currency. C is incorrect because Eurocommercial paper may be issued on an interest-bearing (or yield) basis or a discount basis.

25. B is correct. With a serial maturity structure, a stated number of bonds mature and are paid off on a predetermined schedule before final maturity. With a sinking fund arrangement, the issuer is required to set aside funds over time to retire the bond issue. Both result in a predetermined portion of the issue being paid off according to a predetermined schedule.

26. A is correct. A sinking fund arrangement is a way to reduce credit risk by making the issuer set aside funds over time to retire the bond issue. B and C are incorrect because a sinking fund arrangement has no effect on inflation risk or interest rate risk.

27. C is correct. Wholesale funds available for banks include central bank funds, interbank funds, and negotiable certificates of deposit. A and B are incorrect because demand deposits (also known as checking accounts) and money market accounts are retail deposits (not wholesale funds).

28. B is correct. A negotiable certificate of deposit (CD) allows any depositor (initial or subsequent) to sell the CD in the open market prior to maturity. A is incorrect because negotiable CDs are mostly available in large (not small) denominations. Large-denomination negotiable CDs are an important source of wholesale funds for banks, whereas small-denomination CDs are not. C is incorrect because a penalty is imposed if the depositor withdraws funds prior to maturity for non-negotiable (instead of negotiable) CDs.

29. B is correct. A repurchase agreement (repo) can be viewed as a collateralized loan where the security sold and subsequently repurchased represents the collateral posted. A and C are incorrect because interbank deposits and negotiable certificates of deposit are unsecured deposits—that is, there is no collateral backing the deposit.

30. A is correct. Repo margins vary by transaction and are negotiated bilaterally between the counterparties.

31. A is correct. The repo margin (the difference between the market value of the underlying collateral and the value of the loan) is a function of the supply and demand conditions of the collateral. The repo margin is typically lower if the underlying collateral is in short supply or if there is a high demand for it. B and C are incorrect because the repo margin is usually higher (not lower) when the maturity of the repurchase agreement is long and when the credit risk associated with the underlying collateral is high.

CHAPTER 3

INTRODUCTION TO FIXED-INCOME VALUATION

SOLUTIONS

1. B is correct. The bond price is closest to 101.36. The price is determined in the following manner:

$$PV = \frac{PMT}{(1+r)^1} + \frac{PMT}{(1+r)^2} + \frac{PMT + FV}{(1+r)^3}$$

where:

PV = present value, or the price of the bond
PMT = coupon payment per period
FV = future value paid at maturity, or the par value of the bond
r = market discount rate, or required rate of return per period

$$PV = \frac{5.5}{(1+0.05)^1} + \frac{5.5}{(1+0.05)^2} + \frac{5.5 + 100}{(1+0.05)^3}$$

$$PV = 5.24 + 4.99 + 91.13 = 101.36$$

2. C is correct. The bond price is closest to 98.11. The formula for calculating the price of this bond is:

$$PV = \frac{PMT}{(1+r)^1} + \frac{PMT + FV}{(1+r)^2}$$

where:

PV = present value, or the price of the bond
PMT = coupon payment per period
FV = future value paid at maturity, or the par value of the bond
r = market discount rate, or required rate of return per period

$$PV = \frac{3}{(1 + 0.04)^1} + \frac{3 + 100}{(1 + 0.04)^2} = 2.88 + 95.23 = 98.11$$

3. A is correct. The bond price is closest to 95.00. The bond has six semi-annual periods. Half of the annual coupon is paid in each period with the required rate of return also being halved. The price is determined in the following manner:

$$PV = \frac{PMT}{(1 + r)^1} + \frac{PMT}{(1 + r)^2} + \frac{PMT}{(1 + r)^3} + \frac{PMT}{(1 + r)^4} + \frac{PMT}{(1 + r)^5} + \frac{PMT + FV}{(1 + r)^6}$$

where:

PV = present value, or the price of the bond
PMT = coupon payment per period
FV = future value paid at maturity, or the par value of the bond
r = market discount rate, or required rate of return per period

$$PV = \frac{4.5}{(1 + 0.055)^1} + \frac{4.5}{(1 + 0.055)^2} + \frac{4.5}{(1 + 0.055)^3} + \frac{4.5}{(1 + 0.055)^4} + \frac{4.5}{(1 + 0.055)^5} + \frac{4.5 + 100}{(1 + 0.055)^6}$$

$PV = 4.27 + 4.04 + 3.83 + 3.63 + 3.44 + 75.79 = 95.00$

4. B is correct. The bond price is closest to 96.28. The formula for calculating this bond price is:

$$PV = \frac{PMT}{(1 + r)^1} + \frac{PMT}{(1 + r)^2} + \frac{PMT}{(1 + r)^3} + \frac{PMT + FV}{(1 + r)^4}$$

where:

PV = present value, or the price of the bond
PMT = coupon payment per period
FV = future value paid at maturity, or the par value of the bond
r = market discount rate, or required rate of return per period

$$PV = \frac{2}{(1 + 0.03)^1} + \frac{2}{(1 + 0.03)^2} + \frac{2}{(1 + 0.03)^3} + \frac{2 + 100}{(1 + 0.03)^4}$$

$PV = 1.94 + 1.89 + 1.83 + 90.62 = 96.28$

5. B is correct. The bond price is closest to 112.54. The formula for calculating this bond price is:

$$PV = \frac{PMT}{(1 + r)^1} + \frac{PMT}{(1 + r)^2} + \frac{PMT}{(1 + r)^3} + \cdots + \frac{PMT + FV}{(1 + r)^{14}}$$

where:

PV = present value, or the price of the bond
PMT = coupon payment per period
FV = future value paid at maturity, or the par value of the bond
r = market discount rate, or required rate of return per period

$$PV = \frac{2.5}{(1 + 0.015)^1} + \frac{2.5}{(1 + 0.015)^2} + \frac{2.5}{(1 + 0.015)^3} + \cdots + \frac{2.5}{(1 + 0.015)^{13}} + \frac{2.5 + 100}{(1 + 0.015)^{14}}$$

$$PV = 2.46 + 2.43 + 2.39 + \cdots + 2.06 + 83.21 = 112.54$$

6. B is correct. The price of the zero-coupon bond is closest to 51.67. The price is determined in the following manner:

$$PV = \frac{100}{(1 + r)^N}$$

where:

PV = present value, or the price of the bond
r = market discount rate, or required rate of return per period
N = number of evenly spaced periods to maturity

$$PV = \frac{100}{(1 + 0.045)^{15}}$$

$$PV = 51.67$$

7. B is correct. The price difference between Bonds A and B is closest to 3.77. One method for calculating the price difference between two bonds with an identical term to maturity is to use the following formula:

$$PV = \frac{PMT}{(1 + r)^1} + \frac{PMT}{(1 + r)^2}$$

where:

PV = price difference
PMT = coupon difference per period
r = market discount rate, or required rate of return per period

In this case the coupon difference is (5% − 3%), or 2%.

$$PV = \frac{2}{(1 + 0.04)^1} + \frac{2}{(1 + 0.04)^2} = 1.92 + 1.85 = 3.77$$

8. A is correct. Bond A offers the lowest yield-to-maturity. When a bond is priced at a premium above par value the yield-to-maturity (YTM), or market discount rate, is less than the coupon rate. Bond A is priced at a premium, so its YTM is below its 5% coupon rate. Bond B is priced at par value so its YTM is equal to its 6% coupon rate. Bond C is priced at a discount below par value, so its YTM is above its 5% coupon rate.

9. B is correct. Bond B will most likely experience the smallest percent change in price if market discount rates increase by 100 basis points. A higher-coupon bond has a smaller percentage price change than a lower-coupon bond when their market discount rates change by the same amount (the coupon effect). Also, a shorter-term bond generally has a smaller percentage price change than a longer-term bond when their market discount rates change by the same amount (the maturity effect). Bond B will experience a smaller percent change in price than Bond A because of the coupon effect. Bond B will also experience a smaller percent change in price than Bond C because of the coupon effect and the maturity effect.

10. B is correct. The bond price is most likely to change by less than 5%. The relationship between bond prices and market discount rate is not linear. The percentage price change is greater in absolute value when the market discount rate goes down than when it goes up by the same amount (the convexity effect). If a 100 basis point decrease in the market discount rate will cause the price of the bond to increase by 5%, then a 100 basis point increase in the market discount rate will cause the price of the bond to decline by an amount less than 5%.

11. B is correct. Generally, for two bonds with the same time-to-maturity, a lower coupon bond will experience a greater percentage price change than a higher coupon bond when their market discount rates change by the same amount. Bond B and Bond C have the same time-to-maturity (5 years); however, Bond B offers a lower coupon rate. Therefore, Bond B will likely experience a greater percentage change in price in comparison to Bond C.

12. A is correct. Bond A will likely experience the greatest percent change in price due to the coupon effect and the maturity effect. For two bonds with the same time-to-maturity, a lower-coupon bond has a greater percentage price change than a higher-coupon bond when their market discount rates change by the same amount. Generally, for the same coupon rate, a longer-term bond has a greater percentage price change than a shorter-term bond when their market discount rates change by the same amount. Relative to Bond C, Bond A and Bond B both offer the same lower coupon rate of 6%; however, Bond A has a longer time-to-maturity than Bond B. Therefore, Bond A will likely experience the greater percentage change in price if the market discount rates for all three bonds increase by 100 basis points.

13. A is correct. The bond price is closest to 101.93. The price is determined in the following manner:

$$PV = \frac{PMT}{\left(1 + Z_1\right)^1} + \frac{PMT + FV}{\left(1 + Z_2\right)^2}$$

where:

PV = present value, or the price of the bond
PMT = coupon payment per period
FV = future value paid at maturity, or the par value of the bond
Z_1 = spot rate, or the zero-coupon yield, for Period 1
Z_2 = spot rate, or the zero-coupon yield, for Period 2

$$PV = \frac{5}{\left(1 + 0.03\right)^1} + \frac{5 + 100}{\left(1 + 0.04\right)^2}$$
$$PV = 4.85 + 97.08 = 101.93$$

14. B is correct. The bond price is closest to 101.46. The price is determined in the following manner:

$$PV = \frac{PMT}{\left(1 + Z_1\right)^1} + \frac{PMT}{\left(1 + Z_2\right)^2} + \frac{PMT + FV}{\left(1 + Z_3\right)^3}$$

where:

PV = present value, or the price of the bond

PMT = coupon payment per period

FV = future value paid at maturity, or the par value of the bond

Z_1 = spot rate, or the zero-coupon yield, or zero rate, for period 1

Z_2 = spot rate, or the zero-coupon yield, or zero rate, for period 2

Z_3 = spot rate, or the zero-coupon yield, or zero rate, for period 3

$$PV = \frac{10}{(1 + 0.08)^1} + \frac{10}{(1 + 0.09)^2} + \frac{10 + 100}{(1 + 0.095)^3}$$

$$PV = 9.26 + 8.42 + 83.78 = 101.46$$

15. B is correct. The bond price is closest to 95.28. The formula for calculating this bond price is:

$$PV = \frac{PMT}{(1 + Z_1)^1} + \frac{PMT}{(1 + Z_2)^2} + \frac{PMT + FV}{(1 + Z_3)^3}$$

where:

PV = present value, or the price of the bond

PMT = coupon payment per period

FV = future value paid at maturity, or the par value of the bond

Z_1 = spot rate, or the zero-coupon yield, or zero rate, for period 1

Z_2 = spot rate, or the zero-coupon yield, or zero rate, for period 2

Z_3 = spot rate, or the zero-coupon yield, or zero rate, for period 3

$$PV = \frac{8}{(1 + 0.08)^1} + \frac{8}{(1 + 0.09)^2} + \frac{8 + 100}{(1 + 0.10)^3}$$

$$PV = 7.41 + 6.73 + 81.14 = 95.28$$

16. C is correct. The bond price is closest to 92.76. The formula for calculating this bond price is:

$$PV = \frac{PMT}{(1 + Z_1)^1} + \frac{PMT}{(1 + Z_2)^2} + \frac{PMT + FV}{(1 + Z_3)^3}$$

where:

PV = present value, or the price of the bond

PMT = coupon payment per period

FV = future value paid at maturity, or the par value of the bond

Z_1 = spot rate, or the zero-coupon yield, or zero rate, for period 1

Z_2 = spot rate, or the zero-coupon yield, or zero rate, for period 2

Z_3 = spot rate, or the zero-coupon yield, or zero rate, for period 3

$$PV = \frac{7}{(1 + 0.08)^1} + \frac{7}{(1 + 0.09)^2} + \frac{7 + 100}{(1 + 0.10)^3}$$

$$PV = 6.48 + 5.89 + 80.39 = 92.76$$

17. B is correct. The yield-to-maturity is closest to 9.92%. The formula for calculating the price of Bond Z is:

$$PV = \frac{PMT}{(1 + Z_1)^1} + \frac{PMT}{(1 + Z_2)^2} + \frac{PMT + FV}{(1 + Z_3)^3}$$

where:

PV = present value, or the price of the bond
PMT = coupon payment per period
FV = future value paid at maturity, or the par value of the bond
Z_1 = spot rate, or the zero-coupon yield, or zero rate, for period 1
Z_2 = spot rate, or the zero-coupon yield, or zero rate, for period 2
Z_3 = spot rate, or the zero-coupon yield, or zero rate, for period 3

$$PV = \frac{6}{(1 + 0.08)^1} + \frac{6}{(1 + 0.09)^2} + \frac{6 + 100}{(1 + 0.10)^3}$$

$$PV = 5.56 + 5.05 + 79.64 = 90.25$$

Using this price, the bond's yield-to-maturity can be calculated as:

$$PV = \frac{PMT}{(1 + r)^1} + \frac{PMT}{(1 + r)^2} + \frac{PMT + FV}{(1 + r)^3}$$

$$90.25 = \frac{6}{(1 + r)^1} + \frac{6}{(1 + r)^2} + \frac{6 + 100}{(1 + r)^3}$$

$$r = 9.92\%$$

18. A is correct. Bond dealers usually quote the flat price. When a trade takes place, the accrued interest is added to the flat price to obtain the full price paid by the buyer and received by the seller on the settlement date. The reason for using the flat price for quotation is to avoid misleading investors about the market price trend for the bond. If the full price were to be quoted by dealers, investors would see the price rise day after day even if the yield-to-maturity did not change. That is because the amount of accrued interest increases each day. Then after the coupon payment is made the quoted price would drop dramatically. Using the flat price for quotation avoids that misrepresentation. The full price, flat price plus accrued interest, is not usually quoted by bond dealers.

19. B is correct. The bond's full price is 103.10. The price is determined in the following manner:

As of the beginning of the coupon period on 10 April 2020, there are 2.5 years (5 semi-annual periods) to maturity. These five semi-annual periods occur on 10 October 2020, 10 April 2021, 10 October 2021, 10 April 2022 and 10 October 2022.

$$PV = \frac{PMT}{(1 + r)^1} + \frac{PMT}{(1 + r)^2} + \frac{PMT}{(1 + r)^3} + \frac{PMT}{(1 + r)^4} + \frac{PMT + FV}{(1 + r)^5}$$

where:

PV = present value
PMT = coupon payment per period
FV = future value paid at maturity, or the par value of the bond
r = market discount rate, or required rate of return per period

$$PV = \frac{2.5}{(1+0.02)^1} + \frac{2.5}{(1+0.02)^2} + \frac{2.5}{(1+0.02)^3} + \frac{2.5}{(1+0.02)^4} + \frac{2.5+100}{(1+0.02)^5}$$

$PV = 2.45 + 2.40 + 2.36 + 2.31 + 92.84 = 102.36$

The accrued interest period is identified as 66/180. The number of days between 10 April 2020 and 16 June 2020 is 66 days based on the 30/360 day count convention. (This is 20 days remaining in April + 30 days in May + 16 days in June = 66 days total.) The number of days between coupon periods is assumed to be 180 days using the 30/360 day convention.

$$PV^{Full} = PV \times (1+r)^{66/180}$$

$$PV^{Full} = 102.36 \times (1.02)^{66/180} = 103.10$$

20. C is correct. The accrued interest per 100 of par value is closest to 0.92. The accrued interest is determined in the following manner: The accrued interest period is identified as 66/180. The number of days between 10 April 2020 and 16 June 2020 is 66 days based on the 30/360 day count convention. (This is 20 days remaining in April + 30 days in May + 16 days in June = 66 days total.) The number of days between coupon periods is assumed to be 180 days using the 30/360 day convention.

$$\text{Accrued interest} = \frac{t}{T} \times PMT$$

where:

t = number of days from the last coupon payment to the settlement date
T = number of days in the coupon period
t/T = fraction of the coupon period that has gone by since the last payment
PMT = coupon payment per period

$$\text{Accrued interest} = \frac{66}{180} \times \frac{5.00}{2} = 0.92$$

21. A is correct. The flat price of 102.18 is determined by subtracting the accrued interest (from Question 20) from the full price (from question 19).

$$PV^{Flat} = PV^{Full} - \text{Accrued Interest}$$
$$PV^{Flat} = 103.10 - 0.92 = 102.18$$

22. B is correct. For bonds not actively traded or not yet issued, matrix pricing is a price estimation process that uses market discount rates based on the quoted prices of similar bonds (similar times-to-maturity, coupon rates, and credit quality).

23. A is correct. Matrix pricing is used in underwriting new bonds to get an estimate of the required yield spread over the benchmark rate. The benchmark rate is typically the yield-to-maturity

on a government bond having the same, or close to the same, time-to-maturity. The spread is the difference between the yield-to-maturity on the new bond and the benchmark rate. The yield spread is the additional compensation required by investors for the difference in the credit risk, liquidity risk, and tax status of the bond relative to the government bond.

In matrix pricing, the market discount rates of comparable bonds and the yield-to-maturity on a government bond having a similar time-to-maturity are not estimated. Rather they are known and used to estimate the required yield spread of a new bond.

24. B is correct. The formula for calculating this bond's yield-to-maturity is:

$$PV = \frac{PMT}{(1+r)^1} + \frac{PMT}{(1+r)^2} + \frac{PMT}{(1+r)^3} + \cdots + \frac{PMT}{(1+r)^{39}} + \frac{PMT + FV}{(1+r)^{40}}$$

where:

PV = present value, or the price of the bond
PMT = coupon payment per period
FV = future value paid at maturity, or the par value of the bond
r = market discount rate, or required rate of return per period

$$111 = \frac{2.5}{(1+r)^1} + \frac{2.5}{(1+r)^2} + \frac{2.5}{(1+r)^3} + \cdots + \frac{2.5}{(1+r)^{39}} + \frac{2.5+100}{(1+r)^{40}}$$

$$r = 0.0209$$

To arrive at the annualized yield-to-maturity, the semi-annual rate of 2.09% must be multiplied by two. Therefore, the yield-to-maturity is equal to 2.09% × 2 = 4.18%.

25. B is correct. The annual yield-to-maturity, stated for a periodicity of 12, is 7.21%. It is calculated as follows:

$$PV = \frac{FV}{(1+r)^N}$$

$$75 = \left(\frac{100}{(1+r)^{4\times12}} \right)$$

$$\frac{100}{75} = (1+r)^{48}$$

$$1.33333 = (1+r)^{48}$$

$$[1.33333]^{1/48} = [(1+r)^{48}]^{1/48}$$

$$1.33333^{02083} = (1+r)$$

$$1.00601 = (1+r)$$

$$1.00601 - 1 = r$$

$$0.00601 = r$$

$$r \times 12 = 0.07212, \text{ or approximately } 7.21\%$$

26. A is correct. The yield-to-maturity, stated for a periodicity of 12 (monthly periodicity), is 3.87%. The formula to convert an annual percentage rate (annual yield-to-maturity) from one periodicity to another is as follows:

$$\left(1 + \frac{APR_m}{m}\right)^m = \left(1 + \frac{APR_n}{n}\right)^n$$

$$\left(1 + \frac{0.03897}{2}\right)^2 = \left(1 + \frac{APR_{12}}{12}\right)^{12}$$

$$(1.01949)^2 = \left(1 + \frac{APR_{12}}{12}\right)^{12}$$

$$1.03935 = \left(1 + \frac{APR_{12}}{12}\right)^{12}$$

$$(1.03935)^{1/12} = \left[\left(1 + \frac{APR_{12}}{12}\right)^{12}\right]^{1/12}$$

$$1.00322 = \left(1 + \frac{APR_{12}}{12}\right)$$

$$1.00322 - 1 = \left(\frac{APR_{12}}{12}\right)$$

$APR_{12} = 0.00322 \times 12 = 0.03865$, or approximately 3.87%.

27. B is correct. The yield-to-maturity is 5.77%. The formula for calculating this bond's yield-to-maturity is:

$$PV = \frac{PMT}{(1 + r)^1} + \frac{PMT}{(1 + r)^2} + \frac{PMT}{(1 + r)^3} + \cdots + \frac{PMT}{(1 + r)^9} + \frac{PMT + FV}{(1 + r)^{10}}$$

where:

PV = present value, or the price of the bond
PMT = coupon payment per period
FV = future value paid at maturity, or the par value of the bond
r = market discount rate, or required rate of return per period

$$101 = \frac{3}{(1 + r)^1} + \frac{3}{(1 + r)^2} + \frac{3}{(1 + r)^3} + \cdots + \frac{3}{(1 + r)^9} + \frac{3 + 100}{(1 + r)^{10}}$$

$r = 0.02883$

To arrive at the annualized yield-to-maturity, the semi-annual rate of 2.883% must be multiplied by two. Therefore, the yield-to-maturity is equal to 2.883% × 2 = 5.77% (rounded).

28. C is correct. The yield-to-first-call is 6.25%. Given the first call date is exactly three years away, the formula for calculating this bond's yield-to-first-call is:

$$PV = \frac{PMT}{(1 + r)^1} + \frac{PMT}{(1 + r)^2} + \frac{PMT}{(1 + r)^3} + \cdots + \frac{PMT}{(1 + r)^5} + \frac{PMT + FV}{(1 + r)^6}$$

where:

PV = present value, or the price of the bond
PMT = coupon payment per period
FV = call price paid at call date
r = market discount rate, or required rate of return per period

$$101 = \frac{3}{(1+r)^1} + \frac{3}{(1+r)^2} + \frac{3}{(1+r)^3} + \cdots + \frac{3}{(1+r)^5} + \frac{3+102}{(1+r)^6}$$

$$r = 0.03123$$

To arrive at the annualized yield-to-first-call, the semi-annual rate of 3.123% must be multiplied by two. Therefore, the yield-to-first-call is equal to 3.123% × 2 = 6.25% (rounded).

29. C is correct. The yield-to-second-call is 5.94%. Given the second call date is exactly four years away, the formula for calculating this bond's yield-to-second-call is:

$$PV = \frac{PMT}{(1+r)^1} + \frac{PMT}{(1+r)^2} + \frac{PMT}{(1+r)^3} + \cdots + \frac{PMT}{(1+r)^7} + \frac{PMT+FV}{(1+r)^8}$$

where:

PV = present value, or the price of the bond
PMT = coupon payment per period
FV = call price paid at call date
r = market discount rate, or required rate of return per period

$$101 = \frac{3}{(1+r)^1} + \frac{3}{(1+r)^2} + \frac{3}{(1+r)^3} + \cdots \frac{3}{(1+r)^7} + \frac{3+101}{(1+r)^8}$$

$$r = 0.0297$$

To arrive at the annualized yield-to-second-call, the semi-annual rate of 2.97% must be multiplied by two. Therefore, the yield-to-second-call is equal to 2.97% × 2 = 5.94%.

30. B is correct. The yield-to-worst is 5.77%. The bond's yield-to-worst is the lowest of the sequence of yields-to-call and the yield-to-maturity. From above, we have the following yield measures for this bond:

Yield-to-first-call: 6.25%
Yield-to-second-call: 5.94%
Yield-to-maturity: 5.77%
Thus, the yield-to-worst is 5.77%.

31. B is correct. The discount or required margin is 236 basis points. Given the floater has a maturity of two years and is linked to 6-month Libor, the formula for calculating discount margin is:

$$PV = \frac{\frac{(\text{Index} + QM) \times FV}{m}}{\left(1 + \frac{\text{Index} + DM}{m}\right)^1} + \frac{\frac{(\text{Index} + QM) \times FV}{m}}{\left(1 + \frac{\text{Index} + DM}{m}\right)^2} + \cdots + \frac{\frac{(\text{Index} + QM) \times FV}{m} + FV}{\left(1 + \frac{\text{Index} + DM}{m}\right)^4}$$

where:

PV = present value, or the price of the floating-rate note = 97
Index = reference rate, stated as an annual percentage rate = 0.01
QM = quoted margin, stated as an annual percentage rate = 0.0080
FV = future value paid at maturity, or the par value of the bond = 100
m = periodicity of the floating-rate note, the number of payment periods per year = 2
DM = discount margin, the required margin stated as an annual percentage rate

Substituting given values in:

$$97 = \frac{\frac{(0.01 + 0.0080) \times 100}{2}}{\left(1 + \frac{0.01 + DM}{2}\right)^1} + \frac{\frac{(0.01 + 0.0080) \times 100}{2}}{\left(1 + \frac{0.01 + DM}{2}\right)^2} + \cdots + \frac{\frac{(0.01 + 0.0080) \times 100}{2} + 100}{\left(1 + \frac{0.01 + DM}{2}\right)^4}$$

$$97 = \frac{0.90}{\left(1 + \frac{0.01 + DM}{2}\right)^1} + \frac{0.90}{\left(1 + \frac{0.01 + DM}{2}\right)^2} + \frac{0.90}{\left(1 + \frac{0.01 + DM}{2}\right)^3} + \frac{0.90 + 100}{\left(1 + \frac{0.01 + DM}{2}\right)^4}$$

To calculate DM, begin by solving for the discount rate per period:

$$97 = \frac{0.90}{(1 + r)^1} + \frac{0.90}{(1 + r)^2} + \frac{0.90}{(1 + r)^3} + \frac{0.90 + 100}{(1 + r)^4}$$

$$r = 0.0168$$

Now, solve for DM:

$$\frac{0.01 + DM}{2} = 0.0168$$

$$DM = 0.0236$$

The discount margin for the floater is equal to 236 basis points.

32. A is correct. FRN X will be priced at a premium on the next reset date because the quoted margin of 0.40% is greater than the discount or required margin of 0.32%. The premium amount is the present value of the extra or "excess" interest payments of 0.08% each quarter (0.40% − 0.32%). FRN Y will be priced at par value on the next reset date since there is no difference between the quoted and discount margins. FRN Z will be priced at a discount since the quoted margin is less than the required margin.

33. C is correct. The bond equivalent yield is closest to 3.78%. It is calculated as:

$$AOR = \left(\frac{Year}{Days}\right) \times \left(\frac{FV - PV}{PV}\right)$$

where:

PV = present value, principal amount, or the price of the money market instrument
FV = future value, or the redemption amount paid at maturity including interest
Days = number of days between settlement and maturity
Year = number of days in the year
AOR = add-on rate, stated as an annual percentage rate (also called bond equivalent yield).

$$AOR = \left(\frac{365}{350}\right) \times \left(\frac{100 - 96.5}{96.5}\right)$$

$$AOR = 1.04286 \times 0.03627$$

$$AOR = 0.03783 \text{ or approximately } 3.78\%$$

34. C is correct. The bond equivalent yield is closest to 4.40%. The present value of the banker's acceptance is calculated as:

$$PV = FV \times \left(1 - \frac{Days}{Year} \times DR\right)$$

where:

      PV = present value, or price of the money market instrument
      FV = future value paid at maturity, or face value of the money market instrument
    Days = number of days between settlement and maturity
    Year = number of days in the year
     DR = discount rate, stated as an annual percentage rate

$$PV = 100 \times \left(1 - \frac{Days}{Year} \times DR\right)$$

$$PV = 100 \times \left(1 - \frac{180}{360} \times 0.0425\right)$$

$$PV = 100 \times (1 - 0.02125)$$

$$PV = 100 \times 0.97875$$

$$PV = 97.875$$

The bond equivalent yield (AOR) is calculated as:

$$AOR = \left(\frac{Year}{Days}\right) \times \left(\frac{FV - PV}{PV}\right)$$

where:

      PV = present value, principal amount, or the price of the money market instrument
      FV = future value, or the redemption amount paid at maturity including interest
    Days = number of days between settlement and maturity
    Year = number of days in the year
   AOR = add-on rate (bond equivalent yield), stated as an annual percentage rate

$$AOR = \left(\frac{365}{180}\right) \times \left(\frac{100 - PV}{PV}\right)$$

$$AOR = \left(\frac{365}{180}\right) \times \left(\frac{100 - 97.875}{97.875}\right)$$

$$AOR = 2.02778 \times 0.02171$$

$$AOR = 0.04402, \text{ or approximately } 4.40\%$$

Note that the PV is calculated using an assumed 360-day year and the AOR (bond equivalent yield) is calculated using a 365-day year.

35. B is correct. All bonds on a par curve are assumed to have similar, not different, credit risk. Par curves are obtained from spot curves and all bonds used to derive the par curve are assumed to have the same credit risk, as well as the same periodicity, currency, liquidity, tax status, and annual yields. A par curve is a sequence of yields-to-maturity such that each bond is priced at par value.

36. B is correct. The spot curve, also known as the strip or zero curve, is the yield curve constructed from a sequence of yields-to-maturities on zero-coupon bonds. The par curve is a sequence of yields-to-maturity such that each bond is priced at par value. The forward curve is constructed using a series of forward rates, each having the same timeframe.

37. B is correct. The forward rate can be interpreted to be the incremental or marginal return for extending the time-to-maturity of an investment for an additional time period. The add-on rate (bond equivalent yield) is a rate quoted for money market instruments such as bank certificates of deposit and indexes such as Libor and Euribor. Yield-to-maturity is the internal rate of return on the bond's cash flows—the uniform interest rate such that when the bond's future cash flows are discounted at that rate, the sum of the present values equals the price of the bond. It is the implied market discount rate.

38. B is correct. The 3 year implied spot rate is closest to 1.94%. It is calculated as the geometric average of the one-year forward rates:

$$(1.0080 \times 1.0112 \times 1.0394) = (1 + z_3)^3$$
$$1.05945 = (1 + z_3)^3$$
$$[1.05945]^{1/3} = [(1 + z_3)^3]^{1/3}$$
$$1.01944 = 1 + z_3$$
$$1.01944 - 1 = z_3$$
$$0.01944 = z_3, z_3 = 1.944\% \text{ or approximately } 1.94\%$$

39. B is correct. The value per 100 of par value is closest to 105.01. Using the forward curve, the bond price is calculated as follows:

$$\frac{3.5}{1.0080} + \frac{103.5}{(1.0080 \times 1.0112)} = 3.47 + 101.54 = 105.01$$

40. C is correct. The spread component of a specific bond's yield-to-maturity is least likely impacted by changes in inflation of its currency of denomination. The effect of changes in macroeconomic factors, such as the expected rate of inflation in the currency of denomination, is seen mostly in changes in the benchmark yield. The spread or risk premium component is impacted by microeconomic factors specific to the bond and bond issuer including tax status and quality rating.

41. A is correct. The I-spread, or interpolated spread, is the yield spread of a specific bond over the standard swap rate in that currency of the same tenor. The yield spread in basis points over an actual or interpolated government bond is known as the G-spread. The Z-spread (zero-volatility spread) is the constant spread that is added to each spot rate such that the present value of the cash flows matches the price of the bond.

42. B is correct. The G-spread is closest to 285 bps. The benchmark rate for UK fixed-rate bonds is the UK government benchmark bond. The euro interest rate spread benchmark

is used to calculate the G-spread for euro-denominated corporate bonds, not UK bonds. The G-spread is calculated as follows:

Yield-to-maturity on the UK corporate bond:

$$100.65 = \frac{5}{(1+r)^1} + \frac{5}{(1+r)^2} + \frac{105}{(1+r)^3}, \ r = 0.04762 \text{ or } 476 \text{ bps}$$

Yield-to-maturity on the UK government benchmark bond:

$$100.25 = \frac{2}{(1+r)^1} + \frac{2}{(1+r)^2} + \frac{102}{(1+r)^3}, \ r = 0.01913 \text{ or } 191 \text{ bps}$$

The G-spread is $476 - 191 = 285$ bps.

43. A is correct. The value of the bond is closest to 92.38. The calculation is:

$$PV = \frac{PMT}{(1+z_1+Z)^1} + \frac{PMT}{(1+z_2+Z)^2} + \frac{PMT+FV}{(1+z_3+Z)^3}$$

$$= \frac{5}{(1+0.0486+0.0234)^1} + \frac{5}{(1+0.0495+0.0234)^2} + \frac{105}{(1+0.0565+0.0234)^3}$$

$$= \frac{5}{1.0720} + \frac{5}{1.15111} + \frac{105}{1.25936} = 4.66 + 4.34 + 83.38 = 92.38$$

44. C is correct. The option value in basis points per year is subtracted from the Z-spread to calculate the option-adjusted spread (OAS). The Z-spread is the constant yield spread over the benchmark spot curve. The I-spread is the yield spread of a specific bond over the standard swap rate in that currency of the same tenor.

CHAPTER 4

INTRODUCTION TO ASSET-BACKED SECURITIES

SOLUTIONS

1. B is correct. Securitization increases the funds available for banks to lend because it allows banks to remove loans from their balance sheets and issue bonds that are backed by those loans. Securitization repackages relatively simple debt obligations, such as bank loans, into more complex, not simpler, structures. Securitization involves transferring ownership of assets from the original owner—in this case, the banks—into a special legal entity. As a result, banks do not maintain ownership of the securitized assets.

2. C is correct. By removing the wall between ultimate investors and originating borrowers, investors can achieve better legal claims on the underlying mortgages and portfolios of receivables. This transparency allows investors to tailor interest rate risk and credit risk to their specific needs.

3. C is correct. Securitization allows for the creation of tradable securities with greater liquidity than the original loans on a bank's balance sheet. Securitization results in lessening the roles of intermediaries, which increases disintermediation. Securitization is a process in which relatively simple debt obligations, such as loans, are repackaged into more complex structures.

4. A is correct. Securitization allows investors to achieve more direct legal claims on loans and portfolios of receivables. As a result, investors can add to their portfolios exposure to the risk–return characteristics provided by a wider range of assets.

   B is incorrect because securitization does not reduce credit risk but, rather, provides a structure to mitigate and redistribute the inherent credit risks of pools of loans and receivables.

   C is incorrect because securitization does not eliminate the timing risks associated with ABS cash flows but, rather, provides a structure to mitigate and redistribute those risks, such as contraction risk and extension risk.

5. A is correct. In a securitization, the special purpose entity (SPE) is the special legal entity responsible for the issuance of the asset-backed securities. The servicer, not the SPE, is responsible for both the collection of payments from the borrowers and the recovery of underlying assets if the borrowers default on their loans.

6. B is correct. In a securitization, the loans or receivables are initially sold by the depositor to the special purpose entity (SPE) that uses them as collateral to issue the ABS.

    A is incorrect because the SPE, often referred to as the issuer, is the purchaser of the collateral rather than the seller of the collateral.

    C is incorrect because the underwriter neither sells nor purchases the collateral in a securitization. The underwriter performs the same functions in a securitization as it does in a standard bond offering.

7. C is correct. The first €25 (€5 + €20) million in default are absorbed by the subordinated classes (C and B). The senior Class A bonds will only experience a loss when defaults exceed €25 million.

8. A is correct. Time tranching is the process in which a set of bond classes or tranches is created that allow investors a choice in the type of prepayment risk, extension or contraction, that they prefer to bear. Senior and subordinated bond classes are used in credit tranching. Credit tranching structures allow investors to choose the amount of credit risk that they prefer to bear. Fully and partially amortizing loans are two types of amortizing loans.

9. B is correct. Credit tranching is a form of credit enhancement called subordination in which bond classes or tranches differ as to how they will share losses resulting from defaults of the borrowers whose loans are part of the collateral. This type of protection is commonly referred to as a waterfall structure because of the cascading flow of payments between bond classes in the event of default.

    A is incorrect because time tranching involves the creation of bond classes that possess different expected maturities rather than bond classes that differ as to how credit losses will be shared. Time tranching involves the redistribution of prepayment risk, whereas credit tranching involves the redistribution of credit risk.

    C is incorrect because although overcollateralization is a form of internal credit enhancement similar to subordination, it is the amount by which the principal amount of the pool of collateral exceeds the principal balance of the securities issued and backed by the collateral pool. Losses are absorbed first by the amount of overcollateralization and then according to the credit tranching structure.

10. A is correct. Time tranching is the creation of bond classes that possess different expected maturities so that prepayment risk can be redistributed among bond classes. When loan agreements provide borrowers the ability to alter payments, in the case of declining interest rates, this prepayment risk increases because borrowers tend to pay off part or all of their loans and refinance at lower interest rates.

    B is incorrect because it is possible, and quite common, for a securitization to have structures with both credit tranching and time tranching.

    C is incorrect because the subordinated structures of junior and senior bond classes differ as to how they will share any losses relative to defaults of the borrowers whose loans are in the collateral pool. Junior classes offer protection for senior classes, with losses first realized by the former. The classes are not distinguished by scheduled repayment terms but, rather, by a loss-sharing hierarchy in the event of borrower default.

11. A is correct. The legal implication of a special purpose entity (SPE), a prerequisite for securitization, is that investors contemplating the purchase of bond classes backed by the assets of the SPE will evaluate the credit risk of those assets independently from the credit rating of the entity that sold the assets to the SPE. This separation of the seller's collateral from its credit rating provides the opportunity for the SPE to access a lower aggregate funding cost than what the seller might otherwise obtain.

B is incorrect because the absolute priority rule, under which senior creditors are paid in full before subordinated creditors, has not always been upheld in bankruptcy reorganizations. There is no assurance that if a corporate bond has collateral, the rights of the bondholders will be respected. It is this uncertainty that creates the dominant influence of credit ratings over collateral in credit spreads.

C is incorrect because corporate bond credit spreads will reflect the seller's credit rating primarily and the collateral slightly. Securitization separates the seller's collateral from its credit rating, effectively altering the influence of collateral on the credit spread.

12. C is correct. In a partially amortizing loan, the sum of all the scheduled principal repayments is less than the amount borrowed. The last payment is for the remaining unpaid mortgage balance and is called the "balloon payment."

13. B is correct. Contraction risk is the risk that when interest rates decline, actual prepayments will be higher than forecasted. Extension risk is the risk that when interest rates rise, prepayments will be lower than forecasted. Yield maintenance results from prepayment penalties; the lender is protected from loss in yield by the imposition of prepayment penalties.

14. A is correct. In a recourse loan, the lender has a claim against the borrower for the shortfall between the amount of the mortgage balance outstanding and the proceeds received from the sale of the property. A prepayment option is a benefit to the borrower and would thus not offer protection to the lender. An interest-only mortgage requires no principal repayment for a number of years and will not protect the lender from strategic default by the borrower.

15. B is correct. Bank Nederlandse has a claim against Marolf for 1.5 million EUR, the shortfall between the amount of the mortgage balance outstanding and the proceeds received from the sale of the property. This indicates that the mortgage loan is a recourse loan. The recourse/non-recourse feature indicates the rights of a lender in foreclosure. If Marolf had a non-recourse loan, the bank would have only been entitled to the proceeds from the sale of the underlying property, or 2.5 million EUR. A bullet loan is a special type of interest-only mortgage for which there are no scheduled principal payments over the entire term of the loan. Since the unpaid balance is less than the original mortgage loan, it is unlikely that Marolf has an interest-only mortgage.

16. A is correct. Because the loan has a non-recourse feature, the lender can only look to the underlying property to recover the outstanding mortgage balance and has no further claim against the borrower. The lender is simply entitled to foreclose on the home and sell it.

17. A is correct. A bullet mortgage is a special type of interest-only mortgage in which there are no scheduled principal repayments over the entire life of the loan. At maturity, a balloon payment is required equal to the original loan amount.

B is incorrect because with a fully amortizing mortgage, the sum of all the scheduled principal repayments during the mortgage's life is such that when the last mortgage payment is made, the loan is fully repaid, with no balloon payment required.

C is incorrect because with a partially amortizing mortgage, the sum of all the scheduled principal repayments is less than the amount borrowed, resulting in a balloon payment equal to the unpaid mortgage balance (rather than the original loan amount).

18. A is correct. In non-recourse loan jurisdictions, the borrower may have an incentive to default on an underwater mortgage and allow the lender to foreclose on the property because the lender has no claim against the borrower for the shortfall. For this reason, such defaults, known as strategic defaults, are more likely in non-recourse jurisdictions and less

likely in recourse jurisdictions, where the lender does have a claim against the borrower for the shortfall.

B is incorrect because strategic defaults in non-recourse jurisdictions do have negative consequences for the defaulting borrowers in the form of a lower credit score and a reduced ability to borrow in the future. These negative consequences can be a deterrent in the incidence of underwater mortgage defaults.

C is incorrect because when a recourse loan defaults, the lender can look to both the property and the borrower to recover the outstanding mortgage balance. In a recourse loan, the lender has a claim against the borrower for the shortfall between the amount of the outstanding mortgage balance and the proceeds received from the sale of the property.

19. A is correct. Non-agency RMBS are credit enhanced, either internally or externally, to make the securities more attractive to investors. The most common forms of internal credit enhancements are senior/subordinated structures, reserve accounts, and overcollateralization. Conforming mortgages are used as collateral for agency (not non-agency) mortgage pass-through securities. An agency RMBS, rather than a non-agency RMBS, issued by a GSE (government sponsored enterprise), is guaranteed by the respective GSE.

20. B is correct. Extension risk is the risk that when interest rate rise, fewer prepayments will occur. Homeowners will be reluctant to give up the benefit of a contractual interest rate that is lower. As a result, the mortgage pass-through security becomes longer in maturity than anticipated at the time of purchase.

21. C is correct. Using CMOs, securities can be created to closely satisfy the asset/liability needs of institutional investors. The creation of a CMO cannot eliminate prepayment risk; it can only distribute the various forms of this risk among various classes of bondholders. The collateral of CMOs are mortgage-related products, not the mortgages themselves.

22. C is correct. For a CMO with multiple sequential-pay tranches, the longest-term tranche will have the lowest contraction (prepayments greater than forecasted) risk because of the protection against this risk offered by the other tranches. The longest-term tranche is likely to have the highest average life and extension risk because it is the last tranche repaid in a sequential-pay tranche.

23. A is correct. PAC tranches have limited (but not complete) protection against both extension risk and contraction risk. This protection is provided by the support tranches. A sequential-pay tranche can protect against either extension risk or contraction risk but not both of these risks. The CMO structure with sequential-pay tranches allows investors concerned about extension risk to invest in shorter-term tranches and those concerned about contraction risk to invest in the longer-term tranches.

24. C is correct. The greater predictability of cash flows provided in the planned amortization class (PAC) tranches comes at the expense of support tranches. As a result, investors in support tranches are exposed to higher extension risk and contraction risk than investors in PAC tranches. Investors will be compensated for bearing this risk because support tranches have a higher expected return than PAC tranches.

25. B is correct. CPR is an annualized rate, which indicates the percentage of the outstanding mortgage pool balance at the beginning of the year that is expected to be prepaid by the end of the year.

26. C is correct. When interest rates decline, a mortgage pass-through security is subject to contraction risk. Contraction risk is the risk that when interest rates decline, actual prepayments will be higher than forecasted because borrowers will refinance at now-available lower interest rates. Thus, a security backed by mortgages will have a shorter maturity than was anticipated when the security was purchased.

27. A is correct. The coupon rate of a mortgage pass-through security is called the pass-through rate, whereas the mortgage rate on the underlying pool of mortgages is calculated as a weighted average coupon rate (WAC). The pass-through rate is lower than the WAC by an amount equal to the servicing fee and other administrative fees.

28. B is correct. The SMM is a monthly measure of the prepayment rate or prepayment speed. Contraction risk is the risk that when interest rates decline, actual prepayments will be higher than forecast. So if contraction risk falls, prepayments are likely to be lower than forecast, which would imply a decrease in the SMM.

    A is incorrect because the SMM is a monthly measure of the prepayment rate or prepayment speed. Extension risk is the risk that when interest rates rise, actual prepayments will be lower than forecast. So if extension risk rises, prepayments are likely to be lower than forecast, which would imply a decrease, not an increase, in the SMM.

    C is incorrect because at 100 PSA, investors can expect prepayments to follow the PSA prepayment benchmark. Based on historical patterns, the PSA standard model assumes that prepayment rates are low for newly initiated mortgages and then speed up as mortgages season. Thus, 100 PSA does not imply that the SMM remains the same but, rather, implies that it will vary over the life of the mortgage.

29. A is correct. If commercial mortgage loans are non-recourse loans, the lender can only look to the income-producing property backing the loan for interest and principal repayment. If there is a default, the lender looks to the proceeds from the sale of the property for repayment and has no recourse against the borrower for any unpaid mortgage loan balance. Call protection and prepayment penalty points protect against prepayment risk.

30. A is correct. With CMBS, investors have considerable call protection. An investor in a RMBS is exposed to considerable prepayment risk, but with CMBS, call protection is available to the investor at the structure and loan level. The call protection results in CMBS trading in the market more like a corporate bond than a RMBS. Both internal credit enhancement and the debt-service-coverage (DSC) ratio address credit risk, not prepayment risk.

31. A is correct. If specific ratios of debt to service coverage are needed, and those ratios cannot be met at the loan level, subordination is used to achieve the desired credit rating. Call protection protects investors against prepayment risk. Balloon payments increase the risk of the underlying loans.

32. B is correct. In a non-recourse CMBS, the lender can look only to the income-producing property backing the loan for interest and principal repayment. If a default occurs, the lender can use only the proceeds from the sale of the property for repayment and has no recourse to the borrower for any unpaid balance.

33. B is correct. A critical feature that differentiates CMBSs from RMBSs is the call protection provided to investors. An investor in a RMBS is exposed to considerable prepayment risk because the borrower has the right to prepay the loan before maturity. CMBSs provide investors with considerable call protection that comes either at the structure level or at the loan level.

34. A is correct. An excess spread account, sometimes called excess interest cash flow, is a form of internal credit enhancement that limits credit risk. It is an amount that can be retained and deposited into a reserve account and that can serve as a first line of protection against losses. An excess spread account does not limit prepayment risk, extension, or contraction.

35. C is correct. During the lockout period, the cash flow that is paid out to owners of credit card receivable asset-backed securities is based only on finance charges collected and fees.

36. C is correct. Because credit card receivable ABSs are backed by non-amortizing loans that do not involve scheduled principal repayments, they are not affected by prepayment risk.

    A is incorrect because auto loan ABSs are affected by prepayment risk since they are backed by amortizing loans involving scheduled principal repayments.

    B is incorrect because residential MBSs are affected by prepayment risk since they are backed by amortizing loans involving scheduled principal repayments.

37. A is correct. In addition to a senior/subordinated (sequential pay) structure, many auto loan ABSs are structured with additional credit enhancement in the form of overcollateralization and a reserve account, often an excess spread account. The excess spread is an amount that can be retained and deposited into a reserve account that can serve as a first line of protection against losses.

    B is incorrect because in an auto loan ABS, losses are typically applied against the excess spread account and the amount of overcollateralization before the waterfall loss absorption of the sequential pay structure.

    C is incorrect because in auto loan ABSs, proceeds from the repossession and resale of autos are prepayment cash flows rather than a form of credit enhancement for loss protection.

38. C is correct. In credit card receivable ABSs, the only way the principal cash flows can be altered is by triggering the early amortization provision. Such provisions are included in the ABS structure to safeguard the credit quality of the issue.

    A is incorrect because expiration of the lockout period does not result in the alteration of principal cash flows but instead defines when principal repayments are distributed to the ABS investors. During the lockout period, principal repayments by cardholders are reinvested. When the lockout period expires, principal repayments by cardholders are distributed to investors.

    B is incorrect because the excess spread account is a credit enhancement for loss absorption. When the excess spread account is depleted, losses are applied against the overcollateralization amount followed by the senior/subordinated structure. The only way principal cash flows can be altered is by triggering the early amortization provision.

39. C is correct. The mezzanine tranche consists of bond classes with credit ratings between senior and subordinated bond classes.

    A is incorrect because the equity tranche falls within and carries the credit rating applicable to the subordinated bond classes.

    B is incorrect because the residual tranche falls within and carries the credit ratings applicable to the subordinated bond classes.

40. C is correct. The key to whether a CDO is viable is whether a structure can be created that offers a competitive return for the subordinated tranche (often referred to as the residual or equity tranche). Investors in a subordinated tranche typically use borrowed funds (the bond classes issued) to generate a return above the funding cost.

    A is incorrect because the viability of a CDO depends on a structure that offers a competitive return for the subordinated tranche rather than the senior tranche.

    B is incorrect because the viability of a CDO depends on a structure that offers a competitive return for the subordinated tranche rather than the mezzanine tranche.

41. A is correct. When the collateral manager fails pre-specified tests, a provision is triggered that requires the payoff of the principal to the senior class until the tests are satisfied. This reduction of the senior class effectively deleverages the CDO because the CDO's cheapest funding source is reduced.

42. B is correct. CMOs are designed to redistribute cash flows of mortgage-related products to different bond classes or tranches through securitization. Although CMOs do not eliminate prepayment risk, they distribute prepayment risk among various classes of bondholders.

CHAPTER 5

UNDERSTANDING FIXED INCOME RISK AND RETURN

SOLUTIONS

1. A is correct. A capital gain is least likely to contribute to the investor's total return. There is no capital gain (or loss) because the bond is held to maturity. The carrying value of the bond at maturity is par value, the same as the redemption amount. When a fixed-rate bond is held to its maturity, the investor receives the principal payment at maturity. This principal payment is a source of return for the investor. A fixed-rate bond pays periodic coupon payments, and the reinvestment of these coupon payments is a source of return for the investor. The investor's total return is the redemption of principal at maturity and the sum of the reinvested coupons.

2. C is correct. Because the fixed-rate bond is held to maturity (a "buy-and-hold" investor), interest rate risk arises entirely from changes in coupon reinvestment rates. Higher interest rates increase income from reinvestment of coupon payments, and lower rates decrease income from coupon reinvestment. There will not be a capital gain or loss because the bond is held until maturity. The carrying value at the maturity date is par value, the same as the redemption amount. The redemption of principal does not expose the investor to interest rate risk. The risk to a bond's principal is credit risk.

3. A is correct. Capital gains (losses) arise if a bond is sold at a price above (below) its constant-yield price trajectory. A point on the trajectory represents the carrying value of the bond at that time. That is, the capital gain/loss is measured from the bond's carrying value, the point on the constant-yield price trajectory, and not from the original purchase price. The carrying value is the original purchase price plus the amortized amount of the discount if the bond is purchased at a price below par value. If the bond is purchased at a price above par value, the carrying value is the original purchase price minus (not plus) the amortized amount of the premium. The amortized amount for each year is the change in the price between two points on the trajectory.

4. C is correct. The future value of reinvested cash flows at 8% after five years is closest to 41.07 per 100 of par value.

$$\left[7\times(1.08)^4\right]+\left[7\times(1.08)^3\right]+\left[7\times(1.08)^2\right]+\left[7\times(1.08)^1\right]+7=41.0662$$

The 6.07 difference between the sum of the coupon payments over the five-year holding period (35) and the future value of the reinvested coupons (41.07) represents the "interest-on-interest" gain from compounding.

5. B is correct. The capital loss is closest to 3.31 per 100 of par value. After five years, the bond has four years remaining until maturity and the sale price of the bond is 96.69, calculated as:

$$\frac{7}{(1.08)^1}+\frac{7}{(1.08)^2}+\frac{7}{(1.08)^3}+\frac{107}{(1.08)^4}=96.69$$

The investor purchased the bond at a price equal to par value (100). Because the bond was purchased at a price equal to its par value, the carrying value is par value. Therefore, the investor experienced a capital loss of $96.69 - 100 = -3.31$.

6. B is correct. The investor's five-year horizon yield is closest to 6.62%. After five years, the sale price of the bond is 96.69 (from problem 5) and the future value of reinvested cash flows at 8% is 41.0662 (from problem 4) per 100 of par value. The total return is 137.76 (= 41.07 + 96.69), resulting in a realized five-year horizon yield of 6.62%:

$$100.00=\frac{137.76}{(1+r)^5},\quad r=0.0662$$

7. A is correct. The bond's approximate modified duration is closest to 2.78. Approximate modified duration is calculated as:

$$\text{ApproxModDur}=\frac{(PV_-)-(PV_+)}{2\times(\Delta\text{Yield})\times(PV_0)}$$

Lower yield-to-maturity by 5 bps to 2.95%:

$$PV_-=\frac{5}{(1+0.0295)^1}+\frac{5}{(1+0.0295)^2}+\frac{5+100}{(1+0.0295)^3}=105.804232$$

Increase yield-to-maturity by 5 bps to 3.05%:

$$PV_+=\frac{5}{(1+0.0305)^1}+\frac{5}{(1+0.0305)^2}+\frac{5+100}{(1+0.0305)^3}=105.510494$$

$PV_0 = 105.657223$, $\Delta\text{Yield} = 0.0005$

$$\text{ApproxModDur}=\frac{105.804232-105.510494}{2\times0.0005\times105.657223}=2.78$$

8. C is correct. A bond's modified duration cannot be larger than its Macaulay duration assuming a positive yield-to-maturity. The formula for modified duration is:

$$\text{ModDur}=\frac{\text{MacDur}}{1+r}$$

where r is the bond's yield-to-maturity per period. Therefore, ModDur will be less than MacDur.

Effective duration is a measure of curve duration. Modified duration is a measure of yield duration.

9. C is correct. The bond's Macaulay duration is closest to 2.83. Macaulay duration (MacDur) is a weighted average of the times to the receipt of cash flow. The weights are the shares of the full price corresponding to each coupon and principal payment.

Period	Cash Flow	Present Value	Weight	Period × Weight
1	6	5.555556	0.058575	0.058575
2	6	5.144033	0.054236	0.108472
3	106	84.146218	0.887190	2.661570
		94.845806	1.000000	2.828617

Thus, the bond's Macaulay duration (MacDur) is 2.83.

Alternatively, Macaulay duration can be calculated using the following closed-form formula:

$$\text{MacDur} = \left\{ \frac{1+r}{r} - \frac{1+r+\left[N \times (c-r)\right]}{c \times \left[(1+r)^N - 1\right] + r} \right\} - (t/T)$$

$$\text{MacDur} = \left\{ \frac{1.08}{0.08} - \frac{1.08 + \left[3 \times (0.06 - 0.08)\right]}{0.06 \times \left[(1.08)^3 - 1\right] + 0.08} \right\} - 0$$

$$\text{MacDur} = 13.50 - 10.67 = 2.83$$

10. A is correct. The interest rate risk of a fixed-rate bond with an embedded call option is best measured by effective duration. A callable bond's future cash flows are uncertain because they are contingent on future interest rates. The issuer's decision to call the bond depends on future interest rates. Therefore, the yield-to-maturity on a callable bond is not well defined. Only effective duration, which takes into consideration the value of the call option, is the appropriate interest rate risk measure. Yield durations like Macaulay and modified durations are not relevant for a callable bond because they assume no changes in cash flows when interest rates change.

11. A is correct. Key rate duration is used to measure a bond's sensitivity to a shift at one or more maturity segments of the yield curve that result in a change to yield curve shape. Modified and effective duration measure a bond's sensitivity to parallel shifts in the entire curve.

12. B is correct. The effective duration of the pension fund's liabilities is closest to 14.99. The effective duration is calculated as follows:

$$\text{EffDur} = \frac{(PV_-) - (PV_+)}{2 \times (\Delta \text{Curve}) \times (PV_0)}$$

$PV_0 = 455.4$, $PV_+ = 373.6$, $PV_- = 510.1$, and $\Delta \text{Curve} = 0.0100$.

$$\text{EffDur} = \frac{510.1 - 373.6}{2 \times 0.0100 \times 455.4} = 14.99$$

13. B is correct. A bond's yield-to-maturity is inversely related to its Macaulay duration: The higher the yield-to-maturity, the lower its Macaulay duration and the lower the interest rate risk. A higher yield-to-maturity decreases the weighted average of the times to the receipt of cash flow, and thus decreases the Macaulay duration.

    A bond's coupon rate is inversely related to its Macaulay duration: The lower the coupon, the greater the weight of the payment of principal at maturity. This results in a higher Macaulay duration. Zero-coupon bonds do not pay periodic coupon payments; therefore, the Macaulay duration of a zero-coupon bond is its time-to-maturity.

14. A is correct. The presence of an embedded put option reduces the effective duration of the bond, especially when rates are rising. If interest rates are low compared with the coupon rate, the value of the put option is low and the impact of the change in the benchmark yield on the bond's price is very similar to the impact on the price of a non-putable bond. But when benchmark interest rates rise, the put option becomes more valuable to the investor. The ability to sell the bond at par value limits the price depreciation as rates rise. The presence of an embedded put option reduces the sensitivity of the bond price to changes in the benchmark yield, assuming no change in credit risk.

15. A is correct. The portfolio's modified duration is closest to 7.62. Portfolio duration is commonly estimated as the market-value-weighted average of the yield durations of the individual bonds that compose the portfolio.

    The total market value of the bond portfolio is 170,000 + 120,000 + 100,000 = 390,000.

    The portfolio duration is 5.42 × (170,000/390,000) + 8.44 × (120,000/390,000) + 10.38 × (100,000/390,000) = 7.62.

16. A is correct. A limitation of calculating a bond portfolio's duration as the weighted average of the yield durations of the individual bonds is that this measure implicitly assumes a parallel shift to the yield curve (all rates change by the same amount in the same direction). In reality, interest rate changes frequently result in a steeper or flatter yield curve. This approximation of the "theoretically correct" portfolio duration is *more* accurate when the yield curve is flatter (less steeply sloped). An advantage of this approach is that it can be used with portfolios that include bonds with embedded options. Bonds with embedded options can be included in the weighted average using the effective durations for these securities.

17. B is correct. Bond B has the greatest money duration per 100 of par value. Money duration (MoneyDur) is calculated as the annual modified duration (AnnModDur) times the full price (PV^{Full}) of the bond including accrued interest. Bond B has the highest money duration per 100 of par value.

$$\text{MoneyDur} = \text{AnnModDur} \times PV^{Full}$$

$$\text{MoneyDur of Bond A} = 5.42 \times 85.00 = 460.70$$

$$\text{MoneyDur of Bond B} = 8.44 \times 80.00 = 675.20$$

$$\text{MoneyDur of Bond C} = 7.54 \times 85.78 = 646.78$$

18. B is correct. The PVBP is closest to 0.0648. The formula for the price value of a basis point is:

$$\text{PVBP} = \frac{(PV_-) - (PV_+)}{2}$$

where:

> PVBP = price value of a basis point
> PV_- = full price calculated by lowering the yield-to-maturity by one basis point
> PV_+ = full price calculated by raising the yield-to-maturity by one basis point

Lowering the yield-to-maturity by one basis point to 4.99% results in a bond price of 85.849134:

$$PV_- = \frac{3}{(1+0.0499)^1} + \cdots + \frac{3+100}{(1+0.0499)^9} = 85.849134$$

Increasing the yield-to-maturity by one basis point to 5.01% results in a bond price of 85.719638:

$$PV_+ = \frac{3}{(1+0.0501)^1} + \cdots + \frac{3+100}{(1+0.0501)^9} = 85.719638$$

$$PVBP = \frac{85.849134 - 85.719638}{2} = 0.06475$$

Alternatively, the PVBP can be derived using modified duration:

$$ApproxModDur = \frac{(PV_-) - (PV_+)}{2 \times (\Delta Yield) \times (PV_0)}$$

$$ApproxModDur = \frac{85.849134 - 85.719638}{2 \times 0.0001 \times 85.784357} = 7.548$$

$$PVBP = 7.548 \times 85.784357 \times 0.0001 = 0.06475$$

19. B is correct. Convexity measures the "second order" effect on a bond's percentage price change given a change in yield-to-maturity. Convexity adjusts the percentage price change estimate provided by modified duration to better approximate the true relationship between a bond's price and its yield-to-maturity, which is a curved line (convex).

    Duration estimates the change in the bond's price along the straight line that is tangent to this curved line ("first order" effect). Yield volatility measures the magnitude of changes in the yields along the yield curve.

20. B is correct. The bond's approximate convexity is closest to 70.906. Approximate convexity (ApproxCon) is calculated using the following formula:

$$ApproxCon = [PV_- + PV_+ - (2 \times PV_0)]/(\Delta Yield^2 \times PV_0)$$

where:

> PV_- = new price when the yield-to-maturity is decreased
> PV_+ = new price when the yield-to-maturity is increased
> PV_0 = original price
> $\Delta Yield$ = change in yield-to-maturity

$$ApproxCon = [98.782 + 98.669 - (2 \times 98.722)]/(0.001^2 \times 98.722) = 70.906$$

21. C is correct. The expected percentage price change is closest to 1.78%. The convexity-adjusted percentage price change for a bond given a change in the yield-to-maturity is estimated by:

$$\%\Delta PV^{Full} \approx [-\text{AnnModDur} \times \Delta\text{Yield}] + [0.5 \times \text{AnnConvexity} \times (\Delta\text{Yield})^2]$$

$$\%\Delta PV^{Full} \approx [-7.020 \times (-0.0025)] + [0.5 \times 65.180 \times (-0.0025)^2] = 0.017754, \text{ or } 1.78\%$$

22. B is correct. The expected percentage price change is closest to −3.49%. The convexity-adjusted percentage price change for a bond given a change in the yield-to-maturity is estimated by:

$$\%\Delta PV^{Full} \approx [-\text{AnnModDur} \times \Delta\text{Yield}] + [0.5 \times \text{AnnConvexity} \times (\Delta\text{Yield})^2]$$

$$\%\Delta PV^{Full} \approx [-7.140 \times 0.005] + [0.5 \times 66.200 \times (0.005)^2] = -0.034873, \text{ or } -3.49\%$$

23. B is correct. If the term structure of yield volatility is downward-sloping, then short-term bond yields-to-maturity have greater volatility than for long-term bonds. Therefore, long-term yields are more stable than short-term yields. Higher volatility in short-term rates does not necessarily mean that the level of short-term rates is higher than long-term rates. With a downward-sloping term structure of yield volatility, short-term bonds will not always experience greater price fluctuation than long-term bonds. The estimated percentage change in a bond's price depends on the modified duration and convexity as well as on the yield-to-maturity change.

24. C is correct. When the holder of a bond experiences a one-time parallel shift in the yield curve, the Macaulay duration statistic identifies the number of years necessary to hold the bond so that the losses (or gains) from coupon reinvestment offset the gains (or losses) from market price changes. The duration gap is the difference between the Macaulay duration and the investment horizon. Modified duration approximates the percentage price change of a bond given a change in its yield-to-maturity.

25. C is correct. The duration gap is equal to the bond's Macaulay duration minus the investment horizon. In this case, the duration gap is positive, and price risk dominates coupon reinvestment risk. The investor risk is to higher rates.

    The investor is hedged against interest rate risk if the duration gap is zero; that is, the investor's investment horizon is equal to the bond's Macaulay duration. The investor is at risk of lower rates only if the duration gap is negative; that is, the investor's investment horizon is greater than the bond's Macaulay duration. In this case, coupon reinvestment risk dominates market price risk.

26. C is correct. The duration gap is closest to 4.158. The duration gap is a bond's Macaulay duration minus the investment horizon. The approximate Macaulay duration is the approximate modified duration times one plus the yield-to-maturity. Here it is 12.158 (= 11.470 × 1.06).

    Given an investment horizon of eight years, the duration gap for this bond at purchase is positive: 12.158 − 8 = 4.158. When the investment horizon is less than the Macaulay duration of the bond, the duration gap is positive, and price risk dominates coupon reinvestment risk.

27. A is correct. The price increase was most likely caused by a decrease in the bond's credit spread. The ratings upgrade most likely reflects a lower expected probability of default and/or a greater level of recovery of assets if default occurs. The decrease in credit risk results in a smaller credit spread. The increase in the bond price reflects a decrease in the yield-to-maturity due to a smaller credit spread. The change in the bond price was not due to a change in liquidity risk or an increase in the benchmark rate.

CHAPTER 6

FUNDAMENTALS OF CREDIT ANALYSIS

SOLUTIONS

1. A is correct. Credit migration risk or downgrade risk refers to the risk that a bond issuer's creditworthiness may deteriorate or migrate lower. The result is that investors view the risk of default to be higher, causing the spread on the issuer's bonds to widen.

2. C is correct. Market liquidity risk refers to the risk that the price at which investors transact may be different from the price indicated in the market. Market liquidity risk is increased by (1) less debt outstanding and/or (2) a lower issue credit rating. Because Stedsmart Ltd is comparable to Fignermo Ltd except for less publicly traded debt outstanding, it should have higher market liquidity risk.

3. A is correct. First mortgage debt is senior secured debt and has the highest priority of claims. First mortgage debt also has the highest expected recovery rate. First mortgage debt refers to the pledge of specific property. Neither senior unsecured nor junior subordinate debt has any claims on specific assets.

4. B is correct. Whether or not secured assets are sufficient for the claims against them does not influence priority of claims. Any deficiency between pledged assets and the claims against them becomes senior unsecured debt and still adheres to the guidelines of priority of claims.

5. C is correct. Both analysts and rating agencies have difficulty foreseeing future debt-financed acquisitions.

6. C is correct. Goodwill is viewed as a lower-quality asset compared with tangible assets that can be sold and more easily converted into cash.

7. C is correct. The value of assets in relation to the level of debt is important to assess the collateral of the company; that is, the quality and value of the assets that support the debt levels of the company.

8. B is correct. The growth prospects of the industry provide the analyst insight regarding the capacity of the company.

9. A is correct. The construction company is both highly leveraged, which increases credit risk, and in a highly cyclical industry, which results in more volatile earnings.

10. B is correct. The interest expense is €113 million and EBITDA = Operating profit + Depreciation and amortization = €894 + 249 million = €1,143 million. EBITDA interest coverage = EBITDA/Interest expense = 1,143/113 = 10.12 times.

11. B is correct. Total debt is €1,613 million with Total capital = Total debt + Shareholders' equity = €1,613 + 4,616 = €6,229 million. The Debt/Capital ratio = 1,613/6,229 = 25.90%.

12. A is correct. If the debt of the company remained unchanged but FFO increased, more cash is available to service debt compared to the previous year. Additionally, the debt/capital ratio has improved. It would imply that the ability of Pay Handle Ltd to service their debt has improved.

13. A is correct. Based on four of the five credit ratios, Grupa Zywiec SA's credit quality is superior to that of the industry.

14. A is correct. Davide Campari-Milano S.p.A. has more financial leverage and less interest coverage than Associated British Foods plc, which implies greater credit risk.

15. A is correct. Low demand implies wider yield spreads, while heavy supply will widen spreads even further.

16. C is correct. Credit risk is the risk of loss resulting from the borrower failing to make full and timely payments of interest and/or principal.

17. C is correct. Market liquidity risk is the risk that the price at which investors can actually transact—buying or selling—may differ from the price indicated in the market.

18. C is correct. Loss severity is the portion of a bond's value (including unpaid interest) an investor loses in the event of default.

19. B is correct. The two components of credit risk are default probability and loss severity. In the event of default, loss severity is the portion of a bond's value (including unpaid interest) an investor loses. A and C are incorrect because spread and market liquidity risk are credit-related risks, not components of credit risk.

20. A is correct. Credit risk has two components: default risk and loss severity. Because default risk is quite low for most high-quality debt issuers, bond investors tend to focus more on this likelihood and less on the potential loss severity.

21. B is correct. The expected loss for a given debt instrument is the default probability multiplied by the loss severity given default. The loss severity is often expressed as (1 − Recovery rate).

22. A is correct. Senior subordinated debt is ranked lower than senior unsecured debt and thus has a lower priority of payment.

23. C is correct. The highest-ranked unsecured debt is senior unsecured debt. Lower-ranked debt includes senior subordinated debt. A and B are incorrect because mortgage debt and second lien loans are secured and higher ranked.

24. C is correct. According to the absolute priority of claims, in the event of bankruptcy, creditors with a secured claim have the right to the value of that specific property before any other claim.

25. A is correct. A second lien has a secured interest in the pledged assets. Second lien debt ranks higher in priority of payment than senior unsecured and senior subordinated debt and thus would most likely have a higher recovery rate.

26. A is correct. Notching is the process for moving ratings up or down relative to the issuer rating when rating agencies consider secondary factors, such as priority of claims in the event of a default and the potential loss severity.

27. C is correct. Structural subordination can arise when a corporation with a holding company structure has debt at both its parent holding company and operating subsidiaries. Debt at the operating subsidiaries is serviced by the cash flow and assets of the subsidiaries before funds are passed to the parent holding company.

28. C is correct. The issuer credit rating usually applies to its senior unsecured debt.

29. A is correct. Second lien debt is secured debt, which is senior to unsecured debt and to subordinated debt.

30. C is correct. An issuer credit rating usually applies to its senior unsecured debt.

31. A is correct. Recognizing different payment priorities, and thus the potential for higher (or lower) loss severity in the event of default, the rating agencies have adopted a notching process whereby their credit ratings on issues can be moved up or down from the issuer rating (senior unsecured).

32. C is correct. As a general rule, the higher the senior unsecured rating, the smaller the notching adjustment. Thus, for corporate bonds rated Aa2/AA, the rating agencies will typically apply smaller rating adjustments, or notches, to the related issue.

33. A is correct. Credit migration is the risk that a bond issuer's creditworthiness deteriorates, or migrates lower. Over time, credit ratings can migrate significantly from what they were at the time a bond was issued. An investor should not assume that an issuer's credit rating will remain the same from the time of purchase through the entire holding period.

34. B is correct. An industry with a high number of suppliers reduces the suppliers' negotiating power, thus helping companies control expenses and aiding in the servicing of debt.

35. A is correct. Credit analysis starts with industry structure—for example, by looking at the major forces of competition, followed by an analysis of industry fundamentals—and then turns to examination of the specific issuer.

36. C is correct. Credit analysts can make judgments about management's character by evaluating the use of aggressive accounting policies, such as timing revenue recognition. This activity is a potential warning flag for other behaviors or actions that may adversely affect an issuer's creditworthiness.

37. B is correct. Capacity refers to the ability of a borrower to service its debt. Capacity is determined through credit analysis of an issuer's industry and of the specific issuer.

38. A is correct. Credit analysts can make judgments about management's character in a number of ways, including by observing its use of aggressive accounting policies and/or tax strategies. An example of this aggressiveness is recognizing revenue prematurely.

39. C is correct. The debt/capital and debt/EBITDA ratios are used to assess a company's leverage. Higher leverage ratios indicate more leverage and thus higher credit risk. Company C's debt/capital (46.3%) and debt/EBITDA (2.5×) leverage ratios are higher than those for Companies A and B.

40. B is correct. The EBITDA/interest expense and EBIT/interest expense ratios are coverage ratios. Coverage ratios measure an issuer's ability to meet its interest payments. A higher ratio indicates better credit quality. Company B's EBITDA/interest expense (62.4×) and EBIT/interest expense (58.2×) coverage ratios are higher than those for Companies A and C.

41. C is correct because Company Y has a higher ratio of free cash flow after dividends to debt than Company X, not lower, as shown in the following table.

$$\text{Free cash flow after dividends as a \% of debt} = \frac{\text{FCF after dividends}}{\text{Debt}}$$

	Company X	Company Y
Cash flow from operations	£3.3	£14.0
Less		
Net capital expenditures	−0.8	−1.1
Dividends	−0.3	−6.1
Free cash flow after dividends	£2.2	£6.8
Debt	£12.2	£29.8
Free cash flow after dividends as a % of debt	(2.2/12.2) × 100	(6.8/29.8) × 100
Free cash flow after dividends as a % of debt	18.0%	22.8%

A is incorrect. Company Y has a lower debt/capital ratio than Company X, as shown in the following table.

$$\text{Debt divided by Capital (\%)} = \frac{\text{Debt}}{(\text{Debt} + \text{Equity})}$$

	Company X	Company Y
Debt	£12.2	£29.8
Capital		
Debt	12.2	29.8
+ Equity	1.3	64.0
Capital	£13.5	£93.8
Debt/Capital (%)	(12.2/13.5) × 100	(29.8/93.8) × 100
Debt/Capital (%)	90.4%	31.8%

B is incorrect because Company Y has a lower debt/EBITDA ratio than Company Y, not higher, as shown in the following table.

	Company X	Company Y
Operating income	£1.1	£13.3
EBIT	£1.1	£13.3
plus		
Depreciation	1.0	3.8
Amortization	0.0	0.0
EBITDA	£2.1	£17.1

	Company X	Company Y
Debt	£12.2	£29.8
Debt/EBITDA	12.2/2.1	29.8/17.1
Debt/EBITDA	5.81	1.74

42. A is correct. Compared with Company Y, based on both their debt/capital ratios and their ratios of free cash flow after dividends to debt, which are measures of leverage commonly used in credit analysis, Company X is more highly leveraged, as shown in the following table.

$$\text{Debt divided by Capital (\%)} = \frac{\text{Debt}}{(\text{Debt} + \text{Equity})}$$

	Company X	Company Y
Debt	£2.2	£29.8
Capital		
Debt	2.2	29.8
+ Equity	4.3	64.0
Capital	£6.5	£93.8
Debt/Capital (%)	(12.2/13.5) × 100	(29.8/93.8) × 100
Debt/Capital (%)	90.4%	31.8%

$$\text{Free cash flow after dividends as a \% of debt} = \frac{\text{FCF after dividends}}{\text{Debt}}$$

	Company X	Company Y
Cash flow from operations	£3.3	£14.0
Less		
Net capital expenditures	−0.8	−1.1
Dividends	−0.3	−6.1
Free cash flow after dividends	£2.2	£6.8
Debt	£12.2	£29.8
Free cash flow after dividends as a % of debt	(2.2/12.2) × 100	(6.8/29.8) × 100
Free cash flow after dividends as a % of debt	18.0%	22.8%

43. B is correct. In weak financial markets, including weak markets for equities, credit spreads will widen.

44. B is correct. Weakening economic conditions will push investors to desire a greater risk premium and drive overall credit spreads wider.

45. C is correct. In periods of heavy new issue supply, credit spreads will widen if demand is insufficient.

46. C is correct. Non-sovereign governments typically must balance their operating budgets and lack the discretion to use monetary policy as many sovereigns can.

47. A is correct. Most investors in investment-grade debt focus on spread risk—that is, the effect of changes in spreads on prices and returns—while in high-yield analysis, the focus on default risk is relatively greater.

48. B is correct. Among the most important considerations in sovereign credit analysis is growth and age distribution of population. A relatively young and growing population contributes to growth in GDP and an expanding tax base and relies less on social services, pensions, and health care relative to an older population.

CHAPTER 7

THE TERM STRUCTURE AND INTEREST RATE DYNAMICS

SOLUTIONS

1. Three forward rates can be calculated from the one-, two-, and three-year spot rates. The rate on a one-year loan that begins at the end of Year 1 can be calculated using the one- and two-year spot rates; in the following equation one would solve for $f(1,1)$:

$$[1 + r(2)]^2 = [1 + r(1)]^1[1 + f(1,1)]^1$$

The rate on a one-year loan that starts at the end of Year 2 can be calculated from the two- and three-year spot rates; in the following equation one would solve for $f(2,1)$:

$$[1 + r(3)]^3 = [1 + r(2)]^2[1 + f(2,1)]^1$$

Additionally, the rate on a two-year loan that begins at the end of Year 1 can be computed from the one- and three-year spot rates; in the following equation one would solve for $f(1,2)$:

$$[1 + r(3)]^3 = [1 + r(1)]^1[1 + f(1,2)]^2$$

2. For the two-year forward rate one year from now of 2%, the two interpretations are as follows:
   - 2% is the rate that will make an investor indifferent between buying a three-year zero-coupon bond or investing in a one-year zero-coupon bond and when it matures reinvesting in a zero-coupon bond that matures in two years.
   - 2% is the rate that can be locked in today by buying a three-year zero-coupon bond rather than investing in a one-year zero-coupon bond and when it matures reinvesting in a zero-coupon bond that matures in two years.
3. A flat yield curve implies that all spot interest rates are the same. When the spot rate is the same for every maturity, successive applications of the forward rate model will show all the forward rates will also be the same and equal to the spot rate.

4. A. The yield to maturity of a coupon bond is the expected rate of return on a bond if the bond is held to maturity, there is no default, and the bond and all coupons are reinvested at the original yield to maturity.

   B. Yes, it is possible. For example, if reinvestment rates for the future coupons are lower than the initial yield to maturity, a bond holder may experience lower realized returns.

5. If forward rates are higher than expected future spot rates the market price of the bond will be lower than the intrinsic value. This is because, everything else held constant, the market is currently discounting the bonds cash flows at a higher rate than the investor's expected future spot rates. The investor can capitalize on this by purchasing the undervalued bond. If expected future spot rates are realized, then bond prices should rise, thus generating gains for the investor.

6. The strategy of riding the yield curve is one in which a bond trader attempts to generate a total return over a given investment horizon that exceeds the return to bond with maturity matched to the horizon. The strategy involves buying a bond with maturity more distant than the investment horizon. Assuming an upward sloping yield curve, if the yield curve does not change level or shape, as the bond approaches maturity (or rolls down the yield curve) it will be priced at successively lower yields. So as long as the bond is held for a period less than maturity, it should generate higher returns because of price gains.

7. Some countries do not have active government bond markets with trading at all maturities. For those countries without a liquid government bond market but with an active swap market, there are typically more points available to construct a swap curve than a government bond yield curve. For those markets, the swap curve may be a superior benchmark.

8. The Z-spread is the constant basis point spread added to the default-free spot curve to correctly price a risky bond. A Z-spread of 100 bps for a particular bond would imply that adding a fixed spread of 100 bps to the points along the spot yield curve will correctly price the bond. A higher Z-spread would imply a riskier bond.

9. The TED spread is the difference between a Libor rate and the US T-Bill rate of matching maturity. It is an indicator of perceived credit risk in the general economy. In particular, because sovereign debt instruments are typically the benchmark for the lowest default risk instruments in a given market, and loans between banks (often at Libor) have some counterparty risk, the TED spread is considered to at least in part reflect default (or counterparty) risk in the banking sector.

10. The local expectations theory asserts that the total return over a one-month horizon for a five-year zero-coupon bond would be the same as for a two-year zero-coupon bond.

11. Both theories attempt to explain the shape of any yield curve in terms of supply and demand for bonds. In segmented market theory, bond market participants are limited to purchase of maturities that match the timing of their liabilities. In the preferred habitat theory, participants have a preferred maturity for asset purchases, but may deviate from it if they feel returns in other maturities offer sufficient compensation for leaving their preferred maturity segment.

12. A. Studies have shown that there have been three factors that affect Treasury returns: (1) changes in the level of the yield curve, (2) changes in the slope of the yield curve, and (3) changes in the curvature of the yield curve. Changes in the level refer to upward or downward shifts in the yield curve. For example, an upward shift in the yield curve is likely to result in lower returns across all maturities. Changes in the slope of the yield curve relate to the steepness of the yield curve. Thus, if the yield curve steepens it is likely to result in higher returns for short maturity bonds and lower returns for

long maturity bonds. An example of a change in the curvature of the yield curve is a situation where rates fall at the short and long end of the yield curve while rising for intermediate maturities. In this situation returns on short and long maturities are likely to rise while declining for intermediate maturity bonds.

B. Empirically, the most important factor is the change in the level of interest rates.

C. Key rate duration and a measure based on sensitivities to level, slope, and curvature movements can address shaping risk, but effective duration cannot.

13. C is correct. There is no spot rate information to provide rates for a loan that terminates in five years. That is, $f(2,3)$ is calculated as follows:

$$f(2,3) = \sqrt[3]{\frac{[1+r(5)]^5}{[1+r(2)]^2}} - 1$$

The equation above indicates that in order to calculate the rate for a three-year loan beginning at the end of two years you need the five-year spot rate $r(5)$ and the two-year spot rate $r(2)$. However, $r(5)$ is not provided.

14. A is correct. The forward rate for a one-year loan beginning in one year $f(1,1)$ is $1.04^2/1.03 - 1 = 5\%$. The rate for a one-year loan beginning in two years $f(2,1)$ is $1.05^3/1.04^2 - 1 = 7\%$. This confirms that an upward-sloping yield curve is consistent with an upward-sloping forward curve.

15. C is correct. If one-period forward rates are decreasing with maturity then the forward curve is downward sloping. This turn implies a downward-sloping yield curve where longer-term spot rates $r(T + T^*)$ are less than shorter-term spot rates $r(T)$.

16. C is correct. From the forward rate model, we have

$$[1 + r(2)]^2 = [1 + r(1)]^1[1 + f(1,1)]^1$$

Using the one- and two-year spot rates, we have

$$(1 + .05)^2 = (1 + .04)^1[1 + f(1,1)]^1, \text{ so } \frac{(1+.05)^2}{(1+.04)^1} - 1 = f(1,1) = 6.010\%$$

17. C is correct. From the forward rate model,

$$[1 + r(3)]^3 = [1 + r(1)]^1[1 + f(1,2)]^2$$

Using the one- and three-year spot rates, we find

$$(1 + 0.06)^3 = (1 + 0.04)^1[1 + f(1,2)]^2, \text{ so } \sqrt{\frac{(1+0.06)^3}{(1+0.04)^1}} - 1 = f(1,2) = 7.014\%$$

18. C is correct. From the forward rate model,

$$[1 + r(3)]^3 = [1 + r(2)]^2[1 + f(2,1)]^1$$

Using the two- and three-year spot rates, we find

$$(1 + 0.06)^3 = (1 + 0.05)^2[1 + f(2,1)]^1, \text{ so } \frac{(1+0.06)^3}{(1+0.05)^2} - 1 = f(2,1) = 8.029\%$$

19. A is correct. We can convert spot rates to spot prices to find $P(3) = \dfrac{1}{(1.06)^3} = 0.8396$. The forward pricing model can be used to find the price of the five-year zero as $P(T^* + T) = P(T^*)F(T^*,T)$, so $P(5) = P(3)F(3,2) = 0.8396 \times 0.8479 = 0.7119$.

20. B is correct. Applying the forward rate model, we find

$$[1 + r(3)]^3 = [1 + r(1)]^1[1 + f(1,1)]^1[1 + f(2,1)]^1$$

So $[1 + r(3)]^3 = (1 + 0.04)^1(1 + 0.06)^1(1 + 0.08)^1$, $\sqrt[3]{1.1906} - 1 = r(3) = 5.987\%$.

21. B is correct. We can convert spot rates to spot prices and use the forward pricing model, so

$$P(1) = \frac{1}{(1.05)^1} = 0.9524.$$ The forward pricing model is $P(T^* + T) = P(T^*)F(T^*, T)$

so $P(2) = P(1)F(1,1) = 0.9524 \times 0.9346 = 0.8901$.

22. A is correct. The swap rate is the interest rate for the fixed-rate leg of an interest rate swap.

23. A is correct. The swap spread = 1.00% – 0.63% = 0.37% or 37 bps.

24. C is correct. The fixed leg of the five-year fixed-for-floating swap will be equal to the five-year Treasury rate plus the swap spread: 2% + 0.5% = 2.5%.

25. A is correct. The TED spread is the difference between the three-month Libor rate and the three-month Treasury bill rate. If the T-bill rate falls and Libor does not change, the TED spread will increase.

26. A is correct. The Z-spread is the single rate that, when added to the rates of the spot yield curve, will provide the correct discount rates to price a particular risky bond.

27. A is correct. The 200 bps Z-spread can be added to the 5% rates from the yield curve to price the bond. The resulting 7% discount rate will be the same for all of the bond's cash flows, since the yield curve is flat. A 7% coupon bond yielding 7% will be priced at par.

28. B is correct. The higher Z-spread for Bond B implies it is riskier than Bond A. The higher discount rate will make the price of Bond B lower than Bond A.

29. A is correct. The Ho–Lee model is arbitrage-free and can be calibrated to closely match the observed term structure.

30. B is correct. The five-year spot rate is determined by using forward substitution and using the known values of the one-year, two-year, three-year, and four-year spot rates as follows:

$$1 = \frac{0.0437}{(1.025)} + \frac{0.0437}{(1.030)^2} + \frac{0.0437}{(1.035)^3} + \frac{0.0437}{(1.040)^4} + \frac{1 + 0.0437}{[1 + r(5)]^5}$$

$$r(5) = \sqrt[5]{\frac{1.0437}{0.8394}} - 1 = 4.453\%$$

31. B is correct. The spot rates imply an upward-sloping yield curve, $r(3) > r(2) > r(1)$. Because nominal yields incorporate a premium for expected inflation, an upward-sloping yield curve is generally interpreted as reflecting a market expectation of increasing, or at least level, future inflation (associated with relatively strong economic growth).

32. C is correct. A one-year loan beginning in three years, or $f(3,1)$, is calculated as follows:

$$[1 + r(3 + 1)]^{(3+1)} = [1 + r(3)]^3[1 + f(3,1)]^1$$

$$[1.040]^4 = [1.035]^3[1 + f(3,1)]^1$$

$$f(3,1) = \frac{(1.04)^4}{(1.035)^3} - 1 = 5.514\%$$

33. C is correct. Exhibit 1 provides five years of par rates, from which the spot rates for $r(1)$, $r(2)$, $r(3)$, $r(4)$, and $r(5)$ can be derived. Thus the forward rate $f(1,4)$ can be calculated as follows:

$$f(1,4) = \sqrt[4]{\frac{[1+r(5)]^5}{[1+r(1)]}} - 1$$

34. C is correct. The yield to maturity, $y(3)$, of Bond Z should be a weighted average of the spot rates used in the valuation of the bond. Because the bond's largest cash flow occurs in Year 3, $r(3)$ will have a greater weight than $r(1)$ and $r(2)$ in determining $y(3)$.

    Using the spot rates:

$$\text{Price} = \frac{\$60}{(1.025)^1} + \frac{\$60}{(1.030)^2} + \frac{\$1,060}{(1.035)^3} = \$1,071.16$$

Using the yield to maturity:

$$\text{Price} = \frac{\$60}{[1+y(3)]^1} + \frac{\$60}{[1+y(3)]^2} + \frac{\$1,060}{[1+y(3)]^3} = \$1,071.16$$

Using a calculator, the compute result is $y(3) = 3.46\%$, which is closest to the three-year spot rate of 3.50%.

35. A is correct. Alexander projects that the spot curve two years from today will be below the current forward curve, which implies that her expected future spot rates beyond two years will be lower than the quoted forward rates. Alexander would perceive Bond Z to be undervalued in the sense that the market is effectively discounting the bond's payments at a higher rate than she would and the bond's market price is below her estimate of intrinsic value.

36. B is correct. Nguyen's strategy is to ride the yield curve, which is appropriate when the yield curve is upward sloping. The yield curve implied by Exhibit 1 is upward sloping, which implies that the three-year forward curve is above the current spot curve. When the yield curve slopes upward, as a bond approaches maturity or "rolls down the yield curve," the bond is valued at successively lower yields and higher prices.

37. B is correct. The forward pricing model is based on the no-arbitrage principle and is used to calculate a bond's forward price based on the spot yield curve. The spot curve is constructed by using annualized rates from option-free and default risk–free zero-coupon bonds.

    Equation 2: $P(T^* + T) = P(T^*)F(T^*,T)$; we need to solve for $F(1,1)$.

    $P(1) = 1/(1 + 0.0225)^1$ and $P(2) = 1/(1 + 0.0270)^2$,

    $F(1,1) = P(2)/P(1) = 0.9481/0.9780 = 0.9694$.

38. C is correct. When the spot curve is upward sloping and its level and shape are expected to remain constant over an investment horizon (Shire Gate Advisers' view), buying bonds with a maturity longer than the investment horizon (i.e., riding the yield curve) will provide a total return greater than the return on a maturity-matching strategy.

39. C is correct. The swap spread is a common way to indicate credit spreads in a market. The four-year swap rate (fixed leg of an interest rate swap) can be used as an indication of the four-year corporate yield. Riding the yield curve by purchasing a four-year zero-coupon bond with a yield of 4.75% {i.e., 4.05% + 0.70%, $[P_4 = 100/(1 + 0.0475)^4 = 83.058]$} and then selling it when it becomes a two-year zero-coupon bond with a yield of 3.00% {i.e., 2.70% + 0.30%, $[P_2 = 100/(1 + 0.0300)^2 = 94.260]$} produces an annual return of 6.53%: $(94.260/83.058)^{0.5} - 1.0 = 0.0653$.

40. B is correct. The Z-spread is the constant basis point spread that is added to the default-free spot curve to price a risky bond. A Z-spread of 65 bps for a particular bond would imply adding a fixed spread of 65 bps to maturities along the spot curve to correctly price the bond. Therefore, for the two-year bond, $r(1) = 2.90\%$ (i.e., 2.25% + 0.65%), $r(2) = 3.35\%$ (i.e., 2.70% + 0.65%), and the price of the bond with an annual coupon of 4.15% is as follows:

$$P = 4.15/(1 + 0.029)^1 + 4.15/(1 + 0.0335)^2 + 100/(1 + 0.0335)^2,$$

$$P = 101.54.$$

41. C is correct. The Libor–OIS spread is considered an indicator of the risk and liquidity of money market securities. This spread measures the difference between Libor and the OIS rate.

42. C is correct. Liquidity preference theory asserts that investors demand a risk premium, in the form of a liquidity premium, to compensate them for the added interest rate risk they face when buying long-maturity bonds. The theory also states that the liquidity premium increases with maturity.

43. C is correct. Both statements are incorrect because Madison incorrectly describes both types of models. Equilibrium term structure models are factor models that seek to describe the dynamics of the term structure by using fundamental economic variables that are assumed to affect interest rates. Arbitrage-free term structure models use observed market prices of a reference set of financial instruments, assumed to be correctly priced, to model the market yield curve.

44. A is correct. Consistent with Madison's statement, equilibrium term structure models require fewer parameters to be estimated relative to arbitrage-free models, and arbitrage-free models allow for time-varying parameters. Consequently, arbitrage-free models can model the market yield curve more precisely than equilibrium models.

45. B is correct. The TED spread, calculated as the difference between Libor and the yield on a T-bill of matching maturity, is an indicator of perceived credit risk in the general economy. An increase (decrease) in the TED spread signals that lenders believe the risk of default on interbank loans is increasing (decreasing). Therefore, the TED spread can be thought of as a measure of counterparty risk.

46. A is correct. Madison's response is correct; research indicates that short-term rate volatility is mostly linked to uncertainty regarding monetary policy, whereas long-term rate volatility is mostly linked to uncertainty regarding the real economy and inflation.

47. B is correct. Because the factors in Exhibit 1 have been standardized to have unit standard deviations, a two standard deviation increase in the steepness factor will lead to the yield on the 20-year bond decreasing by 0.6030%, calculated as follows:

Change in 20-year bond yield = $-0.3015\% \times 2 = -0.6030\%$.

48. C is correct. Because the factors in Exhibit 1 have been standardized to have unit standard deviations, a one standard deviation decrease in both the level factor and the curvature factor will lead to the yield on the five-year bond increasing by 0.0389%, calculated as follows:

$$\text{Change in five-year bond yield} = 0.4352\% - 0.3963\% = 0.0389\%.$$

49. C is correct. The assistant states that bootstrapping entails *backward* substitution using par yields to solve for zero-coupon rates one by one, in order from latest to earliest maturities. Bootstrapping entails *forward* substitution, however, using par yields to solve for zero-coupon rates one by one, in order from earliest to latest maturities.

50. C is correct. Country C's private sector is much bigger than the public sector, and the government bond market in Country C currently lacks liquidity. Under such circumstances, the swap curve is a more relevant benchmark for interest rates.

51. C is correct. Although swap spreads provide a convenient way to measure risk, a more accurate measure of credit and liquidity risk is called the zero-spread (Z-spread). It is the constant spread that, added to the implied spot yield curve, makes the discounted cash flows of a bond equal to its current market price. Bonds 1, 2, and 3 are otherwise similar but have Z-spreads of 0.55%, 1.52%, and 1.76%, respectively. Bond 3 has the highest Z-spread, implying that this bond has the greatest credit and liquidity risk.

52. B is correct. The historical three-year swap spread for Country B was the lowest six months ago. Swap spread is defined as the spread paid by the fixed-rate payer of an interest rate swap over the rate of the "on the run" (most recently issued) government bond security with the same maturity as the swap. The lower (higher) the swap spread, the lower (higher) the return that investors require for credit and/or liquidity risks.

    The fixed rate of the three-year fixed-for-floating Libor swap was 0.01% six months ago, and the three-year government bond yield was –0.08% six months ago. Thus the swap spread six months ago was 0.01% – (–0.08%) = 0.09%.

    One month ago, the fixed rate of the three-year fixed-for-floating Libor swap was 0.16%, and the three-year government bond yield was –0.10%. Thus the swap spread one month ago was 0.16% – (–0.10%) = 0.26%.

    Twelve months ago, the fixed rate of the three-year fixed-for-floating Libor swap was 0.71%, and the three-year government bond yield was –0.07%. Thus, the swap spread 12 months ago was 0.71% – (–0.07%) = 0.78%.

53. A is correct. Country A's yield curve is upward sloping—a condition for the strategy—and more so than Country B's.

54. B is correct. The yield curve for Country B is currently upward sloping, but Tyo expects a reversal in the slope of the current yield curve. This means she expects the resulting yield curve for Country B to slope downward, which implies that the resulting forward curve would lie below the spot yield curve. The forward curve lies below the spot curve in scenarios in which the spot curve is downward sloping; the forward curve lies above the spot curve in scenarios in which the spot curve is upward sloping.

    A is incorrect because the yield curve for Country A is currently upward sloping and Tyo expects that the yield curve will maintain its shape and level. That expectation implies that the resulting forward curve would be above the spot yield curve.

    C is incorrect because the yield curve for Country C is currently downward sloping and Tyo expects a reversal in the slope of the current yield curve. This means she expects the resulting yield curve for Country C to slope upward, which implies that the resulting forward curve would be above the spot yield curve.

55. A is correct. Tyo's projected spot curve assumes that future spot rates reflect, or will be equal to, the current forward rates for all respective maturities. This assumption implies that the bonds for Country A are fairly valued because the market is effectively discounting the bond's payments at spot rates that match those projected by Tyo.

    B and C are incorrect because Tyo's projected spot curves for the two countries do not match the current forward rates for all respective maturities. In the case of Country B, she expects future spot rates to be higher (than the current forward rates that the market is using to discount the bond's payments). For Country C, she expects future spot rates to be lower (than the current forward rates). Hence, she perceives the Country B bond to be currently overvalued and the Country C bond to be undervalued.

56. C is correct. Liquidity preference theory suggests that liquidity premiums exist to compensate investors for the added interest rate risk that they face when lending long term and that these premiums increase with maturity. Tyo and her assistant are assuming that liquidity premiums exist.

57. A is correct. From the forward rate model, $f(3,2)$ is found as follows:

$$[1 + r(5)]^5 = [1 + r(3)]^3[1 + f(3,2)]^2$$

Using the three-year and five-year spot rates, we find

$$(1 + 0.107)^5 = (1 + 0.118)^3[1 + f(3,2)]^2, \text{ so}$$

$$\sqrt{\frac{(1+0.107)^5}{(1+0.118)^3}} - 1 = f(3,2) = 9.07\%$$

CHAPTER 8

THE ARBITRAGE-FREE VALUATION FRAMEWORK

SOLUTIONS

1. A is correct. This is the same bond being sold at three different prices so an arbitrage opportunity exists by buying the bond from the exchange where it is priced lowest and immediately selling it on the exchange that has the highest price. Accordingly, an investor would maximize profit from the arbitrage opportunity by buying the bond on the Frankfurt exchange (which has the lowest price of €103.7565) and selling it on the Eurex exchange (which has the highest price of €103.7956) to generate a risk-free profit of €0.0391 (as mentioned, ignoring transaction costs) per €100 par.

   B is incorrect because buying on NYSE Euronext and selling on Eurex would result in an €0.0141 profit per €100 par (€103.7956 – €103.7815 = €0.0141), which is not the maximum arbitrage profit available. A greater profit would be realized if the bond were purchased in Frankfurt and sold on Eurex.

   C is incorrect because buying on Frankfurt and selling on NYSE Euronext would result in an €0.0250 profit per €100 par (€103.7815 – €103.7565 = €0.0250). A greater profit would be realized if the bond were purchased in Frankfurt and sold on Eurex.

2. C is correct. The bond from Exhibit 1 is selling for its calculated value on the NYSE Euronext exchange. The arbitrage-free value of a bond is the present value of its cash flows discounted by the spot rate for zero coupon bonds maturing on the same date as each cash flow. The value of this bond, 103.7815, is calculated as follows:

	Year 1	Year 2	Year 3	Total PV
Yield to maturity	1.2500%	1.500%	1.700%	
Spot rate[1]	1.2500%	1.5019%	1.7049%	
Cash flow	3.00	3.00	103.00	
Present value of payment[2]	2.9630	2.9119	97.9066	103.7815

(continued)

(Continued)

	Eurex	NYSE Euronext	Frankfurt
Price	€103.7956	€103.7815	€103.7565
Mispricing (per 100 par value)	0.141	0	–0.025

Notes:

[1] Spot rates calculated using bootstrapping; for example: Year 2 spot rate (z_2): 100 = 1.5/1.0125 + 101.5/$(1 + z_2)^2$ = 0.015019.

[2] Present value calculated using the formula PV = FV/$(1 + r)^n$, where n = number of years until cash flow, FV = cash flow amount, and r = spot rate.

A is incorrect because the price on the Eurex exchange, €103.7956, was calculated using the yield to maturity rate to discount the cash flows when the spot rates should have been used. C is incorrect because the price on the Frankfurt exchange, €103.7565, uses the Year 3 spot rate to discount all the cash flows.

3. C is correct. Because Node 2–2 is the middle node rate in Year 2, it will be close to the implied one-year forward rate two years from now (as derived from the spot curve). Node 4–1 should be equal to the product of Node 4–5 and $e^{0.8}$. Last, Node 3–2 cannot be derived from Node 2–2; it can be derived from any other Year 3 node; for example, Node 3–2 can be derived from Node 3–4 (equal to the product of Node 3–4 and $e^{4\sigma}$).

4. A is correct. The value of a bond at a particular node, in this case Node 1–2, can be derived by determining the present value of the coupon payment and expected future bond values to the right of that node on the tree. In this case, those two nodes are the middle node in Year 2, equal to 101.5168, and the lower node in Year 2, equal to 102.1350. The coupon payment is 2.5. The bond value at Node 1–2 is calculated as follows:

$$\text{Value} = \frac{2.5 + (0.5 \times 101.5816 + 0.5 \times 102.1350)}{1.014925}$$

$$= 102.7917$$

5. A is correct. Calibrating a binomial interest rate tree to match a specific term structure is important because we can use the known valuation of a benchmark bond from the spot rate pricing to verify the accuracy of the rates shown in the binomial interest rate tree. Once its accuracy is confirmed, the interest rate tree can then be used to value bonds with embedded options. While discounting with spot rates will produce arbitrage-free valuations for option-free bonds, this spot rate method will not work for bonds with embedded options where expected future cash flows are interest-rate dependent (as rate changes impact the likelihood of options being exercised). The interest rate tree allows for the alternative paths that a bond with embedded options might take.

B is incorrect because calibration does not identify mispriced benchmark bonds. In fact, benchmark bonds are employed to prove the accuracy of the binomial interest rate tree, as they are assumed to be correctly priced by the market.

C is incorrect because the calibration of the binomial interest rate tree is designed to produce an arbitrage-free valuation approach and such an approach does not allow a market participant to realize arbitrage profits though stripping and reconstitution.

6. A is correct. Volatility is one of the two key assumptions required to estimate rates for the binomial interest rate tree. Increasing the volatility from 10% to 15% would cause the possible forward rates to spread out on the tree as it increases the exponent in the relationship multiple between nodes ($e^{x\sigma}$, where x = 2 times the number of nodes above the

lowest node in a given year in the interest rate tree). Conversely, using a lower estimate of volatility would cause the forward rates to narrow or converge to the implied forward rates from the prevailing yield curve.

B is incorrect because volatility is a key assumption in the binomial interest rate tree model. Any change in volatility will cause a change in the implied forward rates.

C is incorrect because increasing the volatility from 10% to 15% causes the possible forward rates to spread out on the tree, not converge to the implied forward rates from the current yield curve. Rates will converge to the implied forward rates when lower estimates of volatility are assumed.

7. B is correct. Bond B's arbitrage-free price is calculated as follows:

$$\frac{3}{1.02} + \frac{103}{1.02^2} = 101.9416$$

which is higher than the bond's market price of 100.9641. Therefore, an arbitrage opportunity exists. Since the bond's value (100.9641) is less than the sum of the values of its discounted cash flows individually (101.9416), a trader would perceive an arbitrage opportunity and could buy the bond while selling claims to the individual cash flows (zeros), capturing the excess value. The arbitrage-free prices of Bond A and Bond C are equal to the market prices of the respective bonds, so there is no arbitrage opportunity for these two bonds:

Bond A:
$$\frac{1}{1.02} + \frac{101}{1.02^2} = 98.0584$$

Bond C:
$$\frac{5}{1.02} + \frac{105}{1.02^2} = 105.8247$$

8. C is correct. The first step in the solution is to find the correct spot rate (zero-coupon rates) for each year's cash flow. The benchmark bonds in Exhibit 2 are conveniently priced at par so the yields to maturity and the coupon rates on the bonds are the same. Because the one-year issue has only one cash flow remaining, the YTM equals the spot rate of 3% (or $z_1 = 3\%$). The spot rates for Year 2 (z_2) and Year 3 (z_3) are calculated as follows:

$$100 = \frac{4}{1.0300} + \frac{104}{(1+z_2)^2}; z_2 = 4.02\%$$

$$100 = \frac{5}{1.0300} + \frac{5}{(1.0402)^2} + \frac{105}{(1+z_3)^3}; z_3 = 5.07\%$$

The correct arbitrage-free price for the Hutto-Barkley Inc. bond is:

$$P_0 = \frac{3}{(1.0300)} + \frac{3}{(1.0402)^2} + \frac{103}{(1.0507)^3} = 94.4828$$

Therefore, the bond is mispriced by 94.9984 – 94.4828 = 0.5156 per 100 of par value.

A is incorrect because the correct spot rates are not calculated and instead the Hutto-Barkley Inc. bond is discounted using the respective YTM for each maturity. Therefore, this leads to an incorrect mispricing of 94.6616 – 94.9984 = –0.3368 per 100 of par value.

B is incorrect because the spot rates are derived using the coupon rate for Year 3 (maturity) instead of using each year's respective coupon rate to employ the bootstrap methodology. This leads to an incorrect mispricing of $94.5302 - 94.9984 = -0.4682$ per 100 of par value.

9. B is correct. The Luna y Estrellas Intl. bond contains an embedded option. Method 1 will produce an arbitrage-free valuation for option-free bonds; however, for bonds with embedded options, changes in future interest rates impact the likelihood the option will be exercised and so impact future cash flows. Therefore, to develop a framework that values bonds with embedded options, interest rates must be allowed to take on different potential values in the future based on some assumed level of volatility (Method 2).

    A and C are incorrect because the Hutto-Barkley Inc. bond and the Peaton Scorpio Motors bond are both option-free bonds and can be valued using either Method 1 or Method 2 to produce an arbitrage-free valuation.

10. B is correct. This is the binomial tree that obtains a bond value of 109.0085.

Valuing a 6%, Three-Year Bond

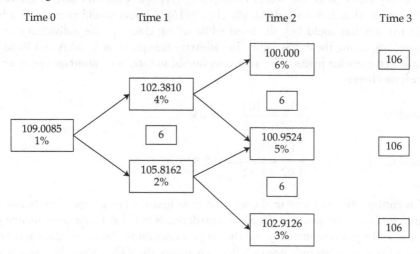

These are the calculations:

$$106/1.06 = 100.0000$$

$$106/1.05 = 100.9524$$

$$106/1.03 = 102.9126$$

$$\frac{6+(0.5\times100.0000+0.5\times100.9524)}{1.04} = 102.3810$$

$$\frac{6+(0.5\times100.9524+0.5\times102.9126)}{1.02} = 105.8162$$

$$\frac{6+(0.5\times102.3810+0.5\times105.8162)}{1.01} = 109.0085$$

A is incorrect because the Time T coupon payment is subtracted from the value in each node calculation for Time T. C is incorrect because it assumes that a coupon is paid at Time 0.

11. B is correct. Based on the dominance principle, an arbitrage opportunity exists. The dominance principle asserts that a financial asset with a risk-free payoff in the future must have a positive price today. Because Asset A and Asset B are both risk-free assets, they should have the same discount rate. Relative to its payoff, Asset A is priced at $500/525, or 0.95238, and Asset B is priced at $1,000/1,100, or 0.90909. Given its higher implied discount rate (10%) and lower corresponding price, Asset B is cheap relative to Asset A, which has a lower implied discount rate (5%) and higher corresponding price.

    The arbitrage opportunity based on dominance is to sell two units of Asset A for $1,000 and buy one unit of Asset B. There is no cash outlay today, and in one year, the portfolio delivers a net cash inflow of $50 [= $1,100 − (2 × $525)].

12. B is correct. Of the three markets, the New York bond has the lowest yield to maturity and, correspondingly, the highest bond price. Similarly, the Hong Kong bond has the highest yield to maturity and the lowest bond price of the three markets. Therefore, the most profitable arbitrage trade would be to buy the bond in Hong Kong and sell it in New York.

13. B is correct. The bond value at the upper node at Time 1 is closest to 99.6255. The cash flow at Time 2 is 102.5, the redemption of par value (100) plus the final coupon payment (2.5). Using backward induction, we calculate the present value of the bond at the upper node of Time 1 as 102.5/1.028853 = 99.6255.

14. B is correct. The price of Bond D is closest to 103.3230 and can be calculated using backward induction.

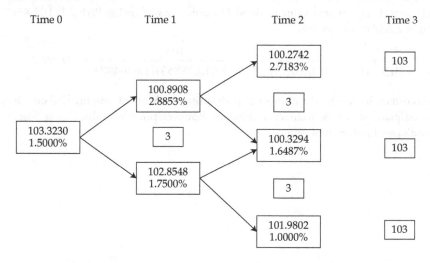

$$\text{Bond value at a node} = \frac{C + (0.5 \times VH + 0.5 \times VL)}{1+i}.$$

Calculations:

The cash flow at Time 3 is 103, the redemption of par value (100) plus the final coupon payment (3).

Time 2 node values:

Upper node: 103/1.027183 = 100.2742

Middle node: 103/1.016487 = 101.3294

Lower node: 103/1.010000 = 101.9802

Working back to Time 1 requires the use of the general expression above.

Time 1 node values:

$$\text{Upper node: } \frac{3+(0.5\times100.2742+0.5\times101.3294)}{1.028853}=100.8908$$

$$\text{Lower node: } \frac{3+(0.5\times101.3294+0.5\times101.9802)}{1.0175}=102.8548$$

$$\text{Time 0 node value: } \frac{3+(0.5\times100.8908+0.5\times102.8548)}{1.015}=103.3230$$

Therefore, the price of the bond is 103.3230.

15. B is correct. Two methods are commonly used to estimate potential interest rate volatility in a binomial interest rate tree. The first method bases estimates on historical interest rate volatility. The second method uses observed market prices of interest rate derivatives.

    Statement 1 is incorrect because there are three requirements to create a binomial interest rate tree, not two. The third requirement is an assumption regarding the interest rate model. Statement 3 is incorrect because the valuation of a bond using spot rates and the valuation of a bond from an interest rate tree will be the same regardless of the volatility assumption used in the model.

16. B is correct. The value of the lower one-period forward rate is closest to 3.5400%, calculated as $0.058365 \times e^{-0.50} = 0.035400$.

17. B is correct. The present value of Bond D's cash flows following Path 2 is 102.8607 and can be calculated as follows:

$$\frac{3}{1.015}+\frac{3}{(1.015)(1.028853)}+\frac{103}{(1.015)(1.028853)(1.016487)}=102.8607$$

18. A is correct. Increasing the number of paths using the Monte Carlo method does increase the estimate's statistical accuracy. It does not, however, provide a value that is closer to the bond's true fundamental value.

CHAPTER 9

VALUATION AND ANALYSIS OF BONDS WITH EMBEDDED OPTIONS

SOLUTIONS

1. C is correct. The call option embedded in Bond 2 can be exercised only at two predetermined dates: 1 October 20X1 and 1 October 20X2. Thus, the call feature is Bermudan style.

2. C is correct. The bond that would most likely protect investors against a significant increase in interest rates is the putable bond, i.e., Bond 3. When interest rates have risen and higher-yield bonds are available, a put option allows the bondholders to put back the bonds to the issuer prior to maturity and to reinvest the proceeds of the retired bonds in higher-yielding bonds.

3. B is correct. A fall in interest rates results in a rise in bond values. For a callable bond such as Bond 2, the upside potential is capped because the issuer is more likely to call the bond. In contrast, the upside potential for a putable bond such as Bond 3 is uncapped. Thus, a fall in interest rates would result in a putable bond having more upside potential than an otherwise identical callable bond. Note that A is incorrect because the effective duration of a putable bond increases, not decreases, with a fall in interest rates—the bond is less likely to be put and thus behaves more like an option-free bond. C is also incorrect because the effective convexity of a putable bond is always positive. It is the effective convexity of a callable bond that will change from positive to negative if interest rates fall and the call option is near the money.

4. A is correct:

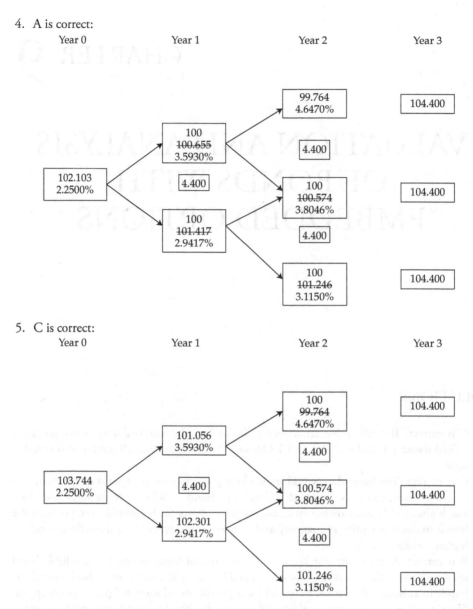

5. C is correct:

6. C is correct. Bond 3 is a putable bond, and the value of a put option increases as interest rates rise. At higher interest rates, the value of the underlying option-free bond (straight bond) declines, but the decline is offset partially by the increase in the value of the embedded put option, which is more likely to be exercised.

7. C is correct. Regardless of the type of option, an increase in interest rate volatility results in an increase in option value. Because the value of a putable bond is equal to the value of the straight bond *plus* the value of the embedded put option, Bond 3 will increase in value if interest rate volatility increases. Put another way, an increase in interest rate volatility will most likely result in more scenarios where the put option is exercised, which increases the values calculated in the interest rate tree and, thus, the value of the putable bond.

8. C is correct. Bond 2 is a callable bond, and the value of the embedded call option increases as the yield curve flattens. When the yield curve is upward sloping, the one-period forward rates on the interest rate tree are high and opportunities for the issuer to call the bond are fewer. When the yield curve flattens or inverts, many nodes on the tree have lower forward rates, which increases the opportunities to call and, thus, the value of the embedded call option.

9. B is correct. The conversion price of a convertible bond is equal to the par value divided by the conversion ratio—that is, $1,000/31= $32.26 per share.

10. B is correct. The conversion value of the bond is 31× $37.50 or $1,162.50, which represents its minimum value. Thus, the convertible bond exhibits mostly stock risk-return characteristics, and a fall in the stock price will result in a fall in the convertible bond price. However, the change in the convertible bond price is less than the change in the stock price because the convertible bond has a floor—that floor is the value of the straight (option-free) bond.

11. C is correct. The option-adjusted spread (OAS) is the constant spread added to all the one-period forward rates that makes the arbitrage-free value of a risky bond equal to its market price. The OAS approach is often used to assess bond relative values. If two bonds have the same characteristics and credit quality, they should have the same OAS. If this is not the case, the bond with the largest OAS (i.e., Bond 2) is likely to be underpriced (cheap) relative to the bond with the smallest OAS (Bond 1).

12. A is correct. The effective duration of a floating-rate bond is close to the time to next reset. As the reset for Bond 6 is annual, the effective duration of this bond is lower than or equal to 1.

13. B is correct. Effective duration indicates the sensitivity of a bond's price to a 100 bps parallel shift of the benchmark yield curve assuming no change in the bond's credit spread. The effective duration of an option-free bond such as Bond 3 changes very little in response to interest rate movements. As interest rates rise, a call option moves out of the money, which increases the value of the callable bond and lengthens its effective duration. In contrast, as interest rates rise, a put option moves into the money, which limits the price depreciation of the putable bond and shortens its effective duration. Thus, the bond whose effective duration will lengthen if interest rates rise is the callable bond, i.e., Bond 4.

14. B is correct. The effective duration of Bond 4 can be calculated using Equation 3 from the reading, where ΔCurve is 20 bps, PV_ is 101.238, and PV+ is 100.478. PV$_0$, the current full price of the bond (i.e., with no shift), is not given but it can be calculated using Exhibit 3 as follows:

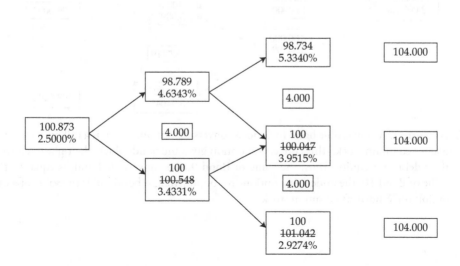

Thus, the effective duration of Bond 4 is:

$$\text{Effective duration} = \frac{101.238 - 100.478}{2 \times (0.0020) \times (100.873)} = 1.88$$

15. A is correct:

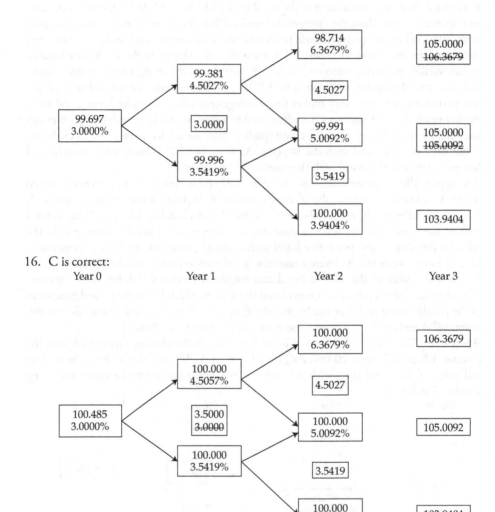

Year 0	Year 1	Year 2	Year 3

16. C is correct:

Year 0	Year 1	Year 2	Year 3

17. B is correct. A convertible bond includes a conversion option, which is a call option on the issuer's common stock. This conversion option gives the bondholders the right to convert their debt into equity. Thus, the value of Bond 9, the convertible bond, is equal to the value of Bond 10, the underlying option-free bond (straight bond), plus the value of a call option on Whorton's common stock.

18. A is correct. The minimum value of a convertible bond is equal to the greater of the conversion value of the convertible bond (i.e., Bond 9) and the current value of the straight bond (i.e., Bond 10).

19. C is correct. The risk–return characteristics of a convertible bond depend on the market price of the issuer's common stock (underlying share price) relative to the bond's conversion price. When the underlying share price is well below the conversion price, the convertible bond exhibits mostly bond risk–return characteristics. In this case, the price of the convertible bond is mainly affected by interest rate movements and the issuer's credit spreads. In contrast, when the underlying share price is above the conversion price, the convertible bond exhibits mostly stock risk–return characteristics. In this case, the price of the convertible bond is mainly affected by the issuer's common stock price movements. The underlying share price ($30) is lower than the conversion price of Bond #9 ($50). Thus, Bond 9 exhibits mostly bond risk–return characteristics and is least affected by Whorton's common stock price movements.

20. C is correct. If the central bank takes actions that lead to lower interest rates, the yields on Alpha's bonds are likely to decrease. If the yield to maturity on Bond 4 (callable) falls below the 1.55% coupon rate, the call option will become valuable and Alpha may call the bond because it is in the money.

    A is incorrect because if the equity market declines, the market value of Alpha stock will also likely decrease. Therefore, Bond 2 (convertible) would have a lower conversion value, and hence, the conversion option likely would not be exercised. Because Bond 2 is currently trading out of the money, it will likely trade further out of the money once the price of Alpha stock decreases.

    B is incorrect because Bond 3 (putable) is more likely to be exercised in an increasing rather than a decreasing interest rate environment.

21. C is correct. All four bonds in Exhibit 2 issued by Alpha Corporation offer the same coupon rate and have the same remaining term to maturity. Bond 4 (callable) most likely has a current price that is less than Bond 1 (straight or option free) because investors are short the call option and must be compensated for bearing call risk. Bond 2 (convertible) most likely has a current price that is greater than Bond 1 because investors are paying for the conversion option embedded in Bond 2 and the option has time value associated with it, even though the option is trading out of the money. Similarly, Bond 3 (putable) most likely has a current price that is greater than Bond 1 because investors are paying for the put option.

22. C is correct. The consensus economic forecast is for interest rates to decrease. In an environment of decreasing interest rates, all bond prices should rise ignoring any price impact resulting from any embedded options. When interest rates fall, the value of the embedded call option in Bond 4 (callable) increases, causing an opposing effect on price. The put option of putable bonds, by contrast, increases in value when interest rates rise rather than decline.

23. C is correct. Bond 4 is a callable bond. Value of an issuer call option = Value of straight bond – Value of callable bond. The value of the straight bond may be calculated using the spot rates or the one-year forward rates.

    Value of an option-free (straight) bond with a 1.55% coupon using spot rates:

    $$1.55/(1.0100)^1 + 1.55/(1.012012)^2 + 101.55/(1.012515)^3 = 100.8789.$$

The value of a callable bond (at par) with no lockout period and a 1.55% coupon rate is 100.5446, as shown in the following table:

	Today	Year 1	Year 2	Year 3
Cash flow		1.55	1.55	100 + 1.55
One-year forward		1.0000%	1.4028%	1.3522%
Value of bond	101.55/1.010000 = 100.5446	101.55/1.014028 = 100.1452 Called at 100	101.55/1.013522 = 100.1952 Called at 100	

The value of the call option = 100.8789 − 100.5446 = 0.3343.

24. B is correct. An increase in interest rate volatility will cause the value of the put and call options embedded in Bond 3 and Bond 4 to increase. Bond 3 (putable) would experience an increase in price because the increased value of the put option increases the bond's value. In contrast, Bond 4 (callable) will experience a price decrease because the increased value of the call option reduces the callable bond's value. Bond 2, an out-of-the-money convertible, will resemble the risk–return characteristics of a straight bond and will thus be unaffected by interest rate volatility.

25. A is correct. All else being equal, the value of a put option decreases as the yield curve moves from being upward sloping to flat to downward sloping (inverted). Alternatively, a call option's value increases as the yield curve flattens and increases further if the yield curve inverts. Therefore, if the yield curve became inverted, the value of the embedded option in Bond 3 (putable) would decrease and the value of the embedded option in Bond 4 (callable) would increase.

26. A is correct. The market price of Bond 4 using the binomial interest rate tree is 100.4578.

The valuation of Bond 4 (callable) with a 1.55% coupon, no lockout periods, and 15% volatility is shown in the following table.

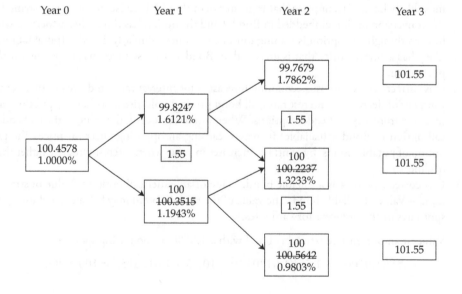

27. B is correct. A bond with a larger option-adjusted spread (OAS) than that of a bond with similar characteristics and credit quality means that the bond is likely underpriced (cheap). Bond 7 (OAS 85 bps) is relatively cheaper than Bond 6 (OAS 65 bps).

   C is incorrect because Bond 8 (CCC) has a lower credit rating than Bond 7 (B) and the OAS alone cannot be used for the relative value comparison. The larger OAS (105 bps) incorporates compensation for the difference between the B and CCC bond credit ratings. Therefore, there is not enough information to draw a conclusion about relative value.

28. B is correct. The AI bond's value if interest rates shift down by 30 bps (PV_) is 100.78:

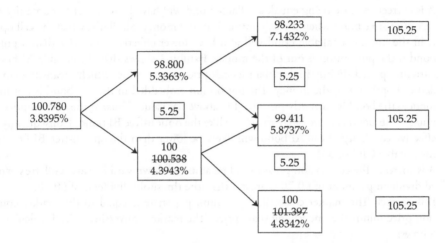

The AI bond's value if interest rates shift up by 30 bps (PV+) is 99.487:

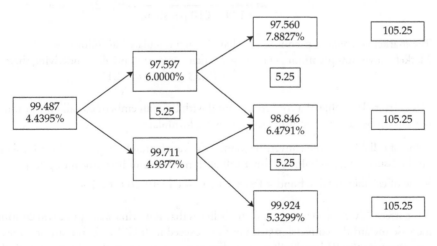

$$\text{Effective duration} = \frac{(PV_-)-(PV_+)}{2\times(\Delta Curve)\times(PV_0)} = \frac{100.780-99.487}{2\times0.003\times100.200} = 2.15$$

29. A is correct. The AI bond is a callable bond and the effective duration of a callable bond decreases when interest rates fall. The reason is that a decline in interest rates may result in the call option moving into the money, which limits the price appreciation of the callable bond. Exhibit 1 also shows that the price of the AI bond is 100.200 and that it is callable at par in one year and two years. Thus, the call option is already in the money and would likely be exercised in response to increases in the AI bond's price.

30. C is correct. The BI bond is an option-free bond and one-sided up-duration and one-sided down-duration will be about equal for option-free bonds.

31. C is correct. The BI bond is an option-free bond. Its longest key rate duration will be in the year of its maturity because the largest cash flow (payment of both coupon and principal) occurs in that year.

32. A is correct. All else being equal, a callable bond will have lower effective convexity than an option-free bond when the call option is in the money. Similarly, when the call option is in the money, a callable bond will also have lower effective convexity than a putable bond if the put option is out of the money. Exhibit 1 shows that the callable AI bond is currently priced slightly higher than its call price of par value, which means the embedded call option is in the money. The put option embedded in the CE bond is not in the money; the bond is currently priced 2.1% above par value. Thus, at the current price, the putable CE bond is more likely to behave like the option-free BI bond. Consequently, the effective convexity of the AI bond will likely be lower than the option-free BI bond and the putable CE bond.

33. A is correct. The conversion price would be adjusted downward because Gillette's expected dividend payment of €0.70 is greater than the threshold dividend of €0.50.

34. B is correct. The market conversion premium per share is equal to the market conversion price minus the underlying share price. The market conversion price is calculated as follows:

$$\text{Market conversion price} = \frac{\text{Convertible bond price}}{\text{Conversion ratio}}$$

$$= \frac{\text{€1,123}}{\text{€1,000/€10 per share}} = \text{€11.23 per share}$$

The market conversion premium per share is then calculated as follows:
Market conversion premium per share = Market conversion price − Underlying share price
$$= \text{€11.23} − \text{€9.10} = \text{€2.13}$$

35. C is correct. The value of a convertible bond with both an embedded call option and a put option can be determined using the following formula:

Value of callable putable convertible bond = Value of straight bond + Value of call option on the issuer's stock − Value of issuer call option + Value of investor put option.

Value of callable putable bond = €978 + €147 − €43 + €26 = €1,108

36. A is correct. Over the next year, Gillette believes that Raffarin's share price will continue to increase toward the conversion price but not exceed it. If Gillette's forecast becomes true, the return on the RI bond will increase but at a lower rate than the increase in Raffarin's share price because the conversion price is not expected to be reached.

CHAPTER 10

CREDIT ANALYSIS MODELS

SOLUTIONS

1. B is correct. The following table shows that the credit valuation adjustment (CVA) for the bond is €36.49, the sum of the present values of expected loss. The steps taken to complete the table are as follows.

   Step 1   Exposure at Date T is $\dfrac{€1,000}{(1 + r)^{4-T}}$, where r is 3%. That is, exposure is computed by discounting the face value of the bond using the risk-free rate and the number of years until maturity.

   Step 2   Recovery = Exposure × Recovery rate

   Step 3   Loss given default (LGD) = Exposure − Recovery

   Step 4   Probability of default (POD) on Date 1 is 1.50%, the assumed hazard rate. The probability of survival (POS) on Date 1 is 98.50%.

   For subsequent dates, POD is calculated as the hazard rate multiplied by the previous date's POS.

   For example, to determine the Date 2 POD (1.4775%), the hazard rate of (1.50%) is multiplied by the Date 1 POS (98.50%).

   Step 5   POS in Dates 2–4 = POS in the previous year − POD

   (That is, POS in Year T = POS in year $[T − 1]$ − POD in Year T.)

   POS can also be determined by subtracting the hazard rate from 100% and raising it to the power of the number of years:

   $$(100\% - 1.5000\%)^1 = 98.5000\%$$

   $$(100\% - 1.5000\%)^2 = 97.0225\%$$

   $$(100\% - 1.5000\%)^3 = 95.5672\%$$

   $$(100\% - 1.5000\%)^4 = 94.1337\%$$

   Step 6   Expected loss = LGD × POD

Step 7   Discount factor (DF) for Date T is $\dfrac{1}{(1+r)^T}$, where r is 3%.

Step 8   PV of expected loss = Expected loss × DF

Date	Exposure	Recovery	LGD	POD	POS	Expected Loss	DF	PV of Expected Loss
0								
1	€915.14	€274.54	€640.60	1.5000%	98.5000%	€9.61	0.970874	€9.33
2	€942.60	€282.78	€659.82	1.4775%	97.0225%	€9.75	0.942596	€9.19
3	€970.87	€291.26	€679.61	1.4553%	95.5672%	€9.89	0.915142	€9.05
4	€1,000.00	€300.00	€700.00	1.4335%	94.1337%	€10.03	0.888487	€8.92
							CVA =	€36.49

Value of the bond if the bond were default free would be 1,000 × DF for Date 4 = €888.49.

Fair value of the bond considering CVA = €888.49 − CVA = €888.49 − €36.49 = €852.00.

Because the market price of the bond (€875) is greater than the fair value of €852, B is correct.

A is incorrect because the market price of the bond differs from its fair value. C is incorrect because although the bond's value if the bond were default free is greater than the market price, the bond has a risk of default, and CVA lowers its fair value to below the market price.

2. B is correct. The recovery rate to be used now in the computation of fair value is 30% × 1.25 = 37.5%, whereas the hazard rate to be used is 1.50% × 1.25 = 1.875%.

Using the steps outlined in the solution to Question 1, the following table is prepared, which shows that the bond's CVA increases to 40.49. Thus, Koning concludes that a change in the probability of default has a greater effect on fair value than a similar change in the recovery rate. The steps taken to complete the table are the same as those in the previous problem. There are no changes in exposures and discount factors in this table.

Date	Exposure	Recovery	LGD	POD	POS	Expected Loss	DF	PV of Expected Loss
0								
1	€915.14	€343.18	€571.96	1.8750%	98.1250%	€10.72	0.970874	€10.41
2	€942.60	€353.47	€589.12	1.8398%	96.2852%	€10.84	0.942596	€10.22
3	€970.87	€364.08	€606.80	1.8053%	94.4798%	€10.95	0.915142	€10.03
4	€1,000.00	€375.00	€625.00	1.7715%	92.7083%	€11.07	0.888487	€9.84
							CVA =	€40.49

Changes in the hazard and recovery rates do not affect the value of the default-free bond. So, it is the same as in the previous question: €888.49.

Fair value of the bond considering CVA = €888.49 − CVA = €888.49 − €40.49 = €848.00

3. A is correct. The following table shows that the CVA for the bond is €42.17, the sum of the present values of expected loss. The steps taken to complete the table are as follows.

Step 1   Exposure at Date 4 is €1,000 + Coupon amount = €1,000 + €60 = €1,060. Exposure at a date T prior to that is Coupon on Date T + PV at Date T of subsequent coupons + PV of €1,000 to be received at Date 4. For example, exposure at Date 2 is

$$€60 + \frac{€60}{1+0.03} + \frac{€60}{(1+0.03)^2} + \frac{€1,000}{(1+0.03)^2} = €60 + \frac{€60}{1+0.03} + \frac{€1,060}{(1+0.03)^2}$$

$$= €1,117.40$$

Steps 2 through 8 are the same as those in the solution to Question 1.

Date	Exposure	Recovery	LGD	POD	POS	Expected Loss	DF	PV of Expected Loss
0								
1	€1,144.86	€343.46	€801.40	1.5000%	98.5000%	€12.02	0.970874	€11.67
2	€1,117.40	€335.22	€782.18	1.4775%	97.0225%	€11.56	0.942596	€10.89
3	€1,089.13	€326.74	€762.39	1.4553%	95.5672%	€11.10	0.915142	€10.15
4	€1,060.00	€318.00	€742.00	1.4335%	94.1337%	€10.64	0.888487	€9.45
							CVA =	€42.17

Value of the bond if the bond were default free would be €60 × DF_1 + €60 × DF_2 + €60 × DF_3 + €1,060 × DF_4 = €1,111.51.

Fair value of the bond considering CVA = €1,111.51 − €42.17 = €1,069.34

4. A is correct. If default occurs on Date 3, the rate of return can be obtained by solving the following equation for internal rate of return (IRR):

$$€1,090 = \frac{€60}{1+\text{IRR}} + \frac{€60}{(1+\text{IRR})^2} + \frac{€326.74}{(1+\text{IRR})^3}$$

In this equation, €60 is the amount of coupon received at Dates 1 and 2 prior to default at Date 3. The amount €326.74 is the recovery at Time 3 (from the CVA table in the solution to the previous question). The solution to the foregoing equation can be obtained using the cash flow IRR function on your calculator.

5. B is correct. For each possible transition, the expected percentage price change, computed as the product of the modified duration and the change in the spread as per Exhibit 7 of the reading, is calculated as follows:

From AA to AAA: −2.75 × (0.60% − 0.90%) = +0.83%

From AA to A: −2.75 × (1.10% − 0.90%) = −0.55%

From AA to BBB: −2.75 × (1.50% − 0.90%) = −1.65%

From AA to BB: −2.75 × (3.40% − 0.90%) = −6.88%

From AA to B: −2.75 × (6.50% − 0.90%) = −15.40%

From AA to C: −2.75 × (9.50% − 0.90%) = −23.65%

The expected percentage change in the value of the AA rated bond is computed by multiplying each expected percentage price change for a possible credit transition by its respective transition probability given in Exhibit 7 of the reading, and summing the products:

$(0.0150 \times 0.83\%) + (0.8800 \times 0\%) + (0.0950 \times -0.55\%) + (0.0075 \times -1.65\%) +$
$(0.0015 \times -6.88\%) + (0.0005 \times -15.40\%) + (0.0003 \times -23.65\%) = -0.0774\%$

Therefore, the expected return on the bond over the next year is its YTM minus 0.0774%, assuming no default.

6. B is correct. Statement B is correct because a reduced-form credit model involves regression analysis using information generally available in the financial markets, such as the measures mentioned in the statement.

   Statement A is incorrect because it is consistent with the use of a structural-form model and not a reduced-form model. It is a structural-form model that is based on the premise that a firm defaults on its debt if the value of its assets falls below its liabilities and that the probability of that event has the characteristics of an option.

   Statement C is incorrect because it is consistent with the use of a structural-form model and not a reduced-form model. A structural-form model involves the estimation of a default barrier, and default occurs if the value of the firm's assets falls below the default barrier.

7. C is correct. Structural models require information best known to the managers of the company. Reduced-form models only require information generally available in financial markets.

   A is literally true but when models were developed is immaterial. Structural models are currently used by commercial banks and credit rating agencies.

   B is incorrect because computer technology facilitates valuation using option pricing models as well as regression analysis.

8. A is correct. The following tree shows the valuation assuming no default of bond B2, which pays a 6% annual coupon.

Date 0	Date 1	Date 2	Date 3	Date 4

The scheduled year-end coupon and principal payments are placed to the right of each forward rate in the tree. For example, the Date 4 values are the principal plus the coupon of 60. The following are the four Date 3 values for the bond, shown above the interest rate at each node:

$$€1,060/1.080804 = €980.75$$

$$€1,060/1.054164 = €1,005.54$$

$$€1,060/1.036307 = €1,022.86$$

$$€1,060/1.024338 = €1,034.81$$

These are the three Date 2 values:

$$\frac{(0.5 \times €980.75 + 0.5 \times €1,005.54) + €60}{1.043999} = €1,008.76$$

$$\frac{(0.5 \times €1,005.54 + 0.5 \times €1,022.86) + €60}{1.029493} = €1,043.43$$

$$\frac{(0.5 \times €1,022.86 + 0.5 \times €1,034.81) + €60}{1.019770} = €1,067.73$$

These are the two Date 1 values:

$$\frac{(0.5 \times €1,008.76 + 0.5 \times €1,043.43) + €60}{1.021180} = €1,063.57$$

$$\frac{(0.5 \times €1,043.43 + 0.5 \times €1,067.73) + €60}{1.014197} = €1,099.96$$

This is the Date 0 value:

$$\frac{(0.5 \times €1,063.57 + 0.5 \times €1,099.96) + €60}{0.997500} = €1,144.63$$

So, the value of the bond assuming no default (VND) is 1,144.63. This value could also have been obtained more directly using the benchmark discount factors from Exhibit 2:

€60 × 1.002506 + €60 × 0.985093 + €60 × 0.955848 + €1,060 × 0.913225 = €1,144.63

The benefit of using the binomial interest rate tree to obtain the VND is that the same tree is used to calculate the expected exposure to default loss.

The credit valuation adjustment table is now prepared following these steps:

Step 1   Compute the expected exposures as described in the following, using the binomial interest rate tree prepared earlier.

The expected exposure for Date 4 is €1,060.

The expected exposure for Date 3 is

[(0.1250 × €980.75) + (0.3750 × €1,005.54) + (0.3750 × €1,022.86) + (0.1250 × €1,034.81)] + 60 = €1,072.60

The expected exposure for Date 2 is

$[(0.25 \times €1,008.76) + (0.50 \times €1,043.43) + (0.25 \times €1,067.73)] + €60 = €1,100.84$

The expected exposure for Date 1 is

$[(0.50 \times €1,063.57) + (0.50 \times €1,099.96)] + 60 = €1,141.76$

Step 2   LGD = Exposure × (1 − Recovery rate)

Step 3   The initial POD, also known as the hazard rate, is provided as 1.50%. For subsequent dates, POD is calculated as the hazard rate multiplied by the previous dates' POS.
For example, to determine the Date 2 POD (1.4775%), the hazard rate (1.5000%) is multiplied by the Date 1 POS (98.5000%).

Step 4   POS is determined by subtracting the hazard rate from 100% and raising it to the power of the number of years:

$$(100\% − 1.5000\%)^1 = 98.5000\%$$

$$(100\% − 1.5000\%)^2 = 97.0225\%$$

$$(100\% − 1.5000\%)^3 = 95.5672\%$$

$$(100\% − 1.5000\%)^4 = 94.1337\%$$

Step 5   Expected loss = LGD × POD

Step 6   Discount factors (DF) in Year T are obtained from Exhibit 2.

Step 7   PV of expected loss = Expected loss × DF

Date	Exposure	LGD	POD	POS	Expected Loss	DF	PV of Expected Loss
0							
1	€1,141.76	€799.23	1.5000%	98.5000%	€11.99	1.002506	€12.02
2	€1,100.84	€770.58	1.4775%	97.0225%	€11.39	0.985093	€11.22
3	€1,072.60	€750.82	1.4553%	95.5672%	€10.93	0.955848	€10.44
4	€1,060.00	€742.00	1.4335%	94.1337%	€10.64	0.913225	€9.71
						CVA =	€43.39

Fair value of the bond considering CVA = €1,144.63 − CVA = €1,144.63 − €43.39 = €1,101.24.

9. A is correct. The corporate bond's fair value is computed in the solution to Question 8 as €1,101.24 The YTM can be obtained by solving the following equation for IRR:

$$€1,101.24 = \frac{€60}{1+IRR} + \frac{€60}{(1+IRR)^2} + \frac{€60}{(1+IRR)^3} + \frac{€1,060}{(1+IRR)^4}$$

The solution to this equation is 3.26%.

Valuation of a four-year, 6% coupon bond under no default (VND) is computed in the solution to Question 8 as 1,144.63. So, the YTM of a theoretical comparable-maturity government bond with the same coupon rate as the corporate bond B2 can be obtained by solving the following equation for IRR:

$$\text{€}1{,}144.63 = \frac{\text{€}60}{1+\text{IRR}} + \frac{\text{€}60}{(1+\text{IRR})^2} + \frac{\text{€}60}{(1+\text{IRR})^3} + \frac{\text{€}1{,}060}{(1+\text{IRR})^4}$$

The solution to this equation is 2.18%. So, the credit spread that the analyst wants to compute is 3.26% − 2.18% = 1.08%, or 108 bps.

B is incorrect, because that is the spread over the four-year government par bond that has a YTM of 2.25% in Exhibit 2: 3.26% − 2.25% = 1.01%, or 101 bps. Although this spread is commonly used in practice, the analyst is interested in finding the spread over a theoretical 6% coupon government bond.

C is incorrect, because that is the YTM of the coupon four-year government bond in Exhibit 2.

10. B is correct. The recovery rate to be used now in the computation of fair value is 30% × 0.75 = 22.500%, whereas the hazard rate to be used is 1.50% × 0.75 = 1.125%.

The tree that shows the valuation assuming no default of bond B2 in the solution to Question 8 will not be affected by the foregoing changes. Accordingly, VND remains €1,144.63.

Following the steps outlined in the solution to Question 8, the following table is prepared, which shows that the CVA for the bond decreases to €36.23. Thus, Ibarra concludes that a decrease in the probability of default has a greater effect on fair value than a similar decrease in the recovery rate. The steps taken to complete the table are the same as those in Question 8. There are no changes in exposures or discount factors in this table.

Date	Exposure	LGD	POD	POS	Expected Loss	DF	PV of Expected Loss
0							
1	€1,141.76	€884.87	1.1250%	98.8750%	€9.95	1.002506	€9.98
2	€1,100.84	€853.15	1.1123%	97.7627%	€9.49	0.985093	€9.35
3	€1,072.60	€831.26	1.0998%	96.6628%	€9.14	0.955848	€8.74
4	€1,060.00	€821.50	1.0875%	95.5754%	€8.93	0.913225	€8.16
						CVA =	€36.23

Fair value of the bond considering CVA = €1,144.63 − CVA = €1,144.63 − €36.23 = €1,108.40

11. A is correct. The following tree shows the valuation assuming no default of floating-rate note (FRN) B4, which has a quoted margin of 4%.

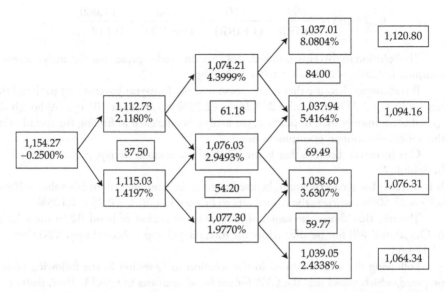

| Date 0 | Date 1 | Date 2 | Date 3 | Date 4 |

The scheduled year-end coupon and principal payments are placed to the right of each forward rate in the tree. For example, the four Date 4 values are the principal plus the coupon.

$$€1,000 \times (1 + 0.080804 + 0.04) = €1,120.80$$

$$€1,000 \times (1 + 0.054164 + 0.04) = €1,094.16$$

$$€1,000 \times (1 + 0.036307 + 0.04) = €1,076.31$$

$$€1,000 \times (1 + 0.024338 + 0.04) = €1,064.34$$

The following are the four Date 3 bond values for the note, shown above the interest rate at each node:

$$€1,120.80/1.080804 = €1,037.01$$

$$€1,094.16/1.054164 = €1,037.94$$

$$€1,076.31/1.036307 = €1,038.60$$

$$€1,064.34/1.024338 = €1,039.05$$

The three Date 3 coupon amounts are computed based on the interest rate at Date 2 plus the quoted margin of 4%:

$$€1,000 \times (0.043999 + 0.04) = €84.00$$

$$€1,000 \times (0.029493 + 0.04) = €69.49$$

$$€1,000 \times (0.019770 + 0.04) = €59.77$$

There are three Date 2 bond values:

$$\frac{(0.5 \times €1,037.01 + 0.5 \times €1,037.94) + €84.00}{1.043999} = €1,074.21$$

$$\frac{(0.5 \times €1,037.94 + 0.5 \times €1,038.60) + €69.49}{1.029493} = €1,076.03$$

$$\frac{(0.5 \times €1,038.60 + 0.5 \times €1,039.05) + €59.77}{1.019770} = €1,077.30$$

The two Date 2 coupon amounts are computed based on the interest rate at Date 1 plus the quoted margin of 4%:

$$€1,000 \times (0.021180 + 0.04) = €61.18$$

$$€1,000 \times (0.014197 + 0.04) = €54.20$$

The Date 1 coupon amount is computed based on the interest rate at Date 0 plus the quoted margin of 4%:

$$€1,000 \times (-0.0025 + 0.04) = €37.50$$

These are the calculations for the bond values for Date 1 and Date 0:

$$\frac{(0.5 \times €1,074.21 + 0.5 \times €1,076.03) + €61.18}{1.021180} = €1,112.73$$

$$\frac{(0.5 \times €1,076.06 + 0.5 \times €1,077.30) + €54.20}{1.014197} = €1,115.00$$

Then, the VND is calculated as follows:

$$\frac{(0.5 \times €1,112.73 + 0.5 \times €1,115.03) + €37.50}{0.9975} = €1,154.27$$

The expected exposures are then computed using the binomial interest rate tree prepared earlier. For example, the expected exposure for Date 4 is computed as follows:

$$[(0.125 \times €1,120.80) + (0.375 \times €1,094.16) + (0.375 \times €1,076.31) + (0.125 \times €1,064.34)] = €1,087.07$$

Similarly, the expected exposure for Date 3 is computed as follows:

$$[(0.125 \times €1,037.01) + (0.375 \times €1,037.94) + (0.375 \times €1,038.60) + (0.125 \times €1,039.05)] + [(0.250 \times €84) + (0.500 \times €69.49) + (0.250 \times €59.77)] = €1,108.90$$

The expected exposures for Dates 2 and 1 are computed similarly, and the credit valuation adjustment table is completed following Steps 2–7 outlined in the solution to Question 8.

Date	Exposure	LGD	POD	POS	Expected Loss	DF	PV of Expected Loss
0							
1	€1,151.38	€805.97	1.5000%	98.5000%	€12.09	1.002506	€12.12
2	€1,133.58	€793.51	1.4775%	97.0225%	€11.72	0.985093	€11.55
3	€1,108.90	€776.23	1.4553%	95.5672%	€11.30	0.955848	€10.80
4	€1,087.07	€760.95	1.4335%	94.1337%	€10.91	0.913225	€9.96
						CVA =	€44.43

Fair value of the FRN considering CVA = €1,154.27 − CVA = €1,154.27 − €44.43 = €1,109.84

Because the market price of €1,070 is less than the estimated fair value, the analyst should recommend adding to existing positions in the FRN.

B and C are incorrect because the FRN is perceived to be undervalued in the market.

12. A is correct. The changing probability of default will not affect the binomial tree prepared in the solution to Question 11. The Date 1 value remains €1,154.27, which is also the VND. The expected exposures, loss given default, and discount factors are also unaffected by the changing probability of default. The following is the completed credit valuation adjustment table.

Date	Exposure	LGD	POD	POS	Expected Loss	DF	PV of Expected Loss
0							
1	€1,151.38	€805.97	1.5000%	98.5000%	€12.09	1.002506	€12.12
2	€1,133.58	€793.51	0.4925%	98.0075%	€3.91	0.985093	€3.85
3	€1,108.90	€776.23	0.4900%	97.5175%	€3.80	0.955848	€3.64
4	€1,087.07	€760.95	0.4876%	97.0299%	€3.71	0.913225	€3.39
						CVA =	€22.99

Thus, CVA decreases to €22.99.

13. C is correct. The credit rating agencies typically make incremental changes as seen in a transition matrix provided in Exhibit 7 of the reading. Ibarra believes the bond to be undervalued, in that her assessment of the probability of default and the recovery rate is more optimistic than that of the agencies. Therefore, she most likely expects the credit rating agencies to put the issuer on a positive watch.

A is incorrect because the bond is perceived to be undervalued, not overvalued. Ibarra is not expecting a credit downgrade.

B is incorrect because it is not the *most likely* expectation. The rating agencies rarely jump an issuer all the way from BBB to AAA. In Exhibit 7, the probability of a BBB rated issuer going from BBB to AAA is 0.02%, whereas it is 4.80% to go from BBB to A.

14. A is correct.

B is incorrect because, although generally true for investment-grade bonds, the statement neglects the fact that high-yield issuers sometimes face a downward-sloping credit term structure. Credit term structures are not *always* upward sloping.

C is incorrect because there is a consistent pattern to the term structure of credit spreads—typically it is upwardly sloped because greater time to maturity is associated with higher projected probabilities of default and lower recovery rates.

15. C is correct. A covered bond is a senior debt obligation of a financial institution that gives recourse to the originator/issuer as well as a predetermined underlying collateral pool. Each specific country or jurisdiction specifies the eligible collateral types as well as the specific structures permissible in the covered bond market. Covered bonds most frequently have either commercial or residential mortgages meeting specific criteria or public sector exposures as underlying collateral.

    A is incorrect. The term "covered" is used in foreign exchange analysis, for instance, "covered interest rate parity." In the context of securitized debt, a covered bond is secured by specific assets in addition to the overall balance sheet of the issuer.

    B is incorrect because a covered bond does not involve a credit default swap. In addition, an issuer is not likely to sell a credit default swap on its own liability.

16. A is correct. Credit spread migration typically reduces the expected return for two reasons. First, the probabilities for rating changes are not symmetrically distributed around the current rating; they are skewed toward a downgrade rather than an upgrade. Second, the increase in the credit spread is much larger for downgrades than is the decrease in the spread for upgrades.

17. A is correct. The expected return on the Entre Corp. bond over the next year is its yield to maturity plus the expected percentage price change in the bond over the next year. In the table below, for each possible transition, the expected percentage price change is the product of the bond's modified duration of 7.54, multiplied by −1, and the change in the spread, weighted by the given probability:

$$
\begin{aligned}
\text{Expected percentage price change} = &\ (0.0002 \times 6.786\%) + (0.0030 \times 4.524\%) + \\
&\ (0.0480 \times 3.016\%) + (0.8573 \times 0.000\%) + \\
&\ (0.0695 \times -14.326\%) + (0.0175 \times -37.700\%) \\
&\ + (0.0045 \times -60.320\%) \\
= &\ -1.76715\%
\end{aligned}
$$

So, the expected return on the Entre Corp. bond is its yield to maturity plus the expected percentage price change due to credit migration:

$$\text{Expected return} = 5.50\% - 1.77\% = 3.73\%$$

	Expected % Price Change (1)	Probability (2)	Expected % Price Change × Probability (1 × 2)
From BBB to AAA	$-7.54 \times (0.60\% - 1.50\%) = 6.786\%$	0.0002	0.00136
From BBB to AA	$-7.54 \times (0.90\% - 1.50\%) = 4.524\%$	0.0030	0.01357
From BBB to A	$-7.54 \times (1.10\% - 1.50\%) = 3.016\%$	0.0480	0.14477
From BBB to BB	$-7.54 \times (3.40\% - 1.50\%) = -14.326\%$	0.0695	−0.99566
From BBB to B	$-7.54 \times (6.50\% - 1.50\%) = -37.700\%$	0.0175	−0.65975
From BBB to CCC, CC, C	$-7.54 \times (9.50\% - 1.50\%) = -60.320\%$	0.0045	−0.27144
		Total:	−1.76715

18. C is correct. The credit spread can be calculated in three steps:

   Step 1   Estimate the value of the three-year VraiRive bond assuming no default. Based on
            Kowalski's assumptions and Exhibits 2 and 3, the value of the three-year VraiRive
            bond assuming no default is 100.0000.

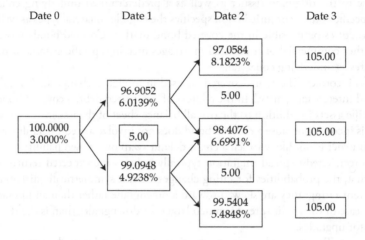

   Supporting calculations:

   The bond value in each node is the value of next period's cash flows discounted by
   the forward rate. For the three nodes on Date 2, the bond values are as follows:

   $$105/1.081823 = 97.0584$$

   $$105/1.066991 = 98.4076$$

   $$105/1.054848 = 99.5404$$

   For the two nodes on Date 1, the two bond values are as follows:

   $$[0.5 \times (97.0584) + 0.5 \times (98.4076) + 5.00]/1.060139 = 96.9052$$

   $$[0.5 \times (98.4076) + 0.5 \times (99.5404) + 5.00]/1.049238 = 99.0948$$

   Finally, for the node on Date 0, the bond value is

   $$[0.5 \times (96.9052) + 0.5 \times (99.0948) + 5.00]/1.030000 = 100.0000$$

   Therefore, the VND for the VraiRive bond is 100.0000.

   Step 2   Calculate the credit valuation adjustment (CVA), and then subtract the CVA
            from the VND from Step 1 to establish the fair value of the bond. The CVA
            equals the sum of the present values of each year's expected loss and is calculated
            as follows:

Date	Expected Exposure	Loss Given Default	Probability of Default	Discount Factor	Present Value of Expected Loss
1	103.0000	68.6667	2.0000%	0.970874	1.3333
2	103.3535	68.9023	1.9600%	0.920560	1.2432
3	105.0000	70.0000	1.9208%	0.862314	1.1594
				CVA =	3.7360

Supporting calculations:

The expected exposures at each date are the bond values at each node, weighted by their risk-neutral probabilities, plus the coupon payment:

Date 1: $0.5 \times (96.9052) + 0.5 \times (99.0948) + 5.00 = 103.0000$

Date 2: $0.25 \times (97.0584) + 0.5 \times (98.4076) + 0.25 \times (99.5404) + 5.00 = 103.3535$

Date 3: 105.0000

The loss given default (LGD) on each date is 2/3 of the expected exposure.
The probability of default (POD) on each date is as follows:

Date 1: 2%

Date 2: $2\% \times (100\% - 2\%) = 1.96\%$

Date 3: $2\% \times (100\% - 2\%)^2 = 1.9208\%$

The discount factor on each date is $1/(1 + \text{spot rate for the date})$ raised to the correct power. Finally, the credit valuation adjustment each year is the product of the LGD times the POD times the discount factor, as shown in the last column of the table. The sum of the three annual CVAs is 3.7360.

So, the fair value of the VraiRive bond is the VND less the CVA, or VND − CVA = $100 - 3.7360 = 96.2640$.

Step 3   Based on the fair value from Step 2, calculate the yield to maturity of the bond, and solve for the credit spread by subtracting the yield to maturity on the benchmark bond from the yield to maturity on the VraiRive bond. The credit spread is equal to the yield to maturity on the VraiRive bond minus the yield to maturity on the three-year benchmark bond (which is 5.0000%). Based on its fair value of 96.2640, the VraiRive bond's yield to maturity (YTM) is

$$96.2640 = \frac{5}{(1+\text{YTM})} + \frac{5}{(1+\text{YTM})^2} + \frac{105}{(1+\text{YTM})^3}$$

Solving for YTM, the yield to maturity is 6.4082%. Therefore, the credit spread on the VraiRive bond is $6.4082\% - 5.0000\% = 1.4082\%$.

19. C is correct. A decrease in the risk-neutral probability of default would decrease the credit valuation adjustment and decrease the credit spread. In contrast, increasing the bond's loss-given-default assumption and increasing the probability-of-default (hazard rate) assumption would increase the credit valuation adjustment and decrease the fair value of the bond (and increase the yield to maturity and the credit spread over its benchmark).

20. A is correct. For investment-grade bonds with the highest credit ratings, credit spreads are extremely low, and credit migration is possible only in one direction given the implied lower bound of zero on credit spreads. As a result, the credit term structure for the most highly rated securities tends to be either flat or slightly upward sloping. Securities with lower credit quality, however, face greater sensitivity to the credit cycle. Credit spreads would decrease, not increase, with the expectation of economic growth. There is a countercyclical relationship between credit spreads and benchmark rates over the business cycle. A strong economic climate is associated with higher benchmark yields but lower credit spreads because the probability of issuers defaulting declines in such good times.

21. A is correct. Positively sloped credit spread curves may arise when a high-quality issuer with a strong competitive position in a stable industry has low leverage, strong cash flow, and a high profit margin. This type of issuer tends to exhibit very low short-term credit

spreads that rise with increasing maturity given greater uncertainty due to the macroeconomic environment, potential adverse changes in the competitive landscape, technological change, or other factors that drive a higher implied probability of default over time. Empirical academic studies also tend to support the view that the credit spread term structure is upward sloping for investment-grade bond portfolios.

22. B is correct. The auto ABS is granular, with many small loans relative to the size of the total portfolio. The auto loans are also homogeneous. These characteristics support using the portfolio-based approach. A loan-by-loan approach would be inefficient because of the large number of basically similar loans; this approach is best for a portfolio of discrete, large loans that are heterogeneous. A statistics-based approach would work for a static book of loans, whereas the auto loan portfolio would be dynamic and would change over time.

23. B is correct. The expected exposure is the projected amount of money that an investor could lose if an event of default occurs, before factoring in possible recovery. The expected exposure for both Bond I and Bond II is $100 + 5 = 105$.

24. C is correct. The loss given default is a positive function of the expected exposure to default loss and a negative function of the recovery rate. Because Bond II has a lower recovery rate than Bond I and the same expected exposure to default loss ($100 + 5 = 105$), it will have a higher loss given default than Bond I will have. The loss given default for Bond I is $105 \times (1 - 0.40) = 63.00$. The loss given default for Bond II is $105 \times (1 - 0.35) = 68.25$.

25. B is correct. In the event of no default, the investor is expected to receive 105. In the event of a default, the investor is expected to receive $105 - [105 \times (1 - 0.40)] = 42$. The expected future value of the bond is, therefore, the weighted average of the no-default and default amounts, or $(105 \times 0.98) + (42 \times 0.02) = 103.74$.

26. B is correct. The risk-neutral default probability, P^*, is calculated using the current price, the expected receipt at maturity with no default (that is, $100 + 5 = 105$), the expected receipt at maturity in the event of a default (that is, $0.40 \times 105 = 42$), and the risk-free rate of interest (0.03):

$$100 = \frac{\left[105 \times \left(1 - P^*\right)\right] + \left(42 \times P^*\right)}{1.03}$$

Solving for P^* gives 0.031746, or 3.1746%.

27. A is correct. The CVA is the sum of the present value of expected losses on the bond, which from Exhibit 2 is 3.3367.

28. C is correct. The expected percentage price change is the product of the negative of the modified duration and the difference between the credit spread in the new rating and the old rating:

Expected percentage price change $= -4.2 \times (0.0175 - 0.01) = -0.0315$, or -3.15%.

29. B is correct. A reduced-form model in credit risk analysis uses historical variables, such as financial ratios and macroeconomic variables, to estimate the default intensity. A structural model for credit risk analysis, in contrast, uses option pricing and relies on a traded market for the issuer's equity.

30. B is correct. Observation 1 is incorrect, but Observation 2 is correct. The actual default probabilities do not include the default risk premium associated with the uncertainty in the timing of the possible default loss. The observed spread over the yield on a risk-free bond in practice does include liquidity and tax considerations, in addition to credit risk.

CHAPTER 11

CREDIT DEFAULT SWAPS

SOLUTIONS

1. A is correct. Deem Advisors would prefer a cash settlement. Deem Advisors owns Bond 2 (trading at 50% of par), which is worth more than the cheapest-to-deliver obligation (Bond 1 trading at 40% of par). Deem Advisors can cash settle for $6 million [= (1 − 40%) × $10 million] on its CDS contract and sell Bond 2 it owns for $5 million, for total proceeds of $11 million. If Deem Advisors were to physically settle the contract, only $10 million would be received, the face amount of the bonds, and they would deliver Bond 2.

   B is incorrect because if Deem Advisors were to physically settle the contract, they would receive only $10 million, which is less than the $11 million that could be obtained from a cash settlement. C is incorrect because Deem Advisors would not be indifferent between settlement protocols as the firm would receive $1 million more with a cash settlement in comparison to a physical settlement.

2. C is correct. A downward-sloping credit curve implies a greater probability of default in the earlier years than in the later years. Downward-sloping curves are less common and often are the result of severe near-term stress in the financial markets.

   A is incorrect because a flat credit curve implies a constant hazard rate (relevant probability of default). B is incorrect because an upward-sloping credit curve implies a greater probability of default in later years.

3. A is correct. UNAB experienced a credit event when it failed to make the scheduled coupon payment on the outstanding subordinated unsecured obligation. Failure to pay, a credit event, occurs when a borrower does not make a scheduled payment of principal or interest on *any* outstanding obligations after a grace period, even without a formal bankruptcy filing.

   B is incorrect because a credit event can occur without filing for bankruptcy. There are three general types of credit events: bankruptcy, failure to pay, and restructuring.

   C is incorrect because a credit event (failure to pay) occurs when a borrower does not make a scheduled payment of principal or interest on *any* outstanding obligations after a grace period, without a formal bankruptcy filing.

4. C is correct. An approximation for the upfront premium is (Credit spread – Fixed coupon rate) × Duration of the CDS. To buy 10-year CDS protection, Deem Advisors would have to pay an approximate upfront premium of 1400 basis points [(700 – 500) × 7], or 14% of the notional.

   A is incorrect because 200 basis points, or 2%, is derived by taking the simple difference between the credit spread and the fixed coupon rate (700 – 500). B is incorrect because 980 basis points, or 9.8%, is the result of dividing the credit spread by the fixed coupon rate and multiplying by the duration of the CDS [(700/500) × 7].

5. B is correct. Deem Advisors purchased protection, and therefore is economically short and benefits from an increase in the company's spread. Since putting on the protection, the credit spread increased by 200 basis points, and Deem Advisors realizes the gain by entering into a new offsetting contract (sells the protection for a higher premium to another party).

   A is incorrect because a decrease (not increase) in the spread would result in a loss for the credit protection buyer. C is incorrect because Deem Advisors, the credit protection buyer, would profit from an increase in the company's credit spread, not break even.

6. A is correct. A difference in credit spreads in the bond market and CDS market is the foundation of the basis trade strategy. If the spread is higher in the bond market than the CDS market, it is said to be a negative basis. In this case, the bond credit spread is currently 4.50% (bond yield minus Libor) and the comparable CDS contract has a credit spread of 4.25%. The credit risk is cheap in the CDS market relative to the bond market. Since the protection and the bond were both purchased, if convergence occurs, the trade will capture the 0.25% differential in the two markets (4.50% – 4.25%).

   B is incorrect because the bond market implies a 4.50% credit risk premium (bond yield minus Libor) and the CDS market implies a 4.25% credit risk premium. Convergence of the bond market credit risk premium and the CDS credit risk premium would result in capturing the differential, 0.25%. The 1.75% is derived by incorrectly subtracting Libor from the credit spread on the CDS (= 4.25% – 2.50%).

   C is incorrect because convergence of the bond market credit risk premium and the CDS credit risk premium would result in capturing the differential, 0.25%. The 2.75% is derived incorrectly by subtracting the credit spread on the CDS from the current bond yield (= 7.00% – 4.25%).

7. C is correct. Parties to CDS contracts generally agree that their contracts will conform to ISDA specifications. These terms are specified in the ISDA master agreement, which the parties to a CDS sign before any transactions are made. Therefore, to satisfy the compliance requirements referenced by Chan, the sovereign wealth fund must sign an ISDA master agreement with SGS.

8. A is correct. A CDS index (e.g., CDX and iTraxx) would allow the SWF to simultaneously fully hedge multiple fixed-income exposures.

9. C is correct. When an entity within an index defaults, that entity is removed from the index and settled as a single-name CDS based on its relative proportion in the index. To qualify as a credit event, the restructuring must be involuntary and forced on the borrower by the creditors. Although the Maxx restructuring would be considered a credit event (default) in the eurozone, in the United States, restructuring is not considered a credit event; therefore, the notional amount of $400 million will not change.

10. A is correct. Based on Exhibit 1, the probability of survival for the first year is 99.78% (100% minus the 0.22% hazard rate). Similarly, the probability of survival for the second and third years is 99.65% (100% minus the 0.35% hazard rate) and 99.50% (100%

minus the 0.50% hazard rate), respectively. Therefore, the probability of survival of the Orion bond through the first three years is equal to $(0.9978) \times (0.9965) \times (0.9950) = 0.9893$, and the probability of default sometime during the first three years is $1 - 0.9893$, or 1.07%.

11. B is correct. The trade assumes that £6 million of five-year CDS protection on Orion is initially sold, so the fund received the premium. Because the credit spread of the Orion CDS narrowed from 150 bps to 100 bps, the CDS position will realize a financial gain. This financial gain is equal to the difference between the upfront premium received on the original CDS position and the upfront premium to be paid on a new, offsetting CDS position. To close the position and monetize this gain, the fund should unwind the position with a new offsetting CDS, thereby buying protection for a lower premium (relative to the original premium collected) in six months.

12. B is correct. The gain on the hypothetical Orion trade is £117,000, calculated as follows.

Approximate profit = Change in credit spread (in bps) × Duration × Notional amount
Approximate profit = (150 bps − 100 bps) × 3.9 × £6 million
Approximate profit = .005 × 3.9 × £6 million
= £117,000

The SWF gains because they sold protection at a spread of 150 bps and closed out the position by buying protection at a lower spread of 100 bps.

13. B is correct. Based on Outlook 1, Chan and Smith anticipate that Italy's economy will weaken. In order to profit from this forecast, one would go short (buy protection) a high-yield Italian CDS (e.g., iTraxx Crossover) index and go long (sell protection) an investment-grade Italian CDS (e.g., iTraxx Main) index.

14. B is correct. To take advantage of Chan's view of the US credit curve steepening in the short term, a curve trade will entail shorting (buying protection) a long-term (20-year) CDX and going long (selling protection) a short-term (2-year) CDX. A steeper curve means that long-term credit risk increases relative to short-term credit risk.

15. B is correct. If Delta Corporation issues significantly more debt, it raises the probability that it may default, thereby increasing the CDS spread. The shares of Zega will be bought at a premium resulting from the unsolicited bid in the market. An equity-versus-credit trade would be to go long (buy) the Zega shares and short (buy protection) the Delta five-year CDS.

CHAPTER 12

OVERVIEW OF FIXED-INCOME PORTFOLIO MANAGEMENT

SOLUTIONS

1. B is correct. Permot has the highest percentage of floating-coupon bonds and inflation-linked bonds. Bonds with floating coupons protect interest income from inflation because the reference rate should adjust for inflation. Inflation-linked bonds protect against inflation by paying a return that is directly linked to an index of consumer prices and adjusting the principal for inflation. Inflation-linked bonds protect both coupon and principal payments against inflation.

   The level of inflation protection for coupons = % portfolio in floating-coupon bonds + % portfolio in inflation-linked bonds:

   Aschel = 2% + 3% = 5%

   Permot = 34% + 28% = 62%

   Rosaiso = 17% + 21% = 38%

   Thus, Permot has the highest level of inflation protection with 62% of its portfolio in floating-coupon and inflation-linked bonds.

2. B is correct. The rolling yield is the sum of the yield income and the rolldown return. Yield income is the sum of the bond's annual current yield and interest on reinvestment income. Perreaux assumes that there is no reinvestment income for any of the three funds, and the yield income for Aschel will be calculated as follows:

   Yield income = Annual average coupon payment/Current bond price
   = $3.63/$117.00
   = 0.0310, or 3.10%

The rolldown return is equal to the bond's percentage price change assuming an unchanged yield curve over the horizon period. The rolldown return will be calculated as follows:

$$\text{Rolldown return} = \frac{\left(\text{Bond price}_{\text{End-of-horizon period}} - \text{Bond price}_{\text{Beginning-of-horizon period}}\right)}{\text{Bond price}_{\text{Beginning-of-horizon period}}}$$

$$= \frac{(\$114.00 - \$117.00)}{\$117.00}$$

$$= -0.0256, \text{ or } -2.56\%$$

Rolling yield = Yield income + Rolldown return = 3.10% − 2.56% = 0.54%

3. B is correct. The return for Aschel is 7.71%, calculated as follows:

$$r_p = \frac{\left(r_I \times (V_E + V_B) - V_B \times r_B\right)}{V_E}$$

$$= r_I + \frac{V_B}{V_E}\left(r_I - r_B\right)$$

$$= 6.20\% + \frac{\$42.00 \text{ million}}{\$94.33 \text{ million}}(6.20\% - 2.80\%)$$

$$= 7.71\%$$

4. C is correct. Rosaiso is the only fund that holds bonds with embedded options. Effective duration should be used for bonds with embedded options. For bonds with embedded options, the duration and convexity measures used to calculate the expected change in price based on the investor's views of yields and yield spreads are effective duration and effective convexity. For bonds without embedded options, convexity and modified duration are used in this calculation.

5. B is correct. Cash flow matching has no yield curve or interest rate assumptions. With this immunization approach, cash flows come from coupon and principal repayments that are expected to match and offset liability cash flows. Because bond cash inflows are scheduled to coincide with liability cash payouts, there is no need for reinvestment of cash flows. Thus, cash flow matching is not affected by interest rate movements. Cash flows coming from coupons and liquidating bond portfolio positions is a key feature of a duration-matching approach.

6. A is correct. The optimal strategy for Villash is the sale of 100% of Bond 1, which Perreaux considers to be overvalued. Because Villash is a tax-exempt foundation, tax considerations are not relevant and Perreaux's investment views drive her trading recommendations.

7. B is correct. The domestic bond portfolio's return objective is to modestly outperform the benchmark. Its risk factors, such as duration, are to closely match the benchmark. Small deviations in sector weights are allowed, and tracking error should be less than 50 bps per year. These features are typical of enhanced indexing.

8. A is correct. Floating-coupon bonds provide inflation protection for the interest income because the reference rate should adjust for inflation. The purchase of fixed-coupon bonds as outlined in Strategy 1 provides no protection against inflation for either interest or principal. Strategy 1 would instead be superior to Strategy 2 in funding future liabilities (better predictability as to the amount of cash flows) and reducing the correlation between the fund's domestic bond portfolio and equity portfolio (better diversification).

9. C is correct. Since the fund's clients are taxable investors, there is value in harvesting tax losses. These losses can be used to offset capital gains within the fund that will otherwise be distributed to the clients and cause them higher tax payments, which decreases the total value of the investment to clients. The fund has to consider the overall value of the investment to its clients, including taxes, which may result in the sale of bonds that are not viewed as overvalued. Tax-exempt investors' decisions are driven by their investment views without regard to offsetting gains and losses for tax purposes.

10. C is correct. Bond 3 is most likely to be the least liquid of the three bonds presented in Exhibit 2 and will thus most likely require the highest liquidity premium. Low credit ratings, longer time since issuance, smaller issuance size, smaller issuance outstanding, and longer time to maturity typically are associated with a lower liquidity (and thus a higher liquidity premium). Bond 3 has the lowest credit quality and the longest time since issuance of the three bonds. Bond 3 also has a smaller issue size and longer time to maturity than Bond 1. The total issuance outstanding for Bond 3 is smaller than that of Bond 2 and equal to that of Bond 1.

11. B is correct. The total expected return is calculated as:

Total expected return = Rolling yield + E(Change in price based on investor's yield and yield spread view) − E(Credit losses) + E(Currency gains or losses)

Rolling yield = Yield income + Rolldown return

Return Component	Formula	Calculation
Yield income	Annual coupon payment/Current bond price	€2.25/€98.45 = 2.29%
+ Rolldown return	$\dfrac{\left(\text{Bond price}_{\text{End-of-horizon period}} - \text{Bond price}_{\text{Beginning-of-horizon period}}\right)}{\text{Bond price}_{\text{Beginning-of-horizon period}}}$	(€98.62 − €98.45)/ €98.45 = 0.17%
= Rolling yield	Yield income + Rolldown return	2.29% + 0.17% = 2.46%
+ E(Change in price based on investor's yield and yield spread view)	$[-\text{MD} \times \Delta\text{Yield}] + [\tfrac{1}{2} \times \text{Convexity} \times (\text{Yield})^2]$	$[-5.19 \times 0.0015]$ $+ [\tfrac{1}{2} \times 22 \times (0.0015)^2]$ = −0.78%
− E(Credit losses)	Given	−0.13%
+ E(Currency gains or losses)	Given	0.65%
= Total expected return		**2.20%**

12. C is correct. The sector weights, risk and return characteristics, and turnover for Manager C differ significantly from those of the index, which is typical of an active management mandate. In particular, Manager C's modified duration of 6.16 represents a much larger deviation from the benchmark index modified duration of 5.22 than that of the other managers, which is a characteristic unique to an active management mandate.

CHAPTER 13

LIABILITY-DRIVEN AND INDEX-BASED STRATEGIES

SOLUTIONS

1. A is correct. Type I liabilities have cash outlays with known amounts and timing. The dates and amounts of Kiest's liabilities are known; therefore, they would be classified as Type I liabilities.

2. C is correct. Structural risk arises from the design of the duration-matching portfolio. It is reduced by minimizing the dispersion of the bond positions, going from a barbell structure to more of a bullet portfolio that concentrates the component bonds' durations around the investment horizon. With bond maturities of 1.5 and 11.5 years, Portfolio C has a definite barbell structure compared with those of Portfolios A and B, and it is thus subject to a greater degree of risk from yield curve twists and non-parallel shifts. In addition, Portfolio C has the highest level of convexity, which increases a portfolio's structural risk.

3. A is correct. The two requirements to achieve immunization for multiple liabilities are for the money duration (or BPV) of the asset and liability to match and for the asset convexity to exceed the convexity of the liability. Although all three portfolios have similar BPVs, Portfolio A is the only portfolio to have a lower convexity than that of the liability portfolio (31.98, versus 33.05 for the $20 million liability portfolio), and thus, it fails to meet one of the two requirements needed for immunization.

4. B is correct. Portfolio B is a laddered portfolio with maturities spread more or less evenly over the yield curve. A desirable aspect of a laddered portfolio is liquidity management. Because there is always a bond close to redemption, the soon-to-mature bond can provide emergency liquidity needs. Barbell portfolios, such as Portfolio C, have maturities only at the short-term and long-term ends and thus are much less desirable for liquidity management.

5. A is correct. Soto believes that any shift in the yield curve will be parallel. Model risk arises whenever assumptions are made about future events and approximations are used to measure key parameters. The risk is that those assumptions turn out to be wrong and the approximations are inaccurate. A non-parallel yield curve shift could occur, resulting in a mismatch of the duration of the immunizing portfolio versus the liability.

6. C is correct. Kiest has a young workforce and thus a long-term investment horizon. The Global Aggregate and Global Aggregate GDP Weighted Indexes have the highest durations (7.73 and 7.71, respectively) and would be appropriate for this group. Hudgens also wants to avoid the "bums" problem, however, which arises as a result of a market-cap-weighted portfolio increasing the weight of a particular issuer or sector that has increasing borrowings. The Global Aggregate Index is a market-cap-weighted index. As a result, the Global Aggregate GDP Weighted Index is the most appropriate selection for Kiest.

7. B is correct. Low tracking error requires an indexing approach. A full replication approach for a broadly diversified bond index would be extremely costly because it requires purchasing all the constituent securities in the index. A more efficient and cost-effective way to track the index is a **stratified sampling** or **cell approach** to indexing, whereby Soto would purchase fewer securities than the index but would match primary risk factors reflected in the index. Closely matching these risk factors could provide low tracking error.

8. B is correct. Although a significant spread between the market price of the underlying fixed-income securities portfolio and an ETF's NAV should drive an authorized participant to engage in arbitrage, many fixed-income securities are either thinly traded or not traded at all. This situation might allow such a divergence to persist.

9. C is correct. Asset–liability management strategies consider both assets and liabilities in the portfolio decision-making process. Mowery notes that DFC's previous fixed-income manager attempted to control for interest rate risk by focusing on both the asset and the liability side of the company's balance sheet. The previous manager thus followed an asset–liability management strategy.

10. C is correct. Approach 1 is a full replication approach, whereas Approach 2 follows a **stratified sampling** approach to indexing. Both full replication and **stratified sampling** can be used to establish a passive exposure to the bond market. Under full replication, the manager buys or sells bonds when there are changes to the index. The larger number of index constituents associated with full replication provides a higher degree of risk diversification compared with a **stratified sampling** approach.

11. C is correct. A stratified sampling approach to indexing is especially useful for investors who consider environmental, social or other factors when selecting a fixed-income portfolio. Environmental, social, and corporate governance (ESG) investing, also called socially responsible investing, refers to the explicit inclusion or exclusion of some sectors, which is more appropriate for a stratified sampling approach to indexing relative to a full index replication strategy. In particular, Approach 2 may be customized to reflect client preferences.

12. B is correct. Immunization is the process of structuring and managing a fixed-income portfolio to minimize the variance in the realized rate of return and to lock in the cash flow yield (internal rate of return) on the portfolio, which in this case is 9.85%.

13. C is correct. Compton is correct that measurement error can arise even in immunization strategies for Type 1 cash flows, which have set amounts and set dates. Also, a parallel shift in yield curves is a sufficient but not a necessary condition to achieve the desired outcome. Non-parallel shifts as well as twists in the yield curve can change the cash flow yield on the immunizing portfolio; however, minimizing the dispersion of cash flows in the asset portfolio mitigates this risk. As a result, both statements are correct.

14. B is correct. In the case of a single liability, immunization is achieved by matching the bond portfolio's Macaulay duration with the horizon date. DFC has a single liability of $500 million due in nine years. Portfolio 2 has a Macaulay duration of 8.9, which is closer to 9 than that of either Portfolio 1 or 3. Therefore, Portfolio 2 will best immunize the portfolio against the liability.

15. C is correct. Structural risk to immunization arises from twists and non-parallel shifts in the yield curve. Structural risk is reduced by minimizing the dispersion of cash flows in the portfolio, which can be accomplished by minimizing the convexity for a given cash flow duration level. Because Portfolio 4 has the lowest convexity compared with the other two portfolios and also has a Macaulay duration close to the liability maturity of nine years, it minimizes structural risk.

16. B is correct. The use of an index as a widely accepted benchmark requires clear, transparent rules for security inclusion and weighting, investability, daily valuation, availability of past returns, and turnover. Because the custom benchmark is valued weekly rather than daily, this characteristic would be inconsistent with an appropriate benchmark.

17. B is correct. DFC has two types of assets, short-term and intermediate-term. For the short-term assets, a benchmark with a short duration is appropriate. For the intermediate-term assets, a benchmark with a longer duration is appropriate. In this situation, DFC may wish to combine several well-defined sub-benchmark categories into an overall blended benchmark (Benchmark 2). The Bloomberg Barclays Short-Term Treasury Index is an appropriate benchmark for the short-term assets, and SD&R uses a 50% weight for this component. The longer-duration Bloomberg Barclays US Corporate Bond Index is an appropriate benchmark for the intermediate-term assets, and SD&R uses a 50% weight for this component. As a result, Compton should recommend proposed Benchmark 2.

18. C is correct. It may be impossible to acquire zero-coupon bonds to precisely match liabilities because the city's liabilities have varying maturities and amounts. In many financial markets, zero-coupon bonds are unavailable.

19. C is correct. An investor having an investment horizon equal to the bond's Macaulay duration is effectively protected, or immunized, from the first change in interest rates, because price and coupon reinvestment effects offset for either higher or lower rates.

20. A is correct. An upward shift in the yield curve reduces the bond's value but increases the reinvestment rate, with these two effects offsetting one another. The price effect and the coupon reinvestment effect cancel each other in the case of an upward shift in the yield curve for an immunized liability.

21. A is correct. Minimizing the convexity of the bond portfolio minimizes the dispersion of the bond portfolio. A non-parallel shift in the yield curve may result in changes in the bond portfolio's cash flow yield. In summary, the characteristics of a bond portfolio structured to immunize a single liability are that it (1) has an initial market value that equals or exceeds the present value of the liability, (2) has a portfolio Macaulay duration that matches the liability's due date, and (3) minimizes the portfolio convexity statistic.

22. C is correct. Under a **stratified sampling** approach to indexing, the index is replicated with fewer than the full set of index constituents but still matches the original index's primary risk factors. This strategy replicates the index performance under different market scenarios more efficiently than the full replication of a pure indexing approach.

23. C is correct. The laddered approach provides both diversification over time and liquidity. Diversification over time offers the investor a balanced position between two sources of interest rate risk: cash flow reinvestment and market price volatility. In practice, perhaps the most desirable aspect of a laddered portfolio is liquidity management, because as time passes, the portfolio will always contain a bond close to maturity.

24.

Template for Question 24

Recommend the portfolio in Exhibit 1 that would *best* achieve the immunization.
(circle one)

Portfolio A
Portfolio B
Portfolio C

Justification:
Portfolio A is the most appropriate portfolio because it is the only one that satisfies the three criteria for immunizing a single future outflow (liability), given that the cash flow yields are sufficiently close in value:

1. Market Value: Portfolio A's initial market value of $235,727 exceeds the outflow's present value of $234,535. Portfolio B is not appropriate because its market value of $233,428 is less than the present value of the future outflow of $234,535. A bond portfolio structured to immunize a single liability must have an initial market value that equals or exceeds the present value of the liability.
2. Macaulay Duration: Portfolio A's Macaulay duration of 9.998 closely matches the 10-year horizon of the outflow. Portfolio C is not appropriate because its Macaulay duration of 9.503 is furthest away from the investment horizon of 10 years.
3. Convexity: Although Portfolio C has the lowest convexity at 108.091, its Macaulay duration does not closely match the outflow amount. Of the remaining two portfolios, Portfolio A has the lower convexity at 119.055; this lower convexity will minimize structural risk.

Default risk (credit risk) is not considered because the portfolios consist of government bonds that presumably have default probabilities approaching zero.

25.

Template for Question 25

Determine the *most appropriate* immunization portfolio in Exhibit 2.
(circle one)

Portfolio 1
Portfolio 2
Portfolio 3

Justification:
Portfolio 2 is the most appropriate immunization portfolio because it is the only one that satisfies the following two criteria for immunizing a portfolio of multiple future outflows:

1. Money Duration: Money durations of all three possible immunizing portfolios match or closely match the money duration of the outflow portfolio. Matching money durations is useful because the market values and cash flow yields of the immunizing portfolio and the outflow portfolio are not necessarily equal.

2. Convexity: Given that the money duration requirement is met by all three possible immunizing portfolios, the portfolio with the lowest convexity that is above the outflow portfolio's convexity of 135.142 should be selected. The dispersion, as measured by convexity, of the immunizing portfolio should be as low as possible subject to being greater than or equal to the dispersion of the outflow portfolio. This will minimize the effect of non-parallel shifts in the yield curve. Portfolio 3's convexity of 132.865 is less than the outflow portfolio's convexity, so Portfolio 3 is not appropriate. Both Portfolio 1 and Portfolio 2 have convexities that exceed the convexity of the outflow portfolio, but Portfolio 2's convexity of 139.851 is lower than Portfolio 1's convexity of 147.640. Therefore, Portfolio 2 is the most appropriate immunizing portfolio.

The immunizing portfolio needs to be greater than the convexity (and dispersion) of the outflow portfolio. But, the convexity of the immunizing portfolio should be minimized in order to minimize dispersion and reduce structural risk.

26. Av's strategy immunizes well for parallel shifts, with little deviation between the outflow portfolio and the immunizing portfolio in market value and BPV. Because the money durations are closely matched, the differences between the outflow portfolio and the immunizing portfolio in market value are small and the duration gaps (as shown by the difference in Δ Portfolio BPVs) between the outflow portfolio and the immunizing portfolio are small for both the upward and downward parallel shifts.

Av's strategy does not immunize well for the non-parallel steepening and flattening twists (i.e., structural risks) shown in Exhibit 3. In those cases, the outflow portfolio and the immunizing portfolio market values deviate substantially and the duration gaps between the outflow portfolio and the immunizing portfolio are large.

CHAPTER 14

YIELD CURVE STRATEGIES

SOLUTIONS

1. C is correct. Last year, McLaughlin expected the yield curve to be stable over the year. Riding the yield curve is a strategy based on the premise that, as a bond ages, it will decline in yield if the yield curve is upward sloping. This is known as "rolldown"; that is, the bond rolls down the (static) curve. Riding the yield curve differs from buy and hold in that the manager is expecting to add to returns by selling the security at a lower yield at the horizon. This strategy may be particularly effective if the portfolio manager targets portions of the yield curve that are relatively steep and where price appreciation resulting from the bond's migration to maturity can be significant. McLaughlin elected to position her portfolio solely in 20-year Treasury bonds, which reflect the steepest part of the yield curve, with the expectation of selling the bonds in one year.

2. A is correct. The expected return on the strategy (riding the curve) is calculated as follows:

$E(R)$	$\approx$	Yield income	(equal to Annual coupon rate/ Current bond price)
	$+$	Rolldown return	[equal to (End bond price − Begin bond price)/Begin bond price]
	$+$	E(Change in price based on investor's views of yields and yield spreads)	
	$-$	E(Credit losses)	
	$+$	E(Currency gains or losses)	

Return Component	Formula*	Portfolio Performance
Yield income	Annual coupon payment/Current bond price	$4/101.7593 = 3.93\%$
+ Rolldown return	$\dfrac{\left(\text{Bond price}_{\text{End-of-horizon}} - \text{Bond price}_{\text{Beginning-of-horizon}}\right)}{\text{Bond price}_{\text{Beginning-of-horizon}}}$	$(109.0629 - 101.7593)/101.7593 = 7.18\%$

(*continued*)

(Continued)

Return Component	Formula*	Portfolio Performance
+ E(Change in price based on investor's views of yields and yield spreads)		0%
= Rolling yield	Yield income + Rolldown return	3.93% + 7.18% = 11.11%
− E(Credit losses)	N/A	−0%
+ E(Currency gains or losses)	Given	−1.50%
= Total expected return		= 9.61%

In this case, the E(Change in price based on investor's views of yields and yield spreads) term is equal to zero because McLaughlin expects the yield curve to remain stable.

3. B is correct. McLaughlin expects the yield curve to experience an increase in the butterfly spread, with the 30-year yield remaining unchanged, which implies that the yield curve will increase its curvature, pinned at the 30-year yield, as shown in Exhibit 1. The barbell portfolio, consisting of 2-year and 30-year bonds, would be expected to perform best. Although the two-year rate is expected to increase, the effective duration of two-year bonds is quite small, resulting in minimal price impact. Similarly, the 30-year yield is expected to remain constant, resulting in minimal price impact as well. Relative to the barbell portfolio, the laddered portfolio has greater exposure to the expected increases in the 5-year and 10-year yields, and the bullet portfolio has greater exposure to the expected increase in the 10-year yield. Therefore, the barbell portfolio would be expected to perform best given McLaughlin's interest rate expectations.

4. C is correct. McLaughlin expects interest rate volatility to be high and the yield curve to experience an increase in the butterfly spread, with the 30-year yield remaining unchanged. Given these expectations, a long barbell (2s and 30s, short bullet [10s]) butterfly trade would be most appropriate. The two-year yield is expected to slightly increase by 0.04%, resulting in minimal price impact given the relatively low duration of two-year bonds. Similarly, the 30-year yield is expected to remain constant, resulting in minimal price impact as well. The 10-year yield (+0.50%) is expected to increase by more than the 5-year yield (+0.40%), and with its higher effective duration, the 10-year would be appropriate for the short bullet part of the butterfly trade.

5. B is correct. McLaughlin expects interest rate volatility to be high and the yield curve to experience an increase in the butterfly spread, with the 30-year yield remaining unchanged. To increase the portfolio's expected return, Donaldson and McLaughlin should buy call options on long-maturity government bond futures to increase convexity.

6. B is correct. Statement 2 is correct: If yields rise, a portfolio of a given duration with higher convexity will experience less of a price decrease than a similar-duration, lower-convexity portfolio. Statement 1 is incorrect, as portfolios with larger convexities often have lower yields. Investors will be willing to pay for increased convexity when they expect yields to change by more than enough to cover the sacrifice in yield.

7. B is correct. A bullet performs well when the yield curve is expected to steepen. Since Prégent's forecast is for long rates to rise and short rates to fall, this strategy will add value

to the French client's portfolio by insulating the portfolio against adverse moves at the long end of the curve. If short rates fall, the bullet portfolio gives up very little in profits given the small magnitude of price changes at the short end of the curve.

8. A is correct. To maintain the effective duration match, the duration of the 10-year bond sale must equal the total weighted duration of the 3-year and long-term bond purchases.

$$9.51 = (\text{Duration of 3-year bond} \times \text{Weight of 3-year bond}) + (\text{Duration of}$$
$$\text{long-term bond} \times \text{Weight of long-term bond})$$
$$x = \text{weight of 3-year bond}$$
$$(1 - x) = \text{weight of long-term bond}$$
$$9.51 = 2.88x + 21.30(1 - x)$$
$$x = 0.64 \text{ or } 64\%$$

The proceeds from the sale of the 10-year Canadian government bond should be allocated 64% to the 3-year bond and 36% to the long-term bond:

$$9.51 = (64\% \times 2.88) + (36\% \times 21.30)$$

Gain in convexity = (Weight of the 3-year) × (Convexity of the
  3-year) + (Weight of the long-term bond) × (Convexity
  of the long-term bond) − (Weight of the 10-year) ×
  (Convexity of the 10-year)
Gain in convexity = $(64\% \times 0.118) + (36\% \times 2.912) - (100\% \times 0.701) =$
  0.42284 or 0.423

9. A is correct. Short maturity at- or near-the-money options on long-term bond futures contain a great deal of convexity. Thus, options increase the convexity of the French client's portfolio. Options are added in anticipation of a significant change in rates. If the yield curve remains stable, the portfolio will experience a loss from both the initial purchase price of the options and the forgone interest income on the liquidated bonds.

10. A is correct. The trades are also called a condor and employ four positions, much like a butterfly with an elongated body. Each pair of duration-neutral trades would result in a profit if the yield curve adds curvature. The trades at the short end of the curve (going long the 1-year bond and short the 3-year bond) would profit if that end of the curve gets steeper. In addition, the trades at the long end of the curve (going short the 10-year bond and long the long-term bond) would profit if that end of the curve becomes flatter.

11. C is correct. In order to take duration-neutral positions that will profit from an increase in the curvature of the yield curve, Hirji should structure a condor. This condor structure has the following positions: long the 2-year bonds, short the 5-year bonds, short the 10-year bonds, and long the long-term bonds. Hirji's allocation to the 2-year bond position is calculated as follows:

The C$150 million long-term bonds have a money duration of C$150 × 1,960 = C$294,000
Allocation to 2-year bond = Money duration of long-term bonds/PVBP of 2-year bond
2-year bond position = C$294,000/197 = 1,492.39 or C$1,492 million

12. C is correct. Hirji proposes an extreme bullet portfolio focusing on the middle of the yield curve. If the forecast is correct and the yield curve loses curvature, the rates at either end of the curve will rise or the intermediate yields will drop. As a result, bonds at the ends of the yield curve will lose value or the intermediate bonds will increase in value. In either case, the bullet portfolio will outperform relative to a more diverse maturity index portfolio like the benchmark.

13. B is correct. The rolling yield of the two portfolios is calculated as follows:

Return Component	Formula	Bullet Portfolio	Barbell Portfolio
Yield income	Annual coupon payment/ Current bond price	1.86/100.00 = 1.86%	1.84/100.00 = 1.84%
+ Rolldown return	(Bond price$_{eh}$ − Bond price$_{bh}$)/Bond price$_{bh}$	(100.38 − 100.00)/100.00 = 0.38%	(100.46 − 100.00)/100.00 = 0.46%
= Rolling yield	Yield income + Rolldown return	= 2.24%	= 2.30%

Difference in Rolling yield = Rolling yield of the bullet portfolio − Rolling yield of the barbell portfolio

$$2.24\% - 2.30\% = -0.06\% \text{ or } -6 \text{ basis points}$$

14. C is correct. The total expected return is calculated as follows:

Return Component	Formula	Barbell Return (C)	Distractor A	Distractor B
Yield income	Annual coupon payment/Current bond price	1.84/100.00 = 1.84%	1.84/100.00 = 1.84%	1.84/100.00 = 1.84%
+ Rolldown return	(Bond price$_{eh}$ − Bond price$_{bh}$)/ Bond price$_{bh}$	(100.46 − 100.00)/100.00 = 0.46%	(100.46 − 100.00)/100.00 = 0.46%	(100.46 − 100.00)/100.00 = 0.46%
= Rolling yield	Yield income + Rolldown return	= 2.30%	= 2.30%	= 2.30%
+ E(change in price based on yield view)	$(-MD_{eh} \times \Delta\text{yield})$ $+ [\frac{1}{2} \times \text{Convexity} \times (\Delta\text{yield})^2]$	[−4.12 × −0.55%] + [½ × 24.98 × (−0.55%)²] = 2.30%	[−4.12 × −0.55%] + [½ × 24.98 × (−0.55%)] = −4.60%	[4.12 × −0.55%] + [½ × 24.98 × (−0.55%)²] = −2.23%
= Total expected return		= 4.60%	= −2.30%	= 0.07%

15. C is correct. Since Abram expects the curve to remain stable, the yield curve is upward sloping and the Fund's duration is neutral to its benchmark. Her best strategy is to ride the yield curve and enhance return by capturing price appreciation as the bonds shorten in maturity.

16. C is correct. If interest rates rise and the yield curve steepens as Edgarton expects, then shortening the Fund's duration from a neutral position to one that is shorter than the benchmark will improve the portfolio's return relative to the benchmark. This duration management strategy will avoid losses from long-term interest rate increases.

17. B is correct. In a stable yield curve environment, holding bonds with higher convexity negatively affects portfolio performance. These bonds have lower yields than bonds with lower convexity, all else being equal. The 5-year US Treasury has higher convexity than the negative convexity 30-year MBS bond. So, by selling the 5-year Treasury and purchasing

the 30-year MBS, Abram will reduce the portfolio's convexity and enhance its yield without violating the duration mandate versus the benchmark.

18. A is correct. Scenario 1 is an extreme barbell and is typically used when the yield curve flattens. In this case, the 30-year bond has larger price gains because of its longer duration and higher convexity relative to other maturities. If the yield curve flattens through rising short-term interest rates, portfolio losses are limited by the lower price sensitivity to the change in yields at the short end of the curve while the benchmark's middle securities will perform poorly.

19. A is correct. To profit from a decrease in yield curve curvature, the correct condor structure will be: short 1s, long 5s, long 10s, and short 30s. The positions of the condor will be: short $338 million 1-year bond, long $71 million 5-year bond, long $38 million 10-year bond, and short $17 million 30-year bond.

    This condor is structured so that it benefits from a decline in curvature, where the middle of the yield curve decreases in yield relative to the short and long ends of the yield curve.

    To determine the positions, we take the maximum allowance of 30-year bonds of $17 million and determine money duration. Money duration is equal to market value × modified duration divided by 100. 30-year bond money duration = $17 million × 19.69/100 = $3,347,300. The market values of the other positions are:

    1-year bond: $3,347,300 × 100/0.99 = $338.11 million or $338 million
    5-year bond: $3,347,300 × 100/4.74 = $70.62 million or $71 million
    10-year bond: $3,347,300 × 100/8.82 = $37.95 million or $38 million

20. C is correct. Given Edgarton's expectation for a steepening yield curve, the best strategy is to shorten the portfolio duration by more heavily weighting shorter maturities. Pro Forma Portfolio 2 shows greater partial duration in the 1- and 3-year maturities relative to the current portfolio and the least combined exposure in the 10- and 30-year maturities of the three portfolios. The predicted change is calculated as follows:

    Predicted change = Portfolio par amount × partial PVBP × (curve shift in bps)/100

21. B is correct. The total expected return is calculated as:

    Total expected return = Yield income + Rolldown return = Rolling yield + E (currency gains or losses)

Return Component	Formula	Buy and Hold Portfolio Performance
Yield income	Annual coupon payment/ Current bond price	1.40/99.75 = 1.40%
+ Rolldown return	(Bond price$_{end\ of\ horizon}$ − Bond price$_{beginning\ of\ horizon}$) ÷ Bond price$_{beginning\ of\ horizon}$	(100 − 99.75)/99.75 = 0.25%
= Rolling yield	Yield income + Rolldown return	1.40 + 0.25 = 1.65%
+ E (currency gains or losses)	Given	−0.57%
= Total expected return		1.08%

22. B is correct. The implied forward rate can be calculated using the yield to maturity (YTM) of the 2-year Ride the Yield Curve and 1-year Buy and Hold portfolios.

$$F_{1,1} = [(1.018)^2/1.0165] - 1 = 1.95\%$$

23. A is correct. Carry trades may or may not involve maturity mismatches. Intra-market carry trades typically do involve different maturities, but inter-market carry trades frequently do not, especially if the currency is not hedged.

    B is incorrect. Carry trades may involve only one yield curve, as is the case for intra-market trades. In addition, if two curves are involved they need not have different slopes provided there is a difference in the level of yields between markets.

    C is incorrect. Inter-market carry trades do not, in general, break even if each yield curve goes to its forward rates. *Intra*-market trades *will* break even if the curve goes to the forward rates because, by construction of the forward rates, all points on the curve will earn the "first-period" rate (that is, the rate for the holding period being considered). *Inter*-market trades need not break even unless the "first-period" rate is the same in the two markets. If the currency exposure is not hedged, then breaking even also requires that there be no change in the currency exchange rate.

24. C is correct. Winslow's Statement VI is *incorrect*. Due to covered interest arbitrage, the relative attractiveness of bonds does not depend on the currency into which they are hedged for comparison. Hence, the ranking of bonds does not depend on the base currency of the portfolio.

    A is incorrect because Winslow's Statement IV is *correct*. Inter-market trades should be assessed on the basis of returns hedged into a common currency. Doing so ensures that they are comparable. Neither local currency returns nor unhedged returns are comparable across markets because they involve different currency exposures/risks.

    B is incorrect because Winslow's Statement V is *correct*. The primary driver of inter-market trades is anticipated changes in yield differentials. Over horizons most relevant for active bond management, the capital gains/losses arising from yield movements generally dominate the income component of return (i.e., carry) and rolling down the curve. Hence, expectations with respect to yield movements are the primary driver of inter-market trade decisions.

25. B is correct. The highest potential return, 0.85%, reflects borrowing USD for 6 months and buying the UK 5-year bond. The carry component of the expected return is actually a *loss* of 0.15% [= (1.10% − 1.40%)/2], but this is more than offset by the 1% expected appreciation of GBP versus USD. A much higher carry component +0.90% = (1.95% − 0.15%)/2 could be obtained by borrowing for 6 months in EUR to buy the US 5-year note, but that advantage would be more than offset by the expected 1% loss from depreciation of the USD (long) against the Euro (short).

    A is incorrect because a higher expected return of 0.85% can be obtained. This answer, +0.275% [= (1.95% − 1.40%)/2], is the highest carry available over the next 6 months within the US market itself (an intra-market carry trade).

    C is incorrect. This answer (+0.90%) is the highest potential carry component of return but ignores the impact of currency exposure (being long the depreciating USD and short the appreciating Euro).

26. B is correct. In order to be duration-neutral and currency-neutral, the trade must lend long/borrow short in one market and do the opposite (lend short/borrow long), with the same maturities, in another market. The best carry is obtained by lending long/borrowing short on the steepest curve and lending short/borrowing long on the flattest curve. The GBP curve is the steepest and the EUR curve is the flattest. The largest yield spread between these markets is 0.55% at the 3-year maturity, and the narrowest spread is 0.35% at the 6-month maturity. Hence, the best trade is to go long the GBP 3-year/short the EUR 3-year and long the EUR 6-month/short the GBP 6-month. This can be implemented in

the swaps market by receiving 3-year fixed/paying 6-month floating in GBP and doing the opposite in EUR (receiving 6-month floating/paying 3-year fixed). The net carry is +0.10% = [(0.95% − 0.50%) + (0.15% − 0.40%)]/2 for six months.

A is incorrect. The FX forward position as stated (pay EUR/receive GBP) corresponds to implicitly borrowing EUR for six months and lending GBP for six months. Correct execution of the trade would require the opposite, receiving EUR and delivering GBP 6 months forward.

C is incorrect. This combination of futures positions does create a duration-neutral, currency-neutral carry trade, but it is not the highest available carry. Since the T-note futures price reflects the pricing of the 5-year note as cheapest to deliver, the long position in this contract is equivalent to buying the 5-year Treasury and financing it for 6 months. This generates net carry of 0.275% = (1.95% − 1.40%)/2. Similarly, the short position in the German note futures is equivalent to being short the 5-year German note and lending the proceeds for 6 months, generating net carry of −0.225% = (0.15% − 0.60%)/2. The combined carry is 0.05%, half of what is available on the position in B.

27. B is correct. Winston should buy the Greek 5-year bond for each portfolio. In the US dollar portfolio, she should leave the currency unhedged, accepting the exposure to the euro, which is projected to appreciate by 1% against the USD. In the UK portfolio, she should hedge the bond's EUR exposure into GBP. In the euro-based portfolio there is no hedging decision to be made because the Greek bond is denominated in EUR.

Because yields are projected to remain unchanged in the US, UK, euro, and Greek markets, the 5-year bonds will still be priced at par in six months when they have 4.5 years to maturity. Hence, the local market return for each of these bonds will equal half of the coupon: 0.975%, 0.55%, 0.30%, and 2.85%, respectively. The Mexican 5-year will be priced to yield 7.0% at the end of the period. Its price will be

$$\sum_{t=1}^{9} \frac{7.25/2}{\left(1+\frac{0.07}{2}\right)^t} + \frac{100}{\left(1+\frac{0.07}{2}\right)^9} = 100.9501$$

Its local market return is therefore 4.576% = (100.9501 + 7.25/2)/100. By covered interest parity, the cost of hedging a bond into a particular currency is the short-term (six months here) rate for the currency into which the bond is hedged minus the short-term rate for the currency in which the bond is denominated. For hedging US, UK, and Mexican bonds into euros for six months the calculation is:

USD into EUR: (0.15% − 1.40%)/2 = −0.625%

GBP into EUR: (0.15% −0.50%)/2 = −0.175%

MXN into EUR: (0.15% − 7.10%)/2 = −3.475%

(Note that a negative number is a cost while a positive number would be a benefit.)

Combining these hedging costs with each bond's local market return, the returns hedged into EUR, which can now be validly compared, are:

US: 0.975% + (−0.625%) = 0.350%

UK: 0.550% + (−0.175%) = 0.375%

MX: 4.576% + (−3.475%) = 1.101%

GR: 2.850% + 0 = 2.850%

EU: 0.300% + 0 = 0.300%

The Greek bond is by far the most attractive investment. This would still be true if returns were hedged into USD or GBP. So, the Greek 5-year should be purchased for each portfolio. Whether or not to actually hedge the currency exposure depends on whether the cost/benefit of hedging is greater than the projected change in the spot exchange rate. For the dollar-denominated portfolio, hedging the Greek bond into USD would "pick up" 0.625% (the opposite of hedging USD into EUR). But EUR is expected to appreciate by 1.0% against the dollar, so it is better to leave the bond unhedged in the USD-denominated portfolio. Hedging EUR into GBP picks up 0.175% of return. Since EUR is projected to remain unchanged against GBP, it is better (from an expected return perspective) to hedge the Greek bond into GBP.

A is incorrect because it can be seen from the explanation for B above that the Greek 5-year bond is by far the most attractive investment, returning 2.85% compared to the Mexican 5-year bond's return of 1.101%. If the returns for these bonds were hedged into USD or GBP (instead of EUR), in each case the return on the Mexican 5-year bond would still be inferior to that of the Greek 5-year bond.

C is incorrect because it can be seen from the explanation for B above that the Greek 5-year bond is by far the most attractive investment, returning 2.85% compared to the Mexican 5-year bond's return of 1.101%. If the returns for these bonds were hedged into USD or GBP (instead of EUR), in each case the return on the Mexican 5-year bond would still be inferior to that of the Greek 5-year bond. Moreover, over the 6-month investment horizon the Mexican peso is expected to depreciate against both the GBP and USD, further impairing the unhedged returns on the Mexican 5-year bond in GBP and USD terms.

28. A is correct. As shown in the previous question, the Greek bond is the most attractive. Although the peso is expected to depreciate by 2% against the EUR and the GBP and by 1% against the USD, this is less than the benefit of hedging EUR into MXN (+3.475%). The net currency component of the expected return is +1.475% = (3.475% − 2.0%) for the EUR and GBP portfolios and +2.475% = (3.475% − 1.0%) for the USD-denominated portfolio. Hedging into GBP would add only 0.175% for any of the portfolios. Hedging into USD would reduce expected return for any of the portfolios because the pickup on the hedge (+0.625%) is less than the expected depreciation (−1.0%) of the USD against the Euro and GBP.

B is incorrect. Hedging the euro-denominated Greek bond into USD would reduce expected return for any of the portfolios because the pickup on the hedge (+0.625%) is less than the expected depreciation of the USD against the euro and GBP.

C is incorrect. As shown above, the Greek bond is more attractive than the Mexican bond.

29.

Template for Question 29

Determine which alternative portfolio in Exhibit 1 would be *most appropriate* for Zhao, given her yield curve forecast. (circle one)

Alternative 1	Alternative 2

Justification:

- Alternative 2 would be most appropriate.
- A barbell portfolio (Alternative 2) has higher convexity than a bullet portfolio (Alternative 1).
- The higher-convexity barbell portfolio (Alternative 2) will likely outperform the bullet portfolio (Alternative 1) if there is an instantaneous downward parallel shift in the yield curve because of the barbell portfolio's greater sensitivity to the expected decline in yields.

Alternative 2 is a barbell structure, and Alternative 1 is a bullet structure. A barbell portfolio has higher convexity than a bullet portfolio. In an instantaneous downward parallel shift, the higher-convexity barbell portfolio will outperform the bullet portfolio because of the barbell portfolio's greater sensitivity to declining yields. Portfolios with higher convexity are most often characterized by lower yields. Investors will be willing to pay for increased convexity when they expect yields to change by more than enough to cover the give-up in yield.

30.

Template for Question 30

Determine which investment would be *most appropriate* for Zhao given her yield curve forecast. (circle one)

Investment 1	Investment 2

Justification:

- Investment 2 is the most appropriate investment choice given Zhao's yield curve forecast.
- Purchasing a near-the-money call option on Treasury bond futures would add convexity and better position the portfolio for the forecasted downward parallel shift in the yield curve.
- Buying an MBS would decrease convexity, which would not be ideal given Zhao's expectation of a downward parallel shift in the yield curve.

In the case of an instantaneous downward parallel shift in the yield curve, a portfolio with added convexity resulting from the purchase of a near-the-money option on Treasury bond futures would increase in value more than a portfolio without the call option. Purchasing an MBS would decrease convexity, which would not be ideal given Zhao's expectation of an instantaneous downward parallel shift in the yield curve.

There would be no significant effect on the portfolio resulting from duration because the durations are closely matched.

31.

Template for Question 31

Determine which portfolio in Exhibit 2 will *most likely* have the *best* performance over the next 12 months given Flander's yield curve forecast. (circle one)

Portfolio A	Portfolio B	Portfolio C

Justification:

- Portfolio C will most likely have the best performance given Flander's yield curve forecast.
- Portfolio C should outperform both Portfolio A and Portfolio B if the yield curve steepens, because of Portfolio C's higher partial PVBPs for short- and intermediate-term bonds.

Portfolio C is expected to outperform Portfolio A and Portfolio B if the yield curve steepens, because of Portfolio C's higher partial PVBPs for short- and intermediate-term bonds.

In Flander's forecast for a yield curve steepening, long yields will remain the same, and short and intermediate rates will decline. The long-term bonds will not change in value, because the long-term yield is not expected to change. A decrease in both the short-term and intermediate-term rates, however, will cause price increases in short-term and inter-mediate-term bonds. Because Portfolio C has the highest partial PVBPs in both short-term and intermediate-term bonds, Portfolio C would have the best performance in this yield curve scenario.

Portfolios A and B would be expected to underperform Portfolio C if the yield curve steepens. Portfolios A and B have lower partial PVBPs for both short-term and interme-diate-term bonds than Portfolio C.

32.

Template for Question 32

Calculate the total expected return for the bullet and barbell portfolios presented in Exhibit 3. **Show** your calculations.

		Portfolio Performance	
Return Component	Formula	Bullet	Barbell
Yield income	Annual Coupon Payment ÷ Current Bond Price The bullet and barbell portfolios contain only zero-coupon bonds, so there is no yield income.	0	0
+ Rolldown return		(99.75 − 98.00)/98.00 = 1.7857%	(100.00 − 98.00)/98.00 = 2.0408%
= Rolling yield	Yield Income + Rolldown Return	0 + 1.7857% = 1.7857%	0 + 2.0408% = 2.0408%
+ E(Change in price based on yield view)		$[-3.95 \times (-0.60\%)] + [\frac{1}{2} \times 19.5 \times (-0.60\%)^2] =$ 2.4051%	$[-3.95 \times (-0.60\%)] + [\frac{1}{2} \times 34 \times (-0.60\%)^2] =$ 2.4312%
= Total expected return		4.1908%	4.4720%

Identify the component factor that contributes most to the overperformance of the higher-performing portfolio.

- The barbell portfolio outperforms the bullet portfolio by approximately 28 bps.
- Rolldown return contributes the majority of barbell outperformance (approximately 25.5 bps of outperformance), likely resulting from strong price appreciation of longer-maturity zeros.
- The greater convexity of the barbell portfolio contributed a small amount (approximately 2.6 bps) of outperformance.

Rolldown return is the component factor that contributes most of the approximately 28 bps of outperformance of the barbell portfolio compared with the bullet portfolio. The bullet and barbell portfolios contain only zero-coupon bonds, so the yield income is zero. Rolldown return (and rolling yield) contributed approximately 25.5 bps of outperformance (i.e., 2.0408% − 1.7857%), and the greater convexity of the barbell portfolio contributed just over 2.6 bps of outperformance (i.e., 2.4312% − 2.4051%).

The strong rolldown contribution is likely driven by the stronger price appreciation (under the stable yield curve assumption) of longer-maturity zeros in the barbell portfolio relative to the price appreciation of the intermediate zeros in the bullet portfolio as the bonds ride the curve over the one-year horizon to a shorter maturity. In this particular case, rolling yield and rolldown return are equal, because yield income is zero.

CHAPTER 15

FIXED-INCOME ACTIVE MANAGEMENT: CREDIT STRATEGIES

SOLUTIONS

1. B is correct. An increase in interest rates results in a decrease in the bond price. An increase in the credit spread also results in a decrease in the bond price. For the EKN bond, its modified duration shows the effect of the 20 bp increase in interest rates. The approximate percentage price change resulting from the increase in interest rates is $-8.47 \times 0.0020 = -1.694\%$. The spread duration shows the effect of the 20 bp increase in the credit spread. The approximate percentage price change resulting from the increase in the credit spread is $-8.47 \times 0.0020 = -1.694\%$. The combined effect is a total change of -3.388%, or a price decrease of roughly 3.4%.

2. A is correct. A bond's empirical duration is often estimated by running a regression of its price returns on changes in a benchmark interest rate.

3. C is correct. The OAS for Bond 2 is close to the bond's other spread levels and thus indicates that there is little embedded optionality in the bond. As a result, Bond 2 is most likely not callable.

4. C is correct. Better-than-expected economic growth is typically associated with narrower credit spreads and lower default rates for high-yield bonds.

5. B is correct. Petit should recommend markets in which yields are expected to decline relative to other markets. As a result, Petit should recommend overweighting US bonds relative to European bonds and overweighting US five-year BB bonds relative to US two-year BB bonds.

6. B is correct. Spread sensitivity is the effect on credit spreads of large withdrawals by investors from credit funds. Spread sensitivity can be measured as the spread widening (in basis points) divided by the percentage outflow from high-yield funds (funds withdrawn divided by assets under management). A decrease in the spread sensitivity to fund outflows would most likely indicate an increase in liquidity.

7. C is correct. Increasing the correlations would likely increase the number of extremely unusual outcomes and, thereby, increase estimated tail risk. Higher correlations in the model increase the dispersion of outcomes (effectively decreasing diversification).

8. A is correct. EM indexes have a higher proportion of commodity producers and banks than developed market indexes have.

9. A is correct. Global credit managers do use currency swaps and invest in pegged currencies to hedge foreign exchange exposures.

10. C is correct. The G-spread is the spread over an actual or interpolated benchmark (usually government) bond. A benefit of the G-spread is that when the maturity of the credit security differs from that of the benchmark bond, the yields of two government bonds can be weighted so that their weighted average maturity matches the credit security's maturity.

11. B is correct. Analyzing expected excess returns against the expected magnitude of the credit-related risks is key to the bottom-up approach. Once the credit universe has been divided into sectors, the investor identifies the bonds with the best relative value within each sector. If Dynamo decides that two issuers have similar credit-related risks, then it will typically compare credit spread measures and buy the bonds of the issuer with the higher spread because those bonds likely have a higher potential for excess returns. For issuers with different credit-related risk, Dynamo must decide whether the additional spread adequately compensates for the additional credit risk.

12. C is correct. When an issuer announces a new corporate bond issue, the issuer's existing bonds often decline in value and their spreads widen. This dynamic is often explained by market participants as an effect of increased supply. A related reason is that because demand is not perfectly elastic, new issues are often given a price concession to entice borrowers to buy the new bonds. This price concession may result in all of an issuer's existing bonds repricing based on the new issue's relatively wider spread. A third reason is that more debt issuance may signal an increase in an issuer's credit risk.

13. C is correct. Bid–offer spreads are larger for high-yield bonds than for investment-grade bonds of similar maturity.

14. A is correct. Investment-grade corporate bonds have meaningful interest rate sensitivity, and therefore, investment-grade portfolio managers usually manage their portfolio durations and yield curve exposures closely. In contrast, high-yield portfolio managers are more likely to focus on credit risk and less likely to focus on interest rate and yield curve dynamics. When default losses are low and credit spreads are relatively tight, however, high-yield bonds tend to behave more like investment-grade bonds—that is, with greater interest rate sensitivity.

15. A is correct. CDOs typically include some form of subordination. With subordination, a CDO has more than one bond class or tranche, including senior bond classes, mezzanine bond classes (which have credit ratings between senior and subordinated bond classes), and subordinated bond classes (often referred to as residual or equity tranches). The correlation of expected defaults on a CDO's collateral affects the relative value between the senior and subordinated tranches of the CDO. As correlations increase, the values of the mezzanine tranches usually increase relative to the values of the senior and equity tranches.

CFA Institute

ABOUT THE CFA PROGRAM

The Chartered Financial Analyst® (CFA®) designation is a globally recognized standard of excellence for measuring the competence and integrity of investment professionals. To earn the CFA charter, candidates must successfully pass through the CFA Program, a global graduate-level self-study program that combines a broad curriculum with professional conduct requirements as preparation for a wide range of investment specialties.

Anchored by a practice-based curriculum, the CFA Program is focused on the knowledge identified by professionals as essential to the investment decision-making process. This body of knowledge maintains current relevance through a regular, extensive survey of practicing CFA charterholders across the globe. The curriculum covers 10 general topic areas, ranging from equity and fixed-income analysis to portfolio management to corporate finance, all with a heavy emphasis on the application of ethics in professional practice. Known for its rigor and breadth, the CFA Program curriculum highlights principles common to every market so that professionals who earn the CFA designation have a thoroughly global investment perspective and a profound understanding of the global marketplace.

www.cfainstitute.org

ABOUT THE
CFA PROGRAM

The Chartered Financial Analyst (CFA) designation is a globally recognized standard of excellence for measuring competence and integrity of investment professionals. To earn the CFA charter, candidates must successfully pass through the CFA Program, a graduate level self-study program that combines a broad curriculum with professional conduct requirements as preparation for a wide range of investment specialties.

Anchored by a practice-based curriculum, the CFA Program is focused on investment knowledge. Beginning with a strong emphasis on the highest ethical standards and a grounding in the global marketplace.